Smaller, Smarter
Home Plans

the Garlinghouse company

212

7

59

133

133

11

39

Smaller, Smarter Home Plans

The Garlinghouse Company

Published by
The Garlinghouse Company

CEO/President
Publisher
D. Jarret Magbee

Graphic Design Consultant
Pamela Stant

Accounting Manager
Monika Jackson

Customer Service Manager
Jean Judd

Designer Relations
Rick Miller

Fulfillment Operations
Andrew Jackson

For Home Plan Orders in United States
2121 Boundary Street, Suite 208
Beaufort, SC 29902
1-800-235-5700

For Home Plan Orders in Canada
102 Ellis Street, Penticton, BC V2A 4L5
1-800-361-7526

Special thanks to the Partnership for Advancing Technology in Housing (PATH) for their insightful editorial content. For more information on topics addressed in *Smaller Smarter Home Plans,* visit www.pathnet.org/homeowners.com.

ON THE COVER: EXTERIOR PHOTO: PLAN #34029, PG. 134
INTERIOR PHOTO: PLAN #65138, PG. 263 FRONT PORCH: PLAN # 19422

CONTENTS

A Smaller, Smarter Home

SENSIBLE SQUARE FOOTAGE. GENEROUS STORAGE SPACE.
LOW MAINTENANCE. ENERGY EFFICIENT.
ALL OF THIS AND MORE COMES TO MIND WHEN WE
THINK OF A SMALLER, SMARTER HOME.

The house designs you'll discover in *Smaller, Smarter Home Plans* were selected not only for their conservative size, but also for their intelligent use of space. A well designed smaller home plan orchestrates the flow of the spaces, making sense of all areas, no matter how compact. It's a design that feels larger than its square footage, with storage space to help eliminate clutter and outdoor living spaces to expand the home to the outside. It's also a home that, most importantly, lives in harmony with your lifestyle.

Smaller, smarter homes are stylish both inside and out, with open room arrangements, tasteful design details and outdoor living areas that expand the sense of space. **Facing page, left and below:** Charming curb appeal and interior views of plan #65431, pg. 182. **Bottom:** Rear covered porch of plan #65001, pg. 38

Beyond the issue of design, you'll find other insights and ideas throughout the following pages that will make your new home live smarter day to day. A smarter home is one that provides a healthy, safe environment for you and your household. Home is —or should be—a place of protection and refuge. Unfortunately, many homes today are anything but safe. Poor indoor air quality is responsible for an array of ailments from allergies to respiratory diseases. A smarter home is one that assures you and your loved ones will breathe easy, and we'll show you how. We'll also explore the elements from which a smarter home is built, such as highly durable materials that require little or no maintenance, and new technologies that can make your new home more energy efficient, comfortable, affordable and environmentally friendly.

Smaller, Smarter Home Plans invites you to view this collection of 339 home plans from North America's leading residential architects and designers. Each of the designs are proven, popular and smartly designed, but a select group stood out as we compiled this book's content. You'll enjoy spending a bit more time with these "Editor's Choice" plans. You can also discover thousands of additional smarter home plans of any size, by visiting us on the web at www.familyhomeplans.com. ∎

visit us

www.familyhomeplans.com

free deck plan

WITH YOUR HOME PLAN PURCHASE

Purchase any home plan from Smaller, Smarter Home Plans and receive a free deck plan of your choice*. Entertain guests, spend time with the family, or just kick back and relax on one of these versatile outdoor living spaces. When ordering your home plan, request the deck plan of your choice.

*While supplies last

Plan ID: **190001**

Easy Patio Deck

• Package Contains 12 Different Sizes

8'x8', 8'x10', 8'x12', 10'x10', 10'x12', 10'x16', 12'x12', 12'x16', 14'x20', 14'x16', 16'x16', 16'x20

Plan ID: **190002**

Easy Raised Deck

• Stair & Railing Plans Included
• Package Contains 8 Different Sizes

8'x8', 8'x10', 8'x12', 10'x10', 10'x12', 10'x16', 12'x12', 12'x16

Smart design makes smaller homes live larger, such as this 1,848 sq. ft. home featured on pages 10-11.

smarter home design

INTELLIGENT, INTUITIVE HOME PLANS, DESIGNED FOR THE WAY YOU LIVE

What makes a home's design "smarter?" Sensible room arrangements? Efficient use of space? Thoughtful traffic patterns? Certainly, these are all characteristics of better quality home plans, but there is much more to consider when it comes to a more intelligent, intuitive design.

Smarter home designs also have the capability to flex and expand as our needs change over time. They allow us our choice of private retreats or interactive areas. They accommodate our every-growing accumulation of "things" with effective storage space. In addition, they live larger than their actual square footage, by expanding living space to the outside.

Beyond the floor plan, a "smarter" design resides in the eye of the beholder. As you consider various home plans, give thought to your lifestyle and how a design should accommodate your needs and wants. Do you prefer the master suite to be secluded on the main floor, or upstairs near secondary bedrooms? Do you entertain formally, or casually? Do you want an open floor plan, or one that allows more private living spaces? One level, or two? The list can go on an on, but in short, a smarter design is one that will live in harmony with you, day after day, for years to come.

Price Code AA 59040

Total Sq. Ft.: 800
Width: 30'
Depth: 36'
Bedrooms: 2
Baths: 1

(For more plan info, visit www.familyhomeplans.com)

The design and layout of this home brings back the memories of days gone by and of places we feel comfortable. Chatting by the warmth of the fireplace in the winter...enjoying the screened-in back porch in the summer...and spending time with your family year-round, make this a most inviting home. A charming home that will fufill many families' needs!

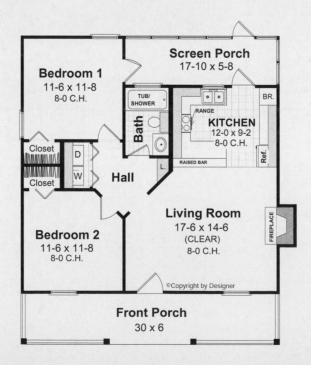

Bedroom 1
11-6 x 11-8
8-0 C.H.

Screen Porch
17-10 x 5-8

TUB/
SHOWER

BR.

Bath

RANGE

KITCHEN
12-0 x 9-2
8-0 C.H.

Ref.

Closet

Closet

D
W

RAISED BAR

L

Hall

FIREPLACE

Bedroom 2
11-6 x 11-8
8-0 C.H.

Living Room
17-6 x 14-6
(CLEAR)
8-0 C.H.

©Copyright by Designer

Front Porch
30 x 6

Price Code AA   40025

Total Sq. Ft.: 923
Width: 32'
Depth: 38'-6"
Bedrooms: 2
Baths: 1

(For more plan info, visit www.familyhomeplans.com)

Front and back porches span the width of this rustic country cottage. The living and dining room provide an open space with cathedral ceilings, while a wood burning fireplace warms this large area. The galley kitchen provides an ample pantry and a window with views to the back yard. The master bedroom includes a full bath which is accessible to the kitchen. Upstairs, the loft bedroom boasts a window seat separating two closets.

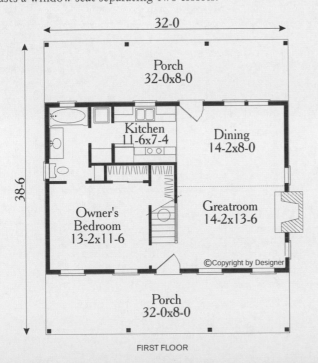

32-0

Porch
32-0x8-0

Kitchen
11-6x7-4

Dining
14-2x8-0

Owner's
Bedroom
13-2x11-6

Greatroom
14-2x13-6

©Copyright by Designer

38-6

Porch
32-0x8-0

FIRST FLOOR

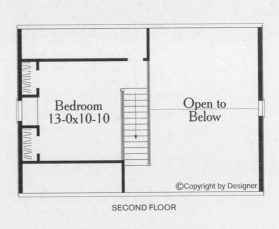

Bedroom
13-0x10-10

Open to
Below

©Copyright by Designer

SECOND FLOOR

beautiful bungalow

Real beauty is versatile, fluid, and often sensible—all the characteristics of this 4-season vacation home design. The main-floor family room with fireplace and soaring cathedral ceiling shares its wide-open atmosphere with an eat-in-kitchen. A large main-floor bedroom with walk-in closet utilizes an adjacent full bath. With two bedrooms on the second floor (or one super-sized bedroom), plus master bath, there's enough comfort to go around. Across the open mezzanine, a snug sitting room warms up with a fireplace. And, the full basement houses a private three-room apartment that nearly mirrors the first level.

Above: Airy, open views in the family room. Top Right: This homeowner chose to relocate the kitchen to the master bedroom's original location. A built-in booth serves casual meals. Middle Right: This dining area occupies the kitchen's original spot. Bottom Right: Views to the entry area from the family room.

FIRST FLOOR

SECOND FLOOR

Price Code A   65015

Total Sq. Ft.: 1,468
Main Level: 958'
Upper Level: 510'
Width 35'
Depth 30'
Bedrooms: 3
Baths: 2
Garage: none

(For more plan info, visit www.familyhomeplans.com)

Price Code AA 65643

Total Sq. Ft.: 984
Width: 33'-9"
Depth: 43'
Bedrooms: 2
Baths: 1.75
Garage: none

(For more plan info, visit www.familyhomeplans.com)

Finished in striking stucco, this charming cottage has classic, space-efficient style. Beyond the columned porch, the angled entry opens to an elegant living room, which boasts a handsome fireplace and a vaulted ceiling. The adjoining dining room is brightened by a trio of French doors, one of which opens to the backyard. The uniquely-shaped kitchen includes a laundry area with access to a covered back porch. The quaint master suite has an angled entrance, while the luxurious master bath offers an oval garden tub and a roomy walk-in closet. The secondary bedroom enjoys a bright boxed-out window and private access to another full bath.

Editor's Choice

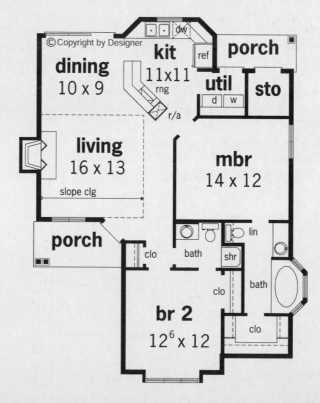

Homes That "Live" With You

Floor plans are more than a cluster of rooms, or an arrangement of spaces. They provide us a glimpse of whether or not the home would accommodate our lifestyles. Consequently, every floor plan has the potential of being perfect or awful, depending on who's viewing it.

The design of your new home should mirror your current lifestyle, as well as anticipate your changing needs in the future. Here are a few personal preferences you'll want to consider.

■ MASTER SUITE: Main floor, or second level. Luxurious. Private location.

■ SECONDARY BEDROOMS: Near the master suite, or set apart. Private or shared baths.

■ ENTERTAINING STYLE: Formal. (formal living and dining rooms) Casual. (great room, eat-in kitchen area, outdoor living areas)

■ KITCHEN: Open to living areas. Sheltered from view. Snack bar. Island. Pantry.

■ LAUNDRY AREA: Large. (with folding counters and utility sink, ironing center) Small. (laundry closet)

■ KID SPACES: (play room, media room, homework/computer area)

■ OFFICE AREA

■ HOBBY AREA

■ WORKSHOP

Price Code A   59043

Total Sq. Ft.: 1,000
Width: 30'
Depth: 38'-4"
Bedrooms: 2
Baths: 2
Garage: none

(For more plan info, visit www.familyhomeplans.com)

Patio
12-8 x 10

Bedroom #1
11-6 x 13
9' Ceiling

Laun.
5-2 x 6

D
W

Breakfast Area
12 x 6
9' Ceiling

Raised Bar

Jet Tub

Bath

Kitchen
12 x 10-4

P

Clos.

Lin.

Raised Bar

Built-Ins

Tub/Shr.

Bath

Clos.

Br.

Hall

Living Room
17-6 x 12-11
(Clear)
9' Ceiling

Gas Logs

Built-Ins

Bedroom #2
11-6 x 13
9' Ceiling

Front Porch
17-10 x 5-0

smart design

Price Code B 75002

Total Sq. Ft.: 1,565
Width: 55'-6"
Depth: 41'-6"
Bedrooms: 3
Baths: 2.5
Garage: 2-car

(For more plan info, visit www.familyhomeplans.com)

A tasteful array of dormered and shuttered windows grace this smartly designed 1½- story home. Inside, an open floor plan marries the great room, kitchen and dining area for a comfortable exchange with friends and family. A covered rear patio, accessed from the dining area, expands the living area of the home. The master suite is tucked away for privacy and features a roomy walk-in closet. Upstairs, bedrooms #2 and #3 share a central bath. A generous bonus room provides unlimited options for flexible use.

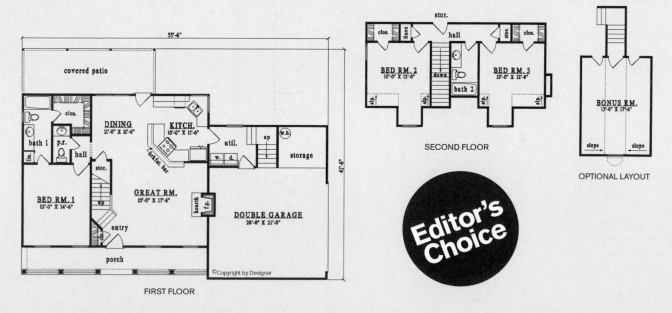

This delightful 1,050 sq. ft. plan is designed as a "starter" home or "empty-nester". It also lends itself well to a vacation atmosphere. A vaulted ceiling gives an airy feeling to the dining and living area. The streamline 9'x11' kitchen has a comfortable work triangle. A cozy fireplace makes the living area really feel like home. A master suite, measuring 11'x12' has a large closet, a French door leading onto a patio and a spacious master bath. The two remaining bedrooms share a hall bath. The washer and dryer are tucked conveniently in a laundry closet.

Price Code A   92438

Total Sq. Ft.: 1,050
Width: 36'
Depth: 42'
Bedrooms: 3
Baths: 2
Garage: 1-car

(For more plan info, visit www.familyhomeplans.com)

Price Code A 55022

Total Sq. Ft.: 1,064
Width: 38'
Depth: 34'
Bedrooms: 2
Baths: 1
Garage: none

(For more plan info, visit www.familyhomeplans.com)

This farmhouse design squeezes space-efficient features into its compact design. A cozy front porch opens into a vaulted great room and its adjoining dining room. Twin dormer windows above flood this area with natural light and accentuate the high ceilings. A warm hearth in the great room adds to its coziness. The U-shaped kitchen has a breakfast bar open to the dining room and a sink overlooking a flower box. A nearby side-door access is found in the handy laundry room. Vaulted bedrooms are positioned along the back of the plan. They contain wall closets and share a full bath with a soaking tub. An open-rail staircase leads to the basement, which can be developed into living or sleeping space at a later time, if needed.

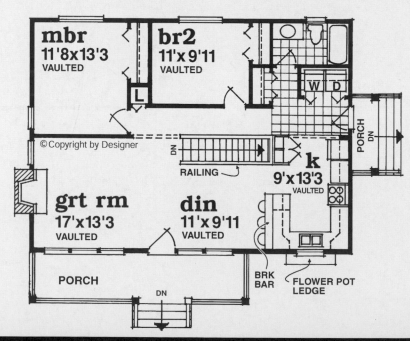

mbr
11'8 x 13'3
VAULTED

br2
11'x 9'11
VAULTED

© Copyright by Designer

W D

DN
RAILING

PORCH
DN

k
9'x 13'3
VAULTED

grt rm
17'x 13'3
VAULTED

din
11'x 9'11
VAULTED

PORCH

DN

BRK BAR

FLOWER POT LEDGE

ORDER NOW! Phone: **1-800-235-5700** Online: **www.FamilyHomePlans.com** Order Code: **H6SSM**

Craftsman styling and a welcoming porch create marvelous curb appeal for this design. A compact footprint allows economy in construction. A volume ceiling in the living and dining rooms and the kitchen make this home live larger than its modest square footage. The kitchen features generous cabinet space and flows directly into the dining room (note the optional buffet) to create a casual country feeling. The master bedroom offers a walk-in closet, a full bath and a bumped-out window overlooking the rear yard. The lower level provides room for an additional bedroom, den, family room and full bath. Choose the unfinished basement or a crawlspace foundation under the living area.

Price Code A 55015

Total Sq. Ft.: 1,108
Width: 38'
Depth: 31'
Bedrooms: 3
Baths: 2
Garage: none

(For more plan info, visit www.familyhomeplans.com)

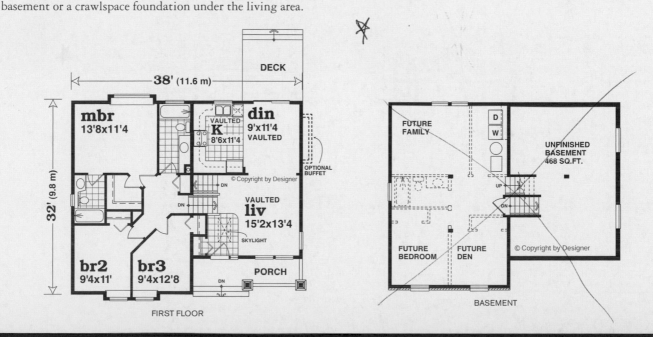

Price Code A   34003

Total Sq. Ft.: 1,146
Width 44'
Depth 28'
Bedrooms: 3
Baths: 2
Garage: none

(For more plan info, visit www.familyhomeplans.com)

A casual front deck, large picture window, and stone chimney are a few of the details that give this 1,146 sq. ft. design its old-world charm. A sloped roof hovers cozily over the living room with fireplace. The kitchen with lunch counter looks into the dining room and out to the back porch as well. Two bright secondary bedrooms are drawn close together for easier access to the full bath and its large linen closet. The master bedroom features double closets, abundant windows and its own windowed bath.

REAR EXTERIOR

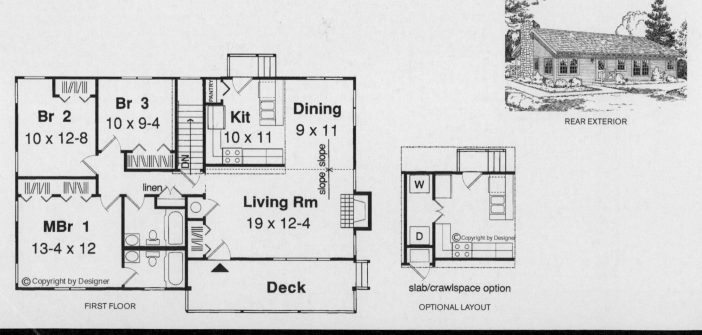

FIRST FLOOR

OPTIONAL LAYOUT

Price Code A   65394

Total Sq. Ft.: 1,147
Width 44'
Depth 30'
Bedrooms: 3
Baths:1

(For more plan info, visit www.familyhomeplans.com)

Two covered porches span the front of this quaint three-bedroom one story home. Inside, the family room provides an intimate setting for family and friends, with the eat-in kitchen politely tucked to the side. All three bedrooms adjoin the family room area and share a centralized bath.

REAR EXTERIOR

9'-0" X 10'-0"
2,70 X 3,00

16'-6" X 15'-4"
4,95 X 4,60

9'-0" X 11'-0"
2,70 X 3,30

© Copyright by Designer

11'-0" X 12'-8"
3,30 X 3,70

14'-4" X 17'-4"
4,30 X 5,20

smart design

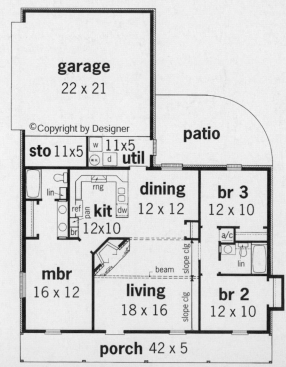

Price Code A   65648

Total Sq. Ft.: 1,191
Width: 44'-5"
Depth: 59'
Bedrooms: 3
Baths: 2
Garage: 2-car

(For more plan info, visit www.familyhomeplans.com)

The efficient layout of this design features an isolated master suite only steps away from the kitchen. The living room has sloped ceilings and a massive stone wood-burning fireplace. The full size front porch is finished with horizontal siding for great looks while the remainder of the exterior is finished with brick for low maintenance. This plan is a super energy saver featuring 2x6 exterior walls.

garage
22 x 21

©Copyright by Designer

patio

sto 11x5   w 11x5
             d   util

dining
12 x 12

br 3
12 x 10

kit
12x10

mbr
16 x 12

living
18 x 16

br 2
12 x 10

porch 42 x 5

Home Design Modification

It's Easier Than You Might Think, to Have It Your Way

One of the biggest advantages of stock home plans is that they are not only affordable, but also changeable. Hopefully, you'll discover a plan that is perfect just as it is. More likely, however, you'll find several designs that come close to what you want, but with a little tweaking, would be exactly right.

Home plan modification, in most cases, is an easy, affordable solution to achieving a home design that meets your needs and wants. Any plan can be changed, and almost any change can be made, so don't ignore plans that aren't 100% on track with what you're seeking.

Here are a few of the most commonly requested home plan changes:

■ Garage: 2-car, to 3-car (or vice versa) Front-load, to Side-load (or vice versa)

■ Foundation: Basement, crawl-space, or slab

■ Master Suite: Usually to enlarge and add amenities

For more information on plan modifications, see page 6 for complete details.

Price Code A   68231

Total Sq. Ft.: 1,195
Width: 40'
Depth: 48'
Bedrooms: 3
Baths: 2
Garage: 2-car

(For more plan info, visit www.familyhomeplans.com)

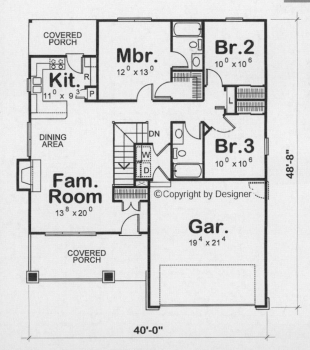

Editor's Choice

© Copyright by Designer

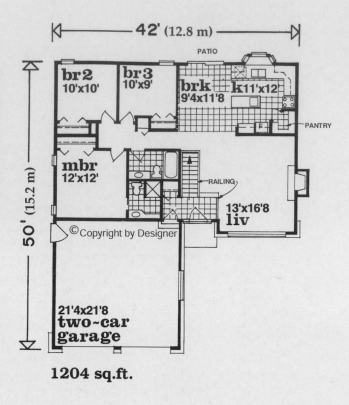

42' (12.8 m)

PATIO

br2 10'x10'
br3 10'x9'
brk 9'4x11'8
k 11'x12

PANTRY

mbr 12'x12'

RAILING

13'x16'8 liv

© Copyright by Designer

50' (15.2 m)

21'4x21'8 two-car garage

1204 sq.ft.

Price Code A 55026

Total Sq. Ft.: 1,204
Width: 43'
Depth: 51'
Bedrooms: 3
Baths: 2
Garage: 2-car

(For more plan info, visit www.familyhomeplans.com)

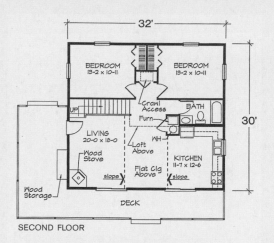

32'

BEDROOM 13-2 x 10-11
BEDROOM 13-2 x 10-11

Crawl Access
Furn
BATH
UP
WH
LIVING 20-0 x 18-0
Loft Above
Wood Stove
Flat Clg Above
KITCHEN 11-7 x 12-6
slope
slope

Wood Storage

30'

DECK

SECOND FLOOR

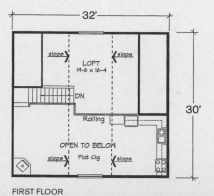

32'

slope
slope
LOFT 19-6 x 16-4

DN

Railing

OPEN TO BELOW
slope
Flat Clg
slope

30'

FIRST FLOOR

Price Code A 20001

Total Sq. Ft.: 1,255
Main Level: 960'
Upper Level: 295'
Bedrooms: 2
Baths: 1
Width: 32'
Depth: 30'
Garage: none

(For more plan info, visit www.familyhomeplans.com)

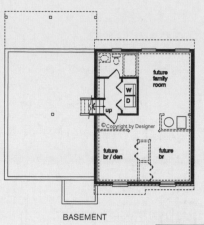

BASEMENT

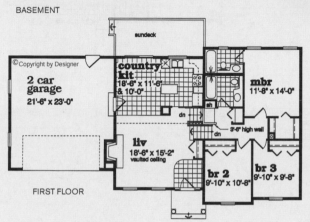

FIRST FLOOR

Price Code A   55029

Total Sq. Ft.: 1,215
Width: 62'
Depth: 34'
Bedrooms: 3
Baths: 2
Garage: 2-car

(For more plan info, visit www.familyhomeplans.com)

ALT. PLAN
CRAWLSPACE OPTION

OPTIONAL LAYOUT

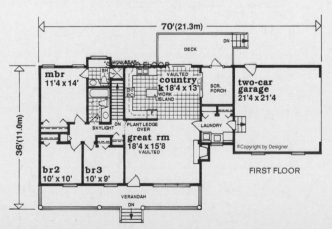

FIRST FLOOR

Price Code A   55017

Total Sq. Ft.: 1,298
Width: 70'
Depth: 36'
Bedrooms: 3
Baths: 2
Garage: 2-car

(For more plan info, visit www.familyhomeplans.com)

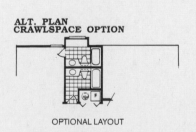

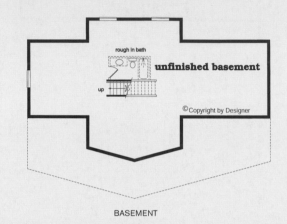

55'6 (16.9m)

30' (9.1m)

br2 9'2x10'4   br3 9'2x10'4

mbr 13'2x11'4

liv 21'x15' VAULTED   din 10'x11'4

k 10' x 11'8

©Copyright by Designer

DECK

1230 sq. ft.   FIRST FLOOR

rough in bath

unfinished basement

up

©Copyright by Designer

BASEMENT

Price Code A   55000

Total Sq. Ft.: 1,230
Width: 55'-6"
Depth: 30'
Bedrooms: 3
Baths: 2
Garage: 1-car

(For more plan info, visit www.familyhomeplans.com)

sto 11 x 6   sto 11 x 6

carport 22 x 22

©Copyright by Designer

dining 10 x 9   kit 9x9   bath   mbr 14 x 13

shvs

living 19 x 17
wood box

shvs

br 2 12 x 10   br 3 12 x 10

porch 44 x 6

Price Code A   65638

Total Sq. Ft.: 1,244
Width: 44'
Depth: 62'
Bedrooms: 3
Baths: 2
Garage: Carport

(For more plan info, visit www.familyhomeplans.com)

ORDER NOW!   Phone: **1-800-235-5700**   Online: **www.FamilyHomePlans.com**   Order Code: **H6SSM**

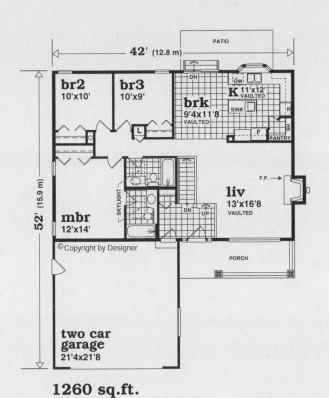

PATIO

42' (12.8 m)

br2
10'x10'

br3
10'x9'

DN

brk
9'4x11'8
VAULTED

K 11'x12'
VAULTED

DW

SINK

PANTRY

F.

SH

R

L

52' (15.9 m)

SKYLIGHT

DN

UP

liv
13'x16'8
VAULTED

F.P. →

mbr
12'x14'

©Copyright by Designer

PORCH

two car garage
21'4x21'8

1260 sq.ft.

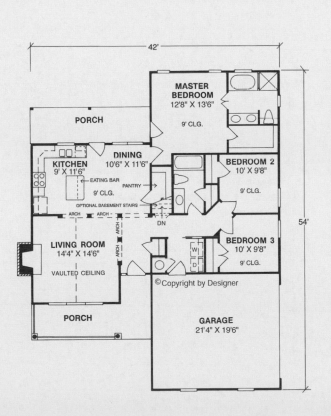

42'

PORCH

MASTER BEDROOM
12'8" X 13'6"
9' CLG.

KITCHEN
9' X 11'6"

EATING BAR
9' CLG.

PANTRY

OPTIONAL BASEMENT STAIRS

DINING
10'6" X 11'6"
9' CLG.

BEDROOM 2
10' X 9'8"
9' CLG.

ARCH   ARCH

ARCH

LIVING ROOM
14'4" X 14'6"

VAULTED CEILING

ARCH

DN

W
D

BEDROOM 3
10' X 9'8"
9' CLG.

©Copyright by Designer

54'

PORCH

GARAGE
21'4" X 19'6"

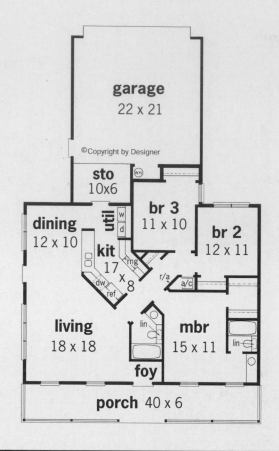

garage
22 x 21

©Copyright by Designer

sto
10x6

util

dining
12 x 10

br 3
11 x 10

br 2
12 x 11

kit
17
x 8

living
18 x 18

lin

mbr
15 x 11

lin

foy

porch 40 x 6

Price Code A   65681

Total Sq. Ft.: 1,266
Width: 40'
Depth: 64'
Bedrooms: 3
Baths: 2
Garage: 2-car

(For more plan info, visit www.familyhomeplans.com)

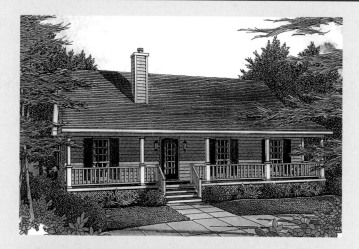

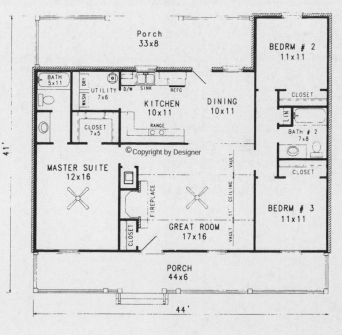

Porch
33x8

BEDRM # 2
11x11

BATH
5x11

UTILITY
7x6

KITCHEN
10x11

DINING
10x11

CLOSET

CLOSET
7x5

RANGE

LIN

BATH # 2
7x8

41'

MASTER SUITE
12x16

©Copyright by Designer

CLOSET

FIREPLACE

GREAT ROOM
17x16

VAULT

VAULT 11' CEILING

VAULT

BEDRM # 3
11x11

CLOSET

PORCH
44x6

44'

Price Code A   96559

Total Sq. Ft.: 1,277
Width: 44'
Depth: 41'
Bedrooms: 3
Baths: 2
Garage: None

(For more plan info, visit www.familyhomeplans.com)

Expandable & Flexible Spaces

Floor plan options that go far beyond the intent of the home's original design

As our lives change, so do our needs for our home's layout.

Below are a few examples of how a home's design might flex and expand to meet your changing needs.

■ Eating areas off the kitchen can easily take the place of formal dining rooms if they are open to main living areas (the family room, great room, etc.)

■ Secondary bedrooms are commonly reconfigured for use as home offices or dens

■ Unfinished attic areas can be finished for use as playrooms, offices, or extensions of walk-in closets.

■ The area beneath front porches or stoops can often be excavated to become wine cellars or safe rooms.

■ A secondary bedroom adjoining the master suite can become a private sitting room retreat or nursery.

■ A third-car bay can be transformed into a workshop or storage area—or may allow the laundry room to expand as a laundry/hobby center

Price Code A   65492

Total Sq. Ft.: 1,281
Width 36'-4"
Depth 52'
Bedrooms: 2
Baths: 1
Garage: 1-car

(For more plan info, visit www.familyhomeplans.com)

REAR EXTERIOR

Editor's Choice

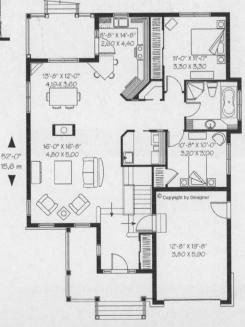

8'-8" X 14'-8"
2,60 X 4,40

11'-0" X 11'-0"
3,30 X 3,30

13'-8" X 12'-0"
4,10 X 3,60

10'-8" X 10'-0"
3,20 X 3,00

16'-0" X 16'-8"
4,80 X 5,00

52'-0"
15,6 m

12'-8" X 19'-8"
3,80 X 5,90

© Copyright by Designer

Price Code A 92431

Total Sq. Ft.: 1,296
Width: 46'
Depth: 42'
Bedrooms: 3
Baths: 2
Garage: 2-car

(For more plan info, visit www.familyhomeplans.com)

BEDROOM 2
11x11

BEDROOM 3
11x10

GARAGE
19x20

FAMILY ROOM
16x20

12' CEILING

DINING

KITCHEN
10x10

MASTER BEDROOM
12x14

OPTIONAL BAY

OPTIONAL MASTER BATH

© Copyright by Designer

Price Code A 55030

Total Sq. Ft.: 1,299
Width: 42'
Depth: 40'
Bedrooms: 3
Baths: 2
Garage: 2-car

(For more plan info, visit www.familyhomeplans.com)

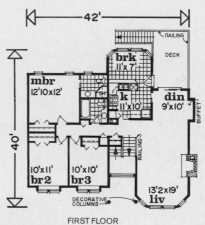

42'

40'

mbr
12'10x12'

brk
11'x7'

DECK

k
11'x10'

din
9'x10'

BUFFET

10'x11'
br2

10'x10'
br3

RAILING

13'2x19'
liv

DECORATIVE COLUMNS

FIRST FLOOR

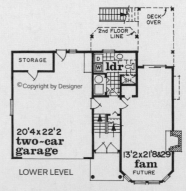

STORAGE

© Copyright by Designer

20'4x22'2
two-car garage

2nd FLOOR LINE

ldr

SH

DECK OVER

13'2x21'8x29'
fam
FUTURE

LOWER LEVEL

ORDER NOW! Phone: **1-800-235-5700** Online: **www.FamilyHomePlans.com** Order Code: **H6SSM**

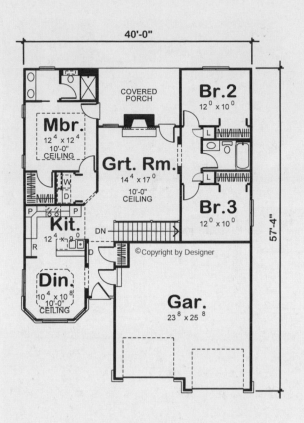

40'-0"

Mbr.
12⁴ x 12⁴
10'-0"
CEILING

COVERED PORCH

Br. 2
12⁰ x 10⁰

Grt. Rm.
14⁴ x 17⁰
10'-0"
CEILING

Br. 3
12⁰ x 10⁰

Kit.
12⁴ x

Din.
10⁴ x 10⁸
10'-0"
CEILING

DN

Gar.
23⁸ x 25⁸

57'-4"

©Copyright by Designer

Price Code A   44008

Total Sq. Ft.: 1,304
Bedrooms: 3
Bathrooms: 2
Width: 40'
Depth: 57'-4"
Garage: 2-car

(For more plan info, visit www.familyhomeplans.com)

Editor's Choice

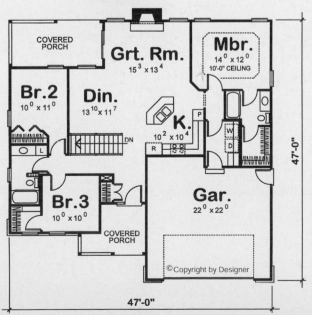

COVERED PORCH

Grt. Rm.
15³ x 13⁴

Mbr.
14⁰ x 12⁰
10'-0" CEILING

Br. 2
10⁰ x 11⁰

Din.
13¹⁰ x 11⁷

K.
10² x 10⁴

DN

Br. 3
10⁰ x 10⁰

Gar.
22⁰ x 22⁰

COVERED PORCH

©Copyright by Designer

47'-0"

47'-0"

Price Code A   68233

Total Sq. Ft.: 1,333
Bedrooms: 3
Bathrooms: 2
Width: 47'
Depth: 47'
Garage: 2-car

(For more plan info, visit www.familyhomeplans.com)

Price Code A   35008

Total Sq. Ft.: 1,291
Main Level: 955'
Upper Level: 336'
Bedrooms: 3
Baths: 1
Width: 24'
Depth: 40'
Garage: none

(For more plan info, visit www.familyhomeplans.com)

Comfortable Three Bedroom. Simple, practical with some lovely features, this home may be the perfect hide-away. The living areas are at the front of the home. The efficient, galley kitchen includes a breakfast bar for informal eating. The living room is equipped with a built-in entertainment center. A laundry area is located near the side door entrance. The full hall bath is located in close proximity to the bedrooms. Overlooking the living room and the dining room is a loft area. There is storage on either side of the loft. With a welcoming country porch, this is a wonderful place to get away from it all.

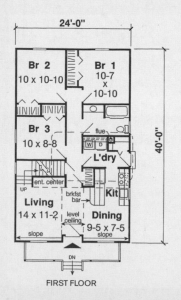

FIRST FLOOR

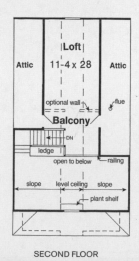

SECOND FLOOR

Slab/ Crawl Space Option

OPTIONAL LAYOUT

Price Code A 24700

Total Sq. Ft.: 1,312
Bedrooms: 3
Baths: 2
Width: 50'
Depth: 40'
Garage: 2-car

(For more plan info, visit www.familyhomeplans.com)

Here, 1,312 sq. ft. exercises the three C's, beautifully—character, comfort, camaraderie. A family-friendly front porch and foyer generate a warm welcome. Special ceiling treatments throughout the interior add elegance. The central living room with great fireplace takes center stage. The private side of the house embraces the master suite with wall-length closet and luxurious bath. Bedrooms #2 and #3 enjoy generous closeting and a shared bath. Plus, there's plenty of potential for converting one of the front bedrooms to a home office. The public side of the home draws family to a hearty kitchen with deck access, and a very special dining room.

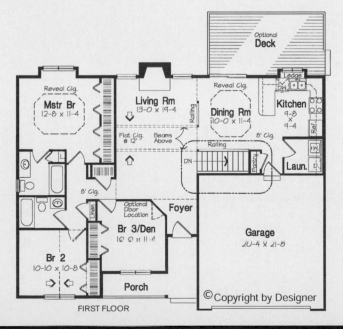

FIRST FLOOR

© Copyright by Designer

OPTIONAL LAYOUT

Price Code A 34600

Total Sq. Ft.: 1,334
Main Level: 1,019'
Upper Level: 315'
Bedrooms: 3
Baths: 2
Width: 36'
Depth: 36'
Garage: none

(For more plan info, visit www.familyhomeplans.com)

Yearning for your little cabin in the woods! With 1,328 sq. ft., it's not terribly little, but it's got all the other classic country charm-including a breezy porch and quaint living room fireplace, and sloped roof, too. The kitchen and dining room pair up so family and good friends can munch and mingle without feeling crowded. Two big bedrooms snuggle up to each other. Each of them owns a large closet, plus windows on two walls that make the most of natural light. Even the bathroom features a window, and a tub tucked beneath it. Small is sweet!

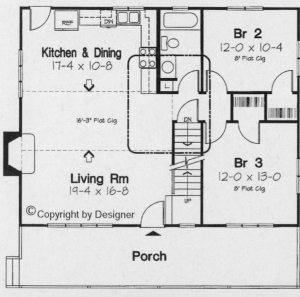

Kitchen & Dining
17-4 x 10-8

16'-3" Flat Clg

Br 2
12-0 x 10-4
8' Flat Clg

Living Rm
19-4 x 16-8

Br 3
12-0 x 13-0
8' Flat Clg

DN

UP

© Copyright by Designer

Porch

FIRST FLOOR

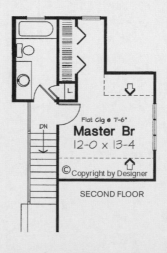

Flat Clg @ 7'-6"

Master Br
12-0 x 13-4

DN

© Copyright by Designer

SECOND FLOOR

FURN WH

Crawl
Space
Access

OPTIONAL LAYOUT

Price Code A   92458

Total Sq. Ft.: 1,343
Width: 50'
Depth: 60'
Bedrooms: 3
Baths: 2
Garage: 2-car

(For more plan info, visit www.familyhomeplans.com)

This lovely 1,343 sq. ft. front porch design is as versatile as it is attractive. It makes a perfect starter home or vacation home and lends itself to narrow lots, with a garage which may easily be reduced in size or omitted entirely. The angled entry opens into a spacious open plan including a dramatic vaulted family room lit by a large "Palladian" style window . The master suite is also vaulted, and includes a luxurious bath, walk-in closet and an inviting screened porch. The two remaining bedrooms share a hall bath and each features a walk-in closet. The washer and dryer are tucked conveniently in a laundry closet.

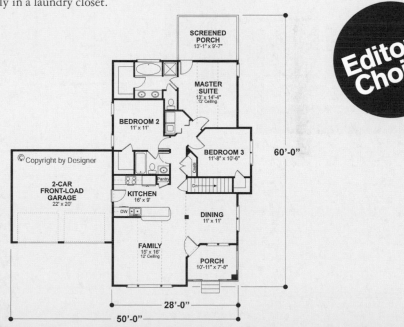

Editor's Choice

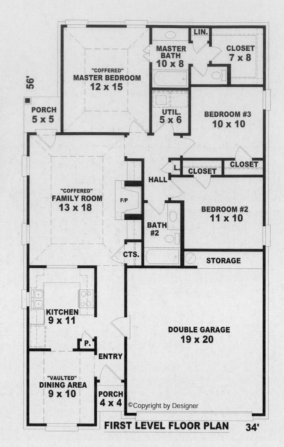

Price Code A 47001

Total Sq. Ft.: 1,363
Width: 34'
Depth: 56'
Bedrooms: 3
Baths: 2
Garage: 2-car

(For more plan info, visit www.familyhomeplans.com)

LIN.
MASTER BATH 10 x 8
CLOSET 7 x 8
"COFFERED" **MASTER BEDROOM 12 x 15**
56'
PORCH 5 x 5
UTIL. 5 x 6
BEDROOM #3 10 x 10
"COFFERED" **FAMILY ROOM 13 x 18**
F/P
HALL
CLOSET **CLOSET**
L.
BATH #2
BEDROOM #2 11 x 10
CTS.
STORAGE
KITCHEN 9 x 11
DOUBLE GARAGE 19 x 20
P.
ENTRY
"VAULTED" **DINING AREA 9 x 10**
PORCH 4 x 4
©Copyright by Designer
FIRST LEVEL FLOOR PLAN 34'

Price Code A 62115

Total Sq. Ft: 1,374
Main Level: 1,070'
Lower Level: 304'
Width: 40'-4"
Depth: 41'-6"
Bedrooms: 4
Baths: 2
Garage: none

(For more plan info, visit www.familyhomeplans.com)

BEDROOM 3 14'-10" X 11'-0"
LOFT 8' CEILING
8' LINE
BEDROOM / STORAGE 11'-0" X 7'-0"
DN
VAULTED CEILING
OPEN TO BELOW
4' WALL
SECOND FLOOR

40'-4"
SUPPLY ROOM
GRILLING PORCH 22'-6" X 8'-0"
CLEANING TABLE
BEDROOM 1 12'-0" X 11'-0"
PAN
KITCHEN 11'-8" X 11'-4"
DW
RG
REF
41'-6"
STACKED W/D
DINING 10'-6" X 11'-4"
VAULTED CEILING
BEDROOM 2 11'-0" X 11'-0"
UP
GREAT ROOM 22'-0" X 14'-4"
COVERED PORCH 18'-0" X 8'-0"
FIRST FLOOR

"Me" Space

A Place in Your Home to Call Your Own

When it comes to choosing home designs, many of us find ourselves doing little more than counting bedrooms, bathrooms and square footage, without considering an aspect of the home that might be most important of all - "me" space.

"Me" space, of course, is your personal get-away place within the home itself. It's a place to unwind from the pace of a hectic day. A place to reflect, refresh and regain your balance in life. "Me" spaces can be found just about anywhere in or around the home.

Some of the most popular "me" spaces are...

- soaking tubs
- master suite sitting areas
- window seats
- sunrooms and 3-season rooms
- dens or home libraries
- covered porches, decks and patios
- workshops or hobby rooms
- exercise rooms

The list could go on and on, but in any case, remember yourself with a "me" space—wherever it might be—as you select your new home's design.

Price Code A   94688

Total Sq. Ft.: 1,363
Width: 30'
Depth: 60'
Bedrooms: 3
Baths: 2
Garage: 2-car

(For more plan info, visit www.familyhomeplans.com)

Editor's Choice

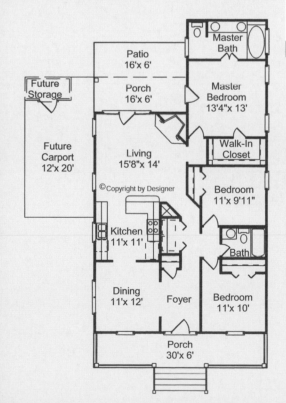

Patio 16'x 6'

Future Storage

Porch 16'x 6'

Master Bath

Master Bedroom 13'4"x 13'

Future Carport 12'x 20'

Living 15'8"x 14'

Walk-In Closet

©Copyright by Designer

Bedroom 11'x 9'11"

Kitchen 11'x 11'

Bath

Dining 11'x 12'

Foyer

Bedroom 11'x 10'

Porch 30'x 6'

Price Code A 24402

Total Sq. Ft.: 1,346
Bedrooms: 3
Baths: 2
Width: 46'-1"
Depth: 53'-1"
Garage: 1-car

(For more plan info, visit www.familyhomeplans.com)

All your preferences—amenities and architectural interest-are spread across one level and 1,346 sq. ft. Cathedral ceilings rise beautifully in both the living and master bedrooms. The dining room has great style plus an exterior deck for after-dinner drinks. The adjacent kitchen is expanded by a casual lunch counter. The master suite is enormously creative and private with personal deck entry, walk-in, and master bath with shower, tub, double vanities. Bedrooms #2 and #3 sleep close together and are across from their shared bath. Families appreciate the roomy garage.

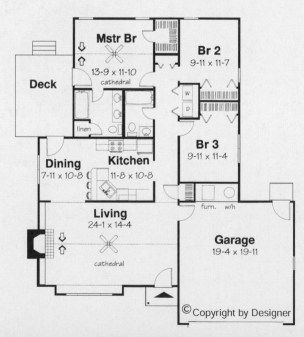

Price Code A 44012

Total Sq. Ft.: 1,372
Main Level: 690'
Upper Level: 682'
Bedrooms: 3
Baths: 2.25
Width: 50'
Depth: 30'
Garage: 2-car

(For more plan info, visit www.familyhomeplans.com)

Efficient use of space is the hallmark of this 1,372 sq. ft. 2-story home. Guests are greeted by immediate views of the living room, with bayed windows and a welcoming fireplace. To the rear, the dining room enjoys views to the outdoors and is situated for open interaction with the kitchen. A mid-level unfinished storage area, accessed on the stairway landing, allows ample space for keeping things in their place and out of the way. Upstairs, an angled central core provides access the master suite and secondary bedrooms.

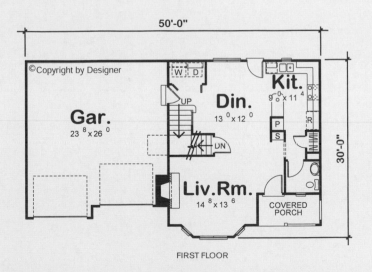

FIRST FLOOR

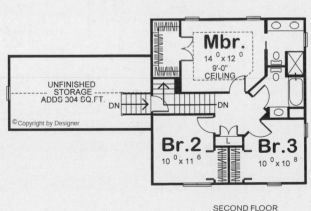

SECOND FLOOR

airy & open, inside and out

Contemporary lifestyles love this open-minded design.
The steep-pitched roof with the aura of an A-frame triggers vacation mode. Double porches with slender pillars interact beautifully with the great outdoors. Inside, a bounty of significantly sized windows and sleek doors with bright sidelights draw the natural light and magnify the view.

Interior

The interior layout—1,480 sq. ft.—opens to a spatially rich arrangement where each of two levels is endowed with its own large bedroom, and private full bath. A cathedral ceiling hovers over the family room with fireplace and open dining area. The country-style kitchen features a crowd-pleasing lunch counter. A nearby smaller bedroom can become a study. The master bedroom owns an enormous walk-in closet and full bath. Upstairs, the secondary bedroom slips easily into its own snug family room and convenient full bath. For an inspired overview, peer from the airy mezzanine into the family room.

Top and Bottom: Light, bright, airy spaces provide the perfect setting for casual dining at the kitchen's comfortable breakfast/lunch counter, or in the spacious dining area, with open views to the family room.

Price Code A   65001

Total Sq. Ft: 1,480
Main Level: 1,024'
Upper Level: 456'
Width 32'
Depth 40'
Bedrooms: 2
Baths: 2
Garage: none

(For more plan info, visit www.familyhomeplans.com)

4,40 X 3,60
14'-8" X 12'-0"

4,20 X 6,80
14'-0" X 22'-8"

4,40 X 3,60
14'-8" X 12'-0"

FIRST FLOOR

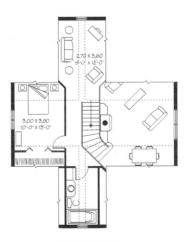

2,70 X 3,60
9'-0" X 12'-0"

3,00 X 3,90
10'-0" X 13'-0"

SECOND FLOOR

OPTIONAL LAYOUT

Deck

Br #2
10-10 x 11-10

Den/Br #3
10-0 x 11-10

Optional Door Location

Dining
11-0 x 11-2

Decor. Ceiling

Kit
10-0 x 11-2

Ldry

Railing

DN

Ret.

Pan.

Solid Wall w/ Opt. Door Location

Plant Ledge

Decor. Ceiling

Living Rm
14-10 x 17-0

10' clg

Garage
20-4 x 21-8

MBr #1
11-7 x 13-0

Seat

©Copyright by Designer

MAIN FLOOR

Price Code A   20156

Total Sq. Ft.: 1,359
Width: 58'
Depth: 34'-4"
Bedrooms: 3
Baths: 2
Garage: 2-Car

(For more plan info, visit www.familyhomeplans.com)

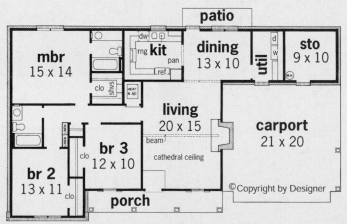

patio

mbr
15 x 14

kit

dw
rng
pan
ref

dining
13 x 10

util
d
w

sto
9 x 10

clo
shvs
HEAT & A/C

living
20 x 15

carport
21 x 20

br 3
12 x 10

beam

cathedral ceiling

br 2
13 x 11

clo

porch

©Copyright by Designer

Price Code A   65617

Total Sq. Ft.: 1,375
Width: 61'
Depth: 35'
Bedrooms: 3
Baths: 2
Garage: 2-car

(For more plan info, visit www.familyhomeplans.com)

Storage Space

Remember, effective storage space is more than counting the number of closets in a home, or having an unfinished space above the garage. With the temptation to put things "out of sight - out of mind," these areas are susceptible to clutter and inefficiency, unless equipped with proper shelving or storage systems.

In addition to closet or attic space, consider these storage options:

■ Space beneath staircases—perfect for built-in storage or even as office nook

■ Shallow cabinets in hallways or on stair landings

■ Cubby holes or lockers in the laundry room for backpacks, boots, hats, etc.

■ Bedroom window seats with built-in storage

■ Built-in "appliance garages" between the kitchen countertops and cabinets

■ Built-in cabinetry and display walls for collectibles, books, etc.

■ Third-car garage bay, finished as a storage room

■ Garage organization and storage systems

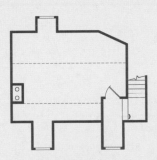

OPTIONAL LAYOUT

Price Code A   99673

Total Sq. Ft.: 1,380
Width: 48'
Depth: 43'-4"
Bedrooms: 3
Baths: 2
Garage: optional

(For more plan info, visit www.familyhomeplans.com)

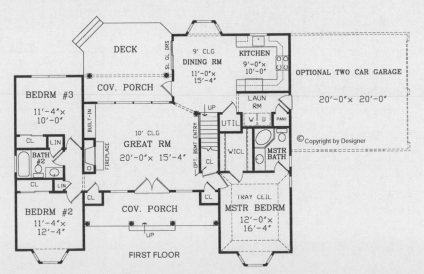

FIRST FLOOR

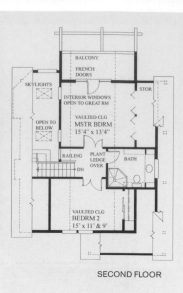

SECOND FLOOR

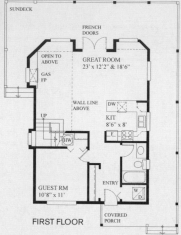

FIRST FLOOR

Price Code A 76012

Total Sq. Ft: 1,370
Main Level: 795'
Lower Level: 575'
Width: 36'
Depth: 46'-6"
Bedrooms: 3
Baths: 2
Garage: none

(For more plan info, visit www.familyhomeplans.com)

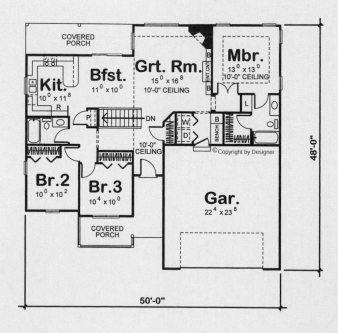

Price Code A 44014

Total Sq. Ft.: 1,381
Bedrooms: 3
Baths: 2
Width: 50'
Depth: 48'
Garage: 2-car

(For more plan info, visit www.familyhomeplans.com)

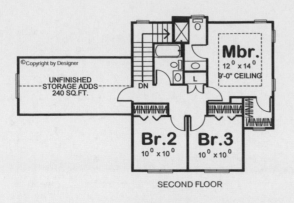

SECOND FLOOR

© Copyright by Designer

UNFINISHED STORAGE ADDS 240 SQ.FT.

Mbr. 12⁰ x 14⁰ 9'-0" CEILING

DN

L

Br.2 10⁰ x 10⁰

Br.3 10⁰ x 10⁰

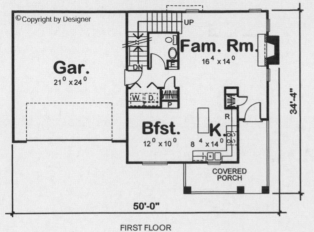

FIRST FLOOR

© Copyright by Designer

UP

Gar. 21⁰ x 24⁰

Fam. Rm. 16⁴ x 14⁰

DN

W. D. P.

Bfst. 12⁰ x 10⁰

K. 8⁴ x 14⁰

R

COVERED PORCH

50'-0"

34'-4"

smart design

Price Code A 44018

Total Sq. Ft.: 1,388
Main Level: 721'
Upper Level: 667'
Bedrooms: 3
Baths: 2.5
Width: 50'
Depth: 34' 4"
Garage: 2-car

(For more plan info, visit www.familyhomeplans.com)

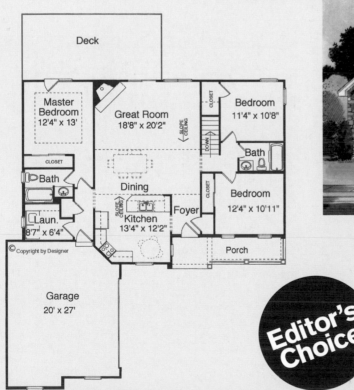

Deck

Master Bedroom 12'4" x 13'

Great Room 18'8" x 20'2"

SLOPE CEILING

CLOSET

Bath

CLOSET

Bedroom 11'4" x 10'8"

DOWN

Bath

Dining

SLOPE CEILING

Kitchen 13'4" x 12'2"

Foyer

CLOSET

Bedroom 12'4" x 10'11"

Laun. 8'7" x 6'4"

© Copyright by Designer

Porch

Garage 20' x 27'

Editor's Choice

Price Code A 50083

Total Sq. Ft.: 1,390
Width: 50'
Depth: 55'-8"
Bedrooms: 3
Baths: 2
Garage: 2-car

(For more plan info, visit www.familyhomeplans.com)

Price Code A   61008

Total Sq. Ft.: 1,387
Bedrooms: 2
Full Baths: 2
Width: 43'
Depth: 63'-10"
Garage: 2-car

(For more plan info, visit www.familyhomeplans.com)

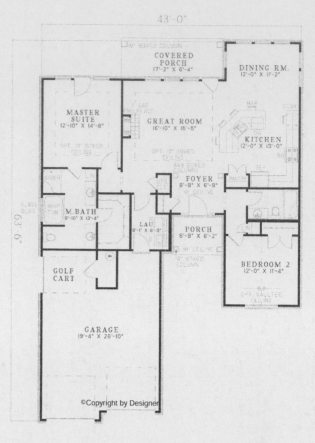

Price Code A   59002

Total Sq. Ft.: 1,400
Width: 54'
Depth: 47'
Bedrooms: 3
Baths: 2.5
Garage: 2-car

(For more plan info, visit www.familyhomeplans.com)

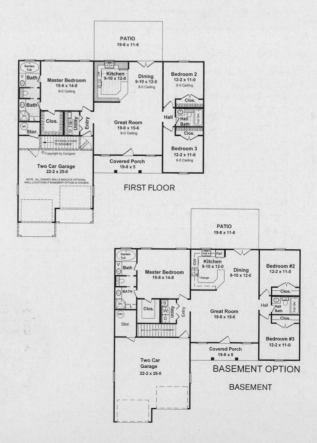

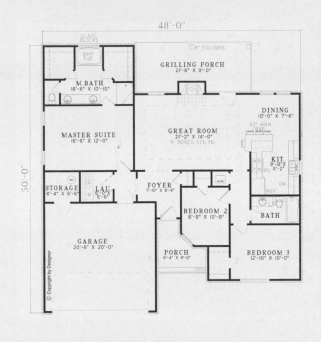

Price Code A 61296

Total Sq. Ft.: 1,407
Width: 48'
Depth: 50'
Bedrooms: 3
Baths: 2
Garage: 2-Car

(For more plan info, visit www.familyhomeplans.com)

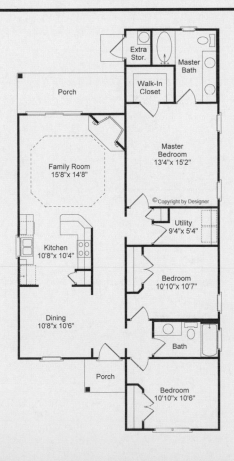

Price Code A 94690

Total Sq. Ft.: 1,401
Width: 30'
Depth: 59'-10"
Bedrooms: 3
Baths: 2
Garage: none

(For more plan info, visit www.familyhomeplans.com)

ORDER NOW! Phone: **1-800-235-5700** Online: **www.FamilyHomePlans.com** Order Code: **H6SSM**

Price Code A 55002

Total Sq. Ft.: 1,405
Width: 62'
Depth: 29'
Bedrooms: 3
Baths: 2
Garage: none

(For more plan info, visit www.familyhomeplans.com)

This three-bedroom leisure home is perfect for the family that spends casual time out of doors. An expansive wall of glass gives a spectacular view to the great room and accentuates the high vaulted ceilings throughout the design. The great room is also warmed by a hearth and is open to the dining room and L-shaped kitchen. A triangular snack bar graces the kitchen and provides space for casual meals. Bedrooms are split, with the master bedroom on the right side of the plan and family bedrooms on the left.

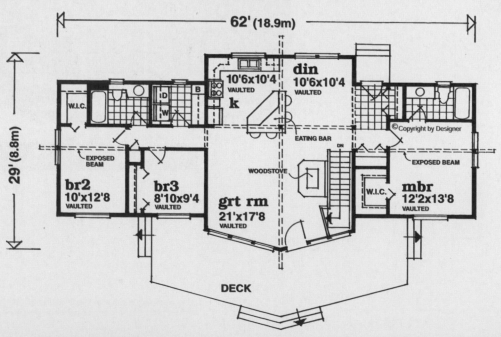

Price Code A | 44007

Total Sq. Ft.: 1,412
Bedrooms: 3
Baths: 1.5
Width: 42'
Depth: 55'-8"
Garage: 2-car

(For more plan info, visit www.familyhomeplans.com)

At just over 1,400 sq. ft., this compact home has plenty to offer. Sleeping areas are segregated, with the master bedroom enjoying privacy from two secondary bedrooms which are accessed through an alcove on the opposite side of the home. The ample great room opens to the kitchen and dining area. Both areas are flooded with natural light from large windows. A rear covered porch, accessed through the dining area, provides an outdoor living space that pleasantly accommodates entertaining or just quiet times to relax.

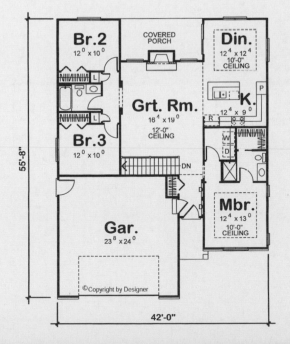

Editor's Choice

smart design

Price Code A 34601

Total Sq. Ft.: 1,415
Main Level: 1,007'
Upper Level: 408'
Bedrooms: 3
Baths: 2
Width 38'-4"
Depth: 36'
Garage: none

(For more plan info, visit www.familyhomeplans.com)

Double dormers and slender pillars across the front porch cinch the beauty of this country charmer. The interior with 1,415 sq. ft. is equally irresistible. A vaulted ceiling in the living room brings in the natural light. A great fireplace warms up the atmosphere. Large windows grace the dining room as it opens into the corner kitchen. Two secondary bedrooms meet on one side of the house and share a full bath complete with laundry facilities. The master bedroom has a walk-in closet, full bath, and the entire second floor all to itself. A nook created by one of the dormers is ideal for a comfy reading chair.

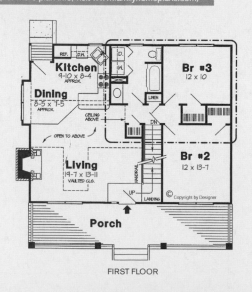

FIRST FLOOR

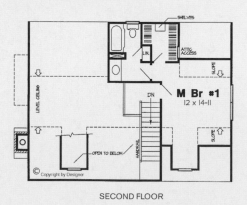

SECOND FLOOR

OPTIONAL LAYOUT

Outdoor Living Areas

Smart Spaces That Bring the Outdoors In—and the Indoors Out

Smart spaces aren't always limited to the inside of the home. As you may well know, outdoor living areas, such as decks, porches and patios are often the most enjoyable spots for entertaining, pursuing pastimes, or just taking it easy.

If you're not the "outdoorsy" type, however, you may prefer a space that provides a sense of the great outdoors from beneath the shelter of your home's roof. Sunrooms and 3-season rooms (unheated sunrooms), are cheerful, versatile spaces that offer an abundance of natural light and expansive views to the outside from within the home itself.

Whether it's a deck, patio or 3-season room, be mindful of how outdoor living spaces can make even the smallest square footage live larger.

Consider the following to enhance the ambiance of your outdoor living areas:

■ Low-maintenance composite decking material
■ Artistic stone or brickwork
■ Fire pits or portable fireplaces
■ Propane patio heaters
■ Fountains or water sculptures
■ Weatherproof music systems
■ Mood lighting

Price Code A   68226

Total Sq. Ft.: 1,416
Width: 49'
Depth: 58'
Bedrooms: 3
Baths: 2
Garage: 2-car

(For more plan info, visit www.familyhomeplans.com)

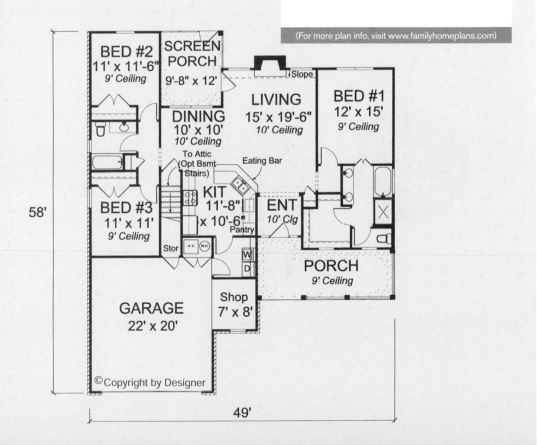

Price Code A 92459

Total Sq. Ft.: 1,420
Width: 50'
Depth: 57'-4"
Bedrooms: 3
Baths: 2
Garage: Optional 2-car

(For more plan info, visit www.familyhomeplans.com)

This inviting 1,420 sq. ft. front porch design is simply irresistible. It makes a perfect starter home or vacation home and lends itself to narrow lots, with its optional garage. The full-width front porch is highlighted by the dramatic radiused entry. The enormous vaulted family room is open to both the dining room and kitchen. The master suite is also vaulted, and includes a luxurious bath, walk-in closet and a striking bow window. The two remaining bedrooms share a hall bath with bedroom 2 offering direct bath access.

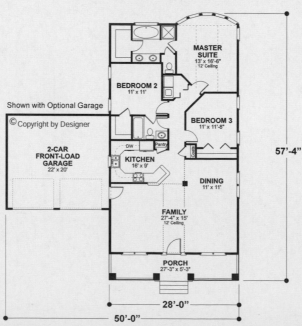

Shown with Optional Garage

© Copyright by Designer

MASTER SUITE
13' x 16'-6"
12' Ceiling

BEDROOM 2
11' x 11'

BEDROOM 3
11' x 11'-8"

2-CAR FRONT-LOAD GARAGE
22' x 20'

DW

Pantry

KITCHEN
16' x 9'

DINING
11' x 11'

FAMILY
27'-4" x 15'
12' Ceiling

PORCH
27'-3" x 5'-3"

57'-4"

28'-0"

50'-0"

Price Code A 65418

Total Sq. Ft.: 1,432
Main Level: 756'
Upper Level: 676'
Width 38'-8"
Depth 32'
Bedrooms: 3
Baths: 1.75
Garage: 1-car

(For more plan info, visit www.familyhomeplans.com)

A front porch and twin gables add charm to this compact two-story home. Inside, all main floor living areas flow together without interruption. A closed foyer helps to maintain energy efficiency and an adjacent bath hides a washer and dryer. The one car garage conveniently accesses the kitchen for short trips inside with groceries. Upstairs, all three bedrooms share a full bath, complete with corner tub and shower.

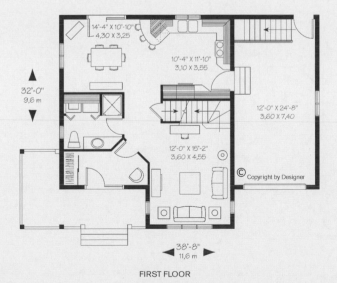

FIRST FLOOR

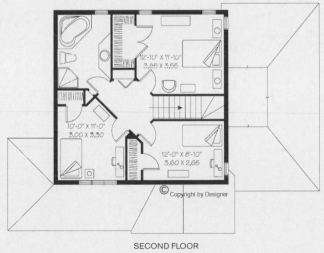

SECOND FLOOR

Price Code A 24711

Total Sq. Ft.: 1,434
Main Level: 1,018'
Upper Level: 416'
Width 73'
Depth 36'
Bedrooms: 3
Baths: 2
Garage: 2-car

(For more plan info, visit www.family homeplans.com)

Get the best of both worlds-a country porch, double front dormers, and 1,434 sq. ft. layout that spoils you with space. The living area reaches high with a soaring ceiling, cozy fireplace, too. It's all open to the kitchen for big-family comfort. A screened porch connects the kitchen/living room to the garage. Bedrooms #2 and #3 are meant to please the kids—roomy closets, window views and nearby full bath with laundry area. The upstairs with balcony overlook is made for mom and dad. The master bedroom features dormer sitting area, a walk-in with shelves, bright master bath, plus attic access.

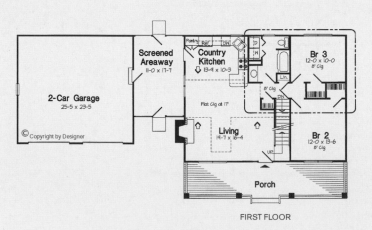

FIRST FLOOR

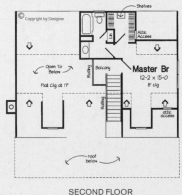

SECOND FLOOR

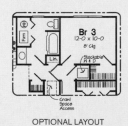

OPTIONAL LAYOUT

Price Code A 50098

Total Sq. Ft.: 1,442
Width 52'-8"
Depth 45'
Bedrooms: 3
Baths: 2
Garage: 2-car

(For more plan info, visit www.familyhomeplans.com)

This delightful home offers space saving convenience and functional living space. The dining area and living room combine to create a great room that is decorated by a gas fireplace and 11'-6" ceiling height, The fully equipped kitchen offers a counter with seating, dishwasher, and built-in microwave. Split bedrooms offer privacy to the master suite, which enjoys a 9' ceiling height, double bowl vanity and compartmented bath. Walk-in closets in the master bedroom and at the garage entry offer great storage. A full basement with access to the rear yard offers the option to expand the square footage of this charming home.

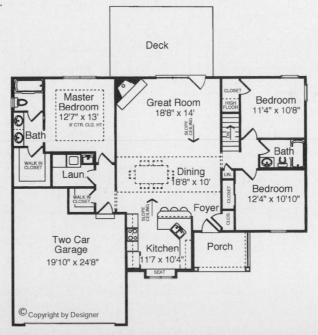

Editor's Choice

Price Code A 97113

Total Finished Sq. Ft.: 1,416
Bedrooms: 3
Full Baths: 2
Garage: 2-car
Width: 48'
Depth: 55'-4"

(For more plan info, visit www.familyhomeplans.com)

In the corner of this home's great room, you'll find a warming direct vent fireplace, ready to add a touch of elegance to any occasion. The dining room, with its cathedral ceiling, is connected to a kitchen with plenty of counter space. Each of the three bedrooms is located right next to a full bath. This home is designed with a basement foundation.

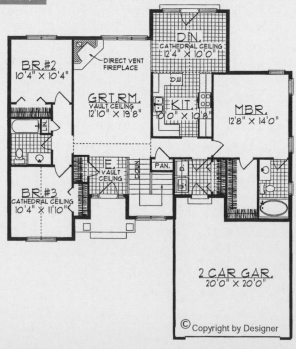

Making Smaller Homes Live Larger

Solutions and Illusions to Enlarge Your Living Space

Smaller homes can feel significantly larger with a bit of attention to the following:

COLOR CHOICES

Select lighter, brighter, cooler colors to visually enlarge smaller rooms. Consult an expert to determine the best choices in tones, shades and sheens.

STORAGE SOLUTIONS

Think beyond closets and unfinished storage areas. Use your creative eye to find nooks and crannies throughout the home that will accommodate built-in cabinets, cubby holes and shelving.

OUTDOOR LIVING AREAS

Take advantage of the additional space offered by decks, patios, porches, 3-season rooms and sun-rooms. Accessorize these areas to be as pleasing and functional as interior rooms.

PROPERLY SIZED FURNISHINGS

Be mindful of the visual impact of your furnishings. Bulky, overstuffed furniture - as opposed to sleeker, streamlined pieces - can tend to make rooms feel smaller.

INTERIOR LIGHTING

Eliminate dark spots with appropriate mood and task lighting. Make every effort to optimize the use of natural light throughout the home, as well as views to the outside.

Price Code A   74001

Total Sq. Ft.: 1,428
Width: 34'
Depth: 42'
Bedrooms: 3
Baths: 2

(For more plan info, visit www.familyhomeplans.com)

Master Br
13-8 x 14
9-0 Ceiling

Bath

Kitchen
13-8 x 12
Sloped Ceiling

Open To Great Room

Dining Area

Br 2
13-8 x 10-1
9-0 Ceiling

Bath

Great Rm
13-8 x 29-4

Optional Fireplace

Living Area
Sloped Ceiling

Den/Br 3
13-8 x 10-8
9-0 Ceiling

Foyer

34'-0"   2'-4"

42'-0"

6'-0"

Front Porch
28 x 6

Price Code A 62131

Total Sq. Ft.: 1,451
Main Level: 868'
Upper Level: 583'
Width: 37'-8"
Depth: 38'-4"
Bedrooms: 3
Baths: 2
Garage: none

(For more plan info, visit www.familyhomeplans.com)

Summertime was always a much anticipated time especially since their new cabin was complete. Set within many acres of a heavily wooded area, the rush of a nearby creek was the most coveted place they knew. As mom and dad fished upstream the kids splashed around on the flat rocks and tiny streams catching tadpoles just the same. Wonderful memories like these are just the beginning of a lifetime full of fun-filled summers and peaceful multi-colored autumn weekends...at Brushy Creek, their most favorite place under the sun.

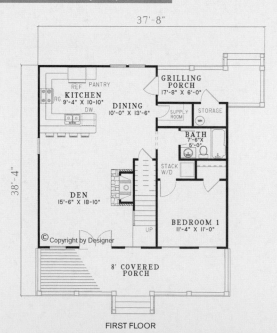

FIRST FLOOR

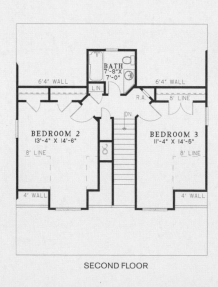

SECOND FLOOR

Price Code A | **82009**

Total Sq. Ft.: 1,452
Width: 48'
Depth: 63'-4"
Bedrooms: 3
Baths: 2
Garage: 2-car

(For more plan info, visit www.familyhomeplans.com)

If you can picture yourself hosting an elegant dinner party surrounded by friends and family, then step into this home. After greeting guests on the covered porch, guide them into the spacious great room. Here, mingling can begin possibly with drinks around the romantic fireplace. Conveniently accessible to the kitchen, you can slip away to check on dinner. A connecting breakfast room can serve as more space. A door opening to a rear grilling porch allows you to prepare dinner with ease. When all the excitement is over, enjoy the privacy of your whirlpool bath.

charming country ranch

There's no reason that a modest, affordable ranch style design can't be adorable and fabulous to live in as well. This lovely home was designed to be all that and more. An open floor plan, with windows in all directions, makes the entire living area feel larger than it is. An optional attached garage is included on the blueprints - or as part of the optional walk-out basement plan as shown.

Left and Bottom: The great room, dining room, kitchen and breakfast area flow together freely to provide comfortable interaction between all living areas. This homeowner relocated the fireplace to the rear wall of the great room and added further definition to the dining area by adding a partial wall. Below: A walk out basement makes the most of this home's sloped building site.

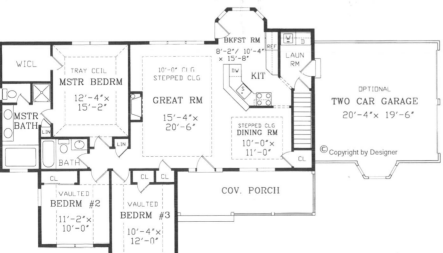

Price Code A   69505

Total Sq. Ft.: 1,489
Width: 72'-3"
Depth: 44'-4"
Bedrooms: 3
Baths: 2
Garage: optional

(For more plan info, visit www.familyhomeplans.com)

Price Code A   55031

Total Sq. Ft.: 1,455
Width: 51'
Depth: 38'
Bedrooms: 3
Baths: 2
Garage: none

(For more plan info, visit www.familyhomeplans.com)

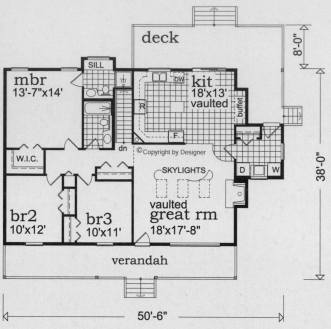

deck

mbr
13'-7"x14'

SILL

kit
18'x13'
vaulted

W.I.C.

8'-0"

buffet

dn

©Copyright by Designer

D   W

38'-0"

SKYLIGHTS

br2
10'x12'

br3
10'x11'

vaulted
great rm
18'x17'-8"

verandah

50'-6"

Price Code A   47005

Total Sq. Ft.: 1,437
Width: 40'
Depth: 48'
Bedrooms: 3
Baths: 2
Garage: none

(For more plan info, visit www.familyhomeplans.com)

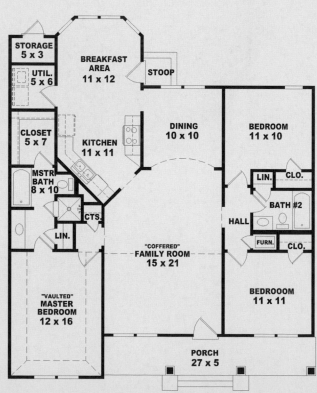

STORAGE
5 x 3

BREAKFAST
AREA
11 x 12

STOOP

UTIL.
5 x 6

CLOSET
5 x 7

KITCHEN
11 x 11

DINING
10 x 10

BEDROOM
11 x 10

LIN.   CLO.

MSTR
BATH
8 x 10

BATH #2

CTS.

HALL

LIN.

FURN.   CLO.

"COFFERED"
FAMILY ROOM
15 x 21

"VAULTED"
MASTER
BEDROOM
12 x 16

BEDROOOM
11 x 11

PORCH
27 x 5

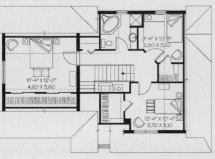

SECOND FLOOR

FIRST FLOOR

◄— 40'-0" —►
12,0 m

Price Code A   65487

Total Sq. Ft.: 1,457
Main Level: 680'
Upper Level: 777'
Width 40'
Depth 30'
Bedrooms: 3
Baths: 2
Garage: 1-car

(For more plan info, visit www.familyhomeplans.com)

Price Code A   96516

Total Sq. Ft.: 1,458
Width: 67'
Depth: 40'
Bedrooms: 3
Baths: 2
Garage: Optional 2-car

(For more plan info, visit www.familyhomeplans.com)

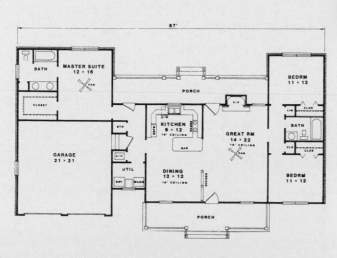

smart design

Price Code A 93165

Total Finished Sq. Ft.: 1,472
Width: 48'
Depth: 56'-4"
Bedrooms: 3
Baths: 2
Garage: 2-car

(For more plan info, visit www.familyhomeplans.com)

Editor's Choice

This brick and siding ranch has much to offer. The foyer leads into the Great room with cathedral ceilings and direct vent corner gas fireplace. There are arched pass-throughs to the kitchen. The kitchen has all of the amenities including plenty of cupboard and counter space. The adjoining dining area has large windows and a glass door leading to the backyard and a screen porch. The private master suite has a large walk-in closet and full bath with corner whirlpool tub and free standing shower. Two more bedrooms can be found off the Great room. Both have large closets and share a full bath. From the two car garage, you will enter into the main floor laundry with a large closet for storage. (This is not to be built within a 20 mile radius of Iowa city, Iowa.)

The Right Home for the Right Site

Tips to Consider when Matching the Plan to the Land

SIZES AND SHAPES

Building sites come in an infinite variety of sizes and shapes. As you narrow your selection of home designs, be mindful of the homes' depths and widths as compared with the dimensions of the lot. Consider local covenants and codes as they relate to side yards and setbacks.

UPS AND DOWNS

In addition to the size and shape of the lot, consider its slope(s) and choose a home design accordingly. If the lot slopes from one side to the other, position the home with the garage on the higher elevation. If the lot slopes front to back, consider modifications to create a walk-out basement.

FRONT OR SIDE LOAD GARAGE?

If you prefer a side load garage, make sure the lot is accommodating, either in its width, or its orientation to a side street. Remember, in most cases, modifications can be made to change any home design from front load to a side load, or vise versa.

Price Code A   97137

Total Finished Sq. Ft.: 1,461
Width: 56'
Depth: 42'
Bedrooms: 3
Full Baths: 2
Garage: 2-car

(For more plan info, visit www.familyhomeplans.com)

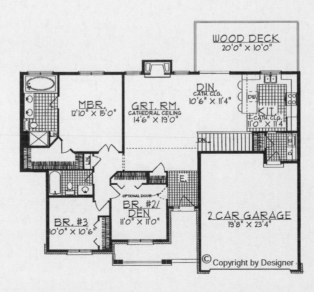

Price Code A 24706

Total Sq. Ft.: 1,407
Main Level: 1,035'
Upper Level: 435'
Width: 35'
Depth: 42'
Bedrooms: 3
Baths: 2
Garage: none

(For more plan info, visit www.familyhomeplans.com)

Victorian flair dazzles the exterior. The company-loving front porch and roof dormer blossom with charm. A modern approach inspires the interior. Porch entry delivers a quaint foyer and living room. A side entry gives quick access to the utility room, a central foyer and the spacious kitchen. The breakfast room brims with a vaulted ceiling, natural light and deck entry. Bedroom #2, with deck view, shares a bath with front-facing Bedroom #3. Here, the cream rises to the top as the master bedroom and master bath own the entire second story. Really dreamy!

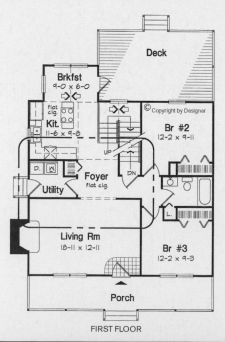

FIRST FLOOR

- Deck
- Brkfst 9-0 x 6-0
- Kit. 11-6 x 9-8
- Br #2 12-2 x 9-11
- Foyer flat clg.
- Utility
- Living Rm 18-11 x 12-11
- Br #3 12-2 x 9-3
- Porch
- UP
- DN
- Copyright by Designer

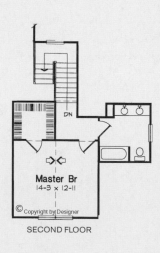

SECOND FLOOR

- Master Br 14-3 x 12-11
- DN
- Copyright by Designer

Alternate Foundation Plan

OPTIONAL LAYOUT

- crawl access
- furn.
- UP
- w/h

And the band plays on... Dixieland, jazz, blues, beach music and
torch songs. The musicians are gathered on the front porch of the Myrtle Grove
making wonderful music for the annual neighborhood picnic. The neighbors
and all their friends rejoice in the first day of summer each year with this
renewing of friendships - both young and old.

Price Code A   86105

Total Sq. Ft: 2,039
Main Level: 1,473'
Upper Level: 566'
Width: 35'-8"
Depth: 86'
Bedrooms: 3
Baths: 2
Garage: 2-car

(For more plan info, visit www.familyhomeplans.com)

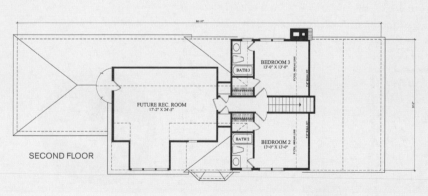

SECOND FLOOR

FIRST FLOOR

Price Code A 55028

Total Sq. Ft.: 1,479
Main Level: 995'
Upper Level: 484'
Width: 38'
Depth: 44'
Bedrooms: 3
Baths: 2.5
Garage: none

(For more plan info, visit www.familyhomeplans.com)

This home's rustic character is defined by cedar lattice, covered columned porches, exposed rafters and multi-pane, double-hung windows. The great room/dining room combination is reached through double doors off the veranda and features a fireplace towering two stories to the lofty ceiling. A U-shaped kitchen contains an angled snack counter that serves this area and loads of space for a breakfast table—or use the handy side porch for alfresco dining. To the rear resides the master bedroom with a full bath and double doors to the veranda. An additional half-bath sits just beyond the laundry room. Upstairs, two family bedrooms and a full bath finish the plan.

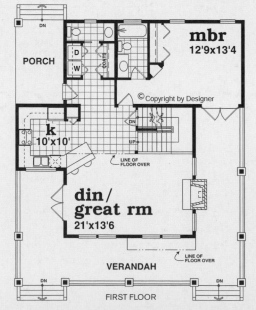

PORCH

DN

D
W

mbr
12'9x13'4

© Copyright by Designer

k
10'x10'

DN
UP

LINE OF
FLOOR OVER

din/
great rm
21'x13'6

LINE OF
FLOOR OVER

VERANDAH

DN   DN

FIRST FLOOR

br3
10'4x10'2

br2
10'4x11'2

DN

RAILING

OPEN TO
GREAT ROOM
BELOW

PLANT LEDGE

SECOND FLOOR

Editor's Choice

Indoor air quality is as essential to your household's well being as proper diet and exercise.

healthy and safe homes

When we think about "home," most of us imagine a place of refuge—a place, where at the end of the day, we and our loved ones are safe and secure, protected from whatever might be lurking on the outside. Ironically, there is something that lurks on the inside of many homes that makes them anything but safe havens—toxic indoor air.

The quality of indoor air has become a more important issue over recent years, as newly built homes have become "tighter" to gain energy efficiency. By nature, older homes "breathe," allowing fresh air inside through tiny cracks and crevices. A tighter home, unless equipped with a special air exchange system, allows little, if any, fresh air inside. As a result, anything that goes into the air, stays in the air: fumes from paints, finishes and cleaning products; allergens such as mold spores and dust; even carbon monoxide and radon—today's second leading cause of lung cancer.

Fortunately, there are simple and practical ways to protect the quality of air inside your home, and you'll discover a number of them throughout the coming pages. There is plenty more to learn, however, and one of the best resources available is the Partnership for Advancing Technology in Housing (PATH). You can find an abundance of helpful tips and information on making your home healthy and safe by visiting their web site at www.pathnet.org/homeowners.

Price Code A 50099

Total Sq. Ft.: 1,483
Width: 70'-2"
Depth: 50'-8"
Bedrooms: 3
Full Baths: 2
Garage: 2-car

(For more plan info, visit www.familyhomeplans.com)

Designed to provide private spaces for each household member, this three bedroom ranch home offers a stylish exterior with brick, stone, cedar shakes, and an inviting covered porch. The interior features a spacious great room, U-shaped kitchen with counter seating and adjacent dining area. The ceiling throughout this space slopes to 13' adding a dramatic effect. The master bedroom suite enjoys a private bath with double bowl vanity; and the walkout basement shows a rec room with wet bar and a fourth bedroom and bath.

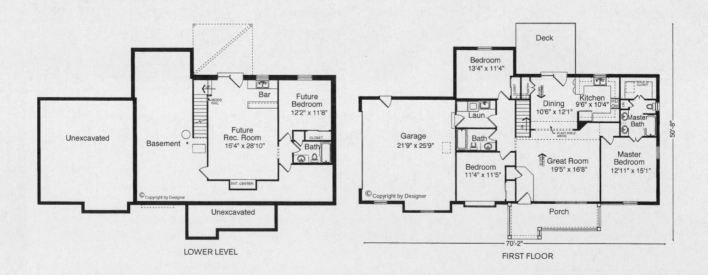

LOWER LEVEL

FIRST FLOOR

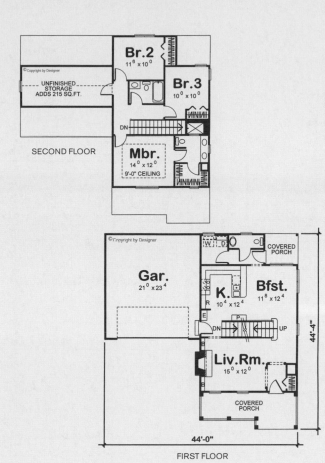

SECOND FLOOR

Br.2
11⁶ x 10⁰

Br.3
10⁰ x 10⁰

©Copyright by Designer

UNFINISHED STORAGE ADDS 215 SQ.FT.

DN

Mbr.
14⁰ x 12⁰
9'-0" CEILING

©Copyright by Designer

Gar.
21⁰ x 23⁴

K.
10⁴ x 12⁴

Bfst.
11⁸ x 12⁴

COVERED PORCH

W D

DN UP

Liv.Rm.
15⁰ x 12⁰

COVERED PORCH

44'-4"

44'-0"

FIRST FLOOR

Price Code A   44017

Total Sq. Ft.: 1,492
Main Level: 762'
Upper Level: 730'
Width: 44'
Depth: 44'-4"
Bedrooms: 3
Baths: 2.25
Garage: 2-car

(For more plan info, visit www.familyhomeplans.com)

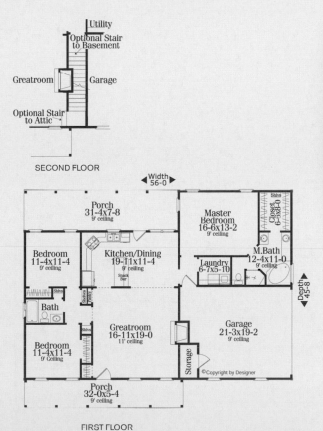

Utility

Optional Stair to Basement

Greatroom   Garage

Optional Stair to Attic

SECOND FLOOR

Width 56-0

Porch
31-4x7-8
9' ceiling

Master Bedroom
16-6x13-2
9' ceiling

Closet
6-5x8-0
Shlvs

Bedroom
11-4x11-4
9' ceiling

Kitchen/Dining
19-11x11-4
9' ceiling

M.Bath
12-4x11-0
9' ceiling

Laundry
6-7x5-10

Snack Bar

Bath

Greatroom
16-11x19-0
11' ceiling

Garage
21-3x19-2
9' ceiling

Bedroom
11-4x11-4
9' Ceiling

Storage

Depth 45-8

Porch
32-0x5-4
9' ceiling

©Copyright by Designer

FIRST FLOOR

Price Code A   40026

Total Sq. Ft.: 1,492
Width: 56'
Depth: 45'-8"
Bedrooms: 3
Baths: 2
Garage: 2-car
Foundation: Slab, Crawlspace, Basement

(For more plan info, visit www.familyhomeplans.com)

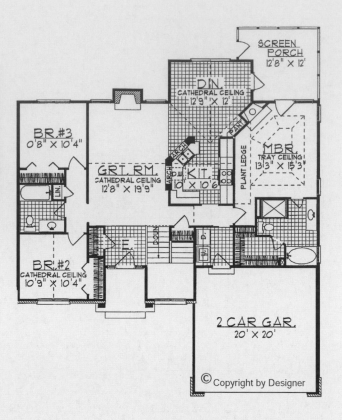

Price Code A 99106

Total Finished Sq. Ft.: 1,495
Width: 48'
Depth: 58'-8"
Bedrooms: 3
Full Baths: 2
Garage: 2-car

(For more plan info, visit www.familyhomeplans.com)

Price Code A 50081

Total Finished Sq. Ft.: 1,498
Width: 66'-4"
Depth: 44'-10"
Bedrooms: 3
Full Baths: 2
Garage: 2-car

(For more plan info, visit www.familyhomeplans.com)

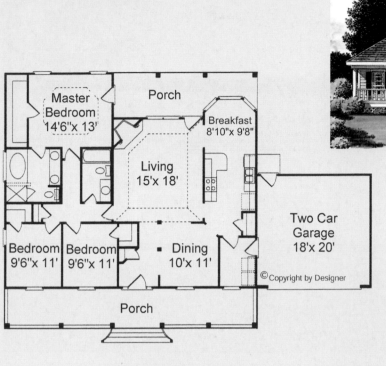

Master Bedroom 14'6"x 13'

Porch

Breakfast 8'10"x 9'8"

Living 15'x 18'

Two Car Garage 18'x 20'

Bedroom 9'6"x 11'

Bedroom 9'6"x 11'

Dining 10'x 11'

© Copyright by Designer

Porch

Price Code A 94517

Total Sq. Ft.: 1,500
Width: 64'
Depth: 45'
Bedrooms: 3
Baths: 2
Garage: 2

(For more plan info, visit www.familyhomeplans.com)

Editor's Choice

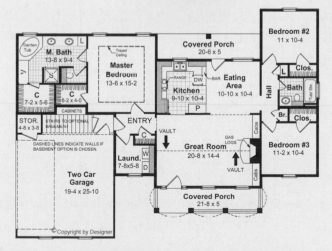

M. Bath 13-8 x 9-4

Master Bedroom 13-6 x 15-2

Trayed Ceiling

Covered Porch 20-6 x 5

Bedroom #2 11 x 10-4

Clos.

C 7-2 x 5-6

C 6-2 x 4-0

RANGE DW BAR

Kitchen 9-10 x 10-4

Eating Area 10-10 x 10-4

Hall

Bath

STOR. 4-8 x 3-8

STAIRS TO OPTIONAL BASEMENT

CABINETS

ENTRY

P

Br. Clos.

DASHED LINES INDICATE WALLS IF BASEMENT OPTION IS CHOSEN.

C

VAULT

Great Room 20-8 x 14-4

GAS LOGS

Bedroom #3 11-2 x 10-4

Two Car Garage 19-4 x 25-10

Laund. 7-8x5-8

W D

VAULT

© Copyright by Designer

Covered Porch 21-8 x 5

Price Code A 59050

Total Sq. Ft.: 1,500
Width: 61'
Depth: 47'-4"
Bedrooms: 3
Baths: 2
Garage: 2-car

(For more plan info, visit www.familyhomeplans.com)

ORDER NOW! Phone: **1-800-235-5700** Online: **www.FamilyHomePlans.com** Order Code: **H6SSM**

Price Code B   59146

Total Sq. Ft.: 1,509
Width: 61'
Depth: 47'-4"
Bedrooms: 3
Bath: 2
Garage: 2-car

(For more plan info, visit www.familyhomeplans.com)

Expansive Master Bedroom. This home provides a very functional split-floor plan layout with many of the features that your family desires. Expansive master bedroom / bath with trayed ceiling and plenty of storage space in the his and her walk-in closets. Large great room with vaulted ceiling and gas log fireplace. Front and rear covered porches. Laundry Room. Open kitchen layout with plenty of counter space for that growing family. Basement foundation option. Great value with a wide variety of innovative features. Make this your home today!

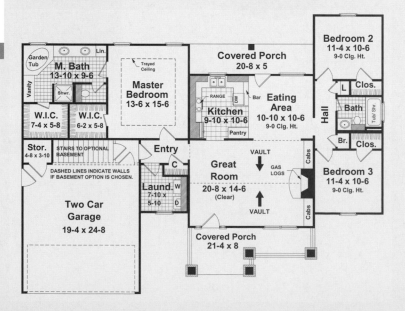

Moisture and Mold Prevention and Control Tips

Molds are part of the natural environment. Outdoors, molds break down dead organic matter such as fallen leaves and dead trees, but indoors, mold growth should be avoided. Molds produce allergens (substances that can cause allergic reactions), irritants, and in some cases, potentially toxic substances (mycotoxins).

Mold may begin growing indoors when mold spores land on surfaces that are wet. There are many types of mold, and none of them will grow without water or moisture.

■ Moisture control is the key to mold control, so when water leaks or spills occur indoors - ACT QUICKLY. If wet or damp materials or areas are dried 24-48 hours after a leak or spill happens, in most cases mold will not grow.

■ Clean and repair roof gutters regularly.

■ Make sure the ground slopes away from the building foundation, so that water does not enter or collect around the foundation.

■ Keep air conditioning drip pans clean and the drain lines unobstructed and flowing properly.

■ Keep indoor humidity low. If possible, keep indoor humidity below 60 percent (ideally between 30 and 50 percent) relative humidity

■ Increase ventilation or air movement by opening doors and/or windows, when practical. Use fans as needed.

■ Cover cold surfaces, such as cold water pipes, with insulation.

Courtesy of the Partnership for Advancing Technology in Housing (PATH) www.pathnet.org/homeowners

Price Code B   40027

Total Sq. Ft.: 1,501
Width: 52'-8"
Depth: 59'-10"
Bedrooms: 3
Baths: 2
Garage: 2-car

(For more plan info, visit www.familyhomeplans.com)

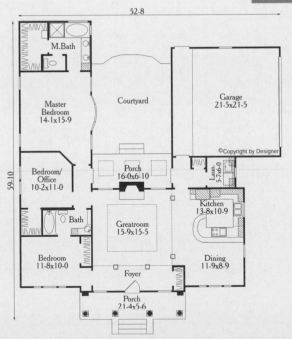

FIRST FLOOR

SECOND FLOOR

Price Code B 93130

Total Sq. Ft.: 1,508
Main Level: 1,508'
Bedrooms: 3
Baths: 2
Width: 52'
Depth: 44'
Garage: 2-car

(For more plan info, visit www.familyhomeplans.com)

This home's gracious foyer has a practical side, with a tiled floor for easy cleanup. A vaulted living room sits beside the stairs, and flows into an elegant corner dining room. The kitchen's pantry and U-shaped counters greatly aid with storage issues. A private full bath and walk-in closet serve the spacious master bedroom, while two secondary bedrooms share a tiled hall bath.

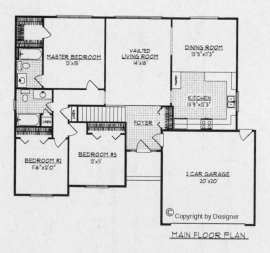

MAIN FLOOR PLAN

Price Code B   50038

Total Sq. Ft.: 1,509
Width: 59'-4"
Depth: 46'-4"
Bedrooms: 3
Baths: 2
Garage: 2-car

(For more plan info, visit www.familyhomeplans.com)

Siding and stone with an arched window and cedar siding create a charming exterior on this one level home. A sloped ceiling in the great room rises 2½ feet above the standard 8 foot ceiling height while a grand opening between the great room and dining area visually expands the living space. A spacious kitchen with an abundance of counter space, a pantry and snack bar create a delightful place to prepare meals. The master bedroom enjoys a private bath with double bowl vanity and large walk-in closet. Two additional bedrooms and a full basement complete this delightful home.

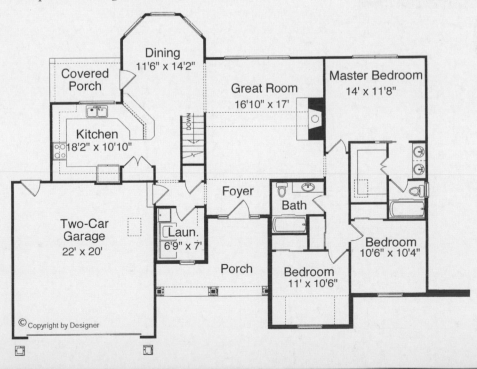

Price Code B 94691

Total Sq. Ft.: 1,510
Width: 38'
Depth: 58'-6"
Bedrooms: 3
Baths: 2
Garage: none

(For more plan info, visit www.familyhomeplans.com)

This 1,510 square foot home is great for a growing family. The facade of the home incorporates low-maintenance vinyl siding and roof gables to provide a homey feel at an affordable cost. Entering the foyer, on the left is a dining room which opens to the kitchen. The kitchen includes an island counter and a breakfast bar. The dining and kitchen both feature tiled floors. The living room includes a tray ceiling and corner fireplace. The living room accesses the rear porch by means of sliding glass doors. The rear porch also features extra storage. To the right of the foyer is a hallway that accesses two bedrooms and a bathroom, which is shared by the two bedrooms. To the right of the living room is a hallway, which accesses the master bedroom. The master bath features his-her walk-in closets, garden tub, standing shower, & dual vanities.

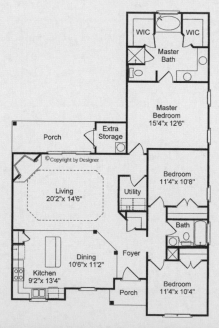

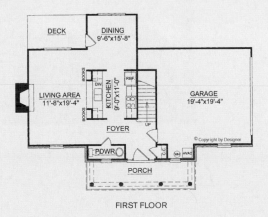

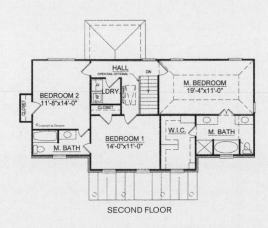

Price Code B 72019

Total Sq. Ft.: 1,515
Main Level: 590'
Upper Level: 925'
Width: 48'
Depth: 30'
Bedrooms: 3
Baths: 2.5
Garage: 2-car

(For more plan info, visit www.familyhomeplans.com)

A covered porch welcomes visitors to this lovely Colonial home. The width of the house creates the look of a much larger residence than its 1,515 square feet. In spite of its conservative size overall however, generously dimensioned rooms and closets, plus a 2-car garage make this home a truly functional plan for a growing family.

FIRST FLOOR

SECOND FLOOR

Price Code B   82026

Total Sq. Ft.: 1,525
Width: 51'-6"
Depth: 49'-10"
Bedrooms: 3
Baths: 2
Garage: 2-car

(For more plan info, visit www.familyhomeplans.com)

Numerous amenities within this traditional home create an attractive design. The great room, complete with fireplace, is the central entertaining area of your home. In your spacious kitchen you will be able to prepare anything your guests desire. Complete with French door access to the great room, you'll find a rear grilling porch—just right for summer barbecues. A convenient computer nook just off the kitchen allows you to monitor the children's activity. You may choose to spend a day lounging in your private master suite complete with whirlpool tub, separate shower and 'his and her' walk-in closets.

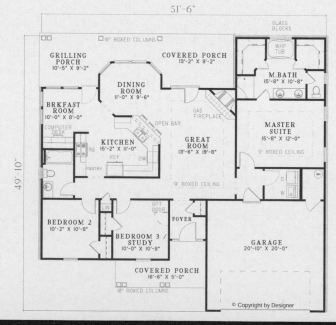

REAR EXTERIOR

Price Code B 65495

Total Sq. Ft.: 1,530
Main Level: 810'
Upper Level: 720'
Width 27'-8"
Depth 32'
Bedrooms: 3
Baths: 2
Garage: none

(For more plan info, visit www.familyhomeplans.com)

A welcoming front porch wraps the front corner of this efficiently designed two-story. At only 1,530 sq. ft., this home provides easy interaction between all areas on the main floor. The closed foyer helps to maintain the inside air temperature and includes a coat closet and sitting area. A snack bar serves casual meals in the kitchen and dining area. Upstairs, all three bedrooms share a full bath, complete with corner tub and shower.

FIRST FLOOR

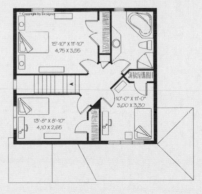

SECOND FLOOR

Price Code B   20083

Total Sq. Ft.: 1,575
Width: 60'
Depth: 42'-10"
Bedrooms: 3
Baths: 2
Garage: 2-car

(For more plan info, visit www.familyhomeplans.com)

One-Level Living with a Twist.

Here's an inviting home with a distinctive difference. Active living areas are wide-open and centrally located. From the foyer, you'll enjoy a full view of the spacious dining, living, and kitchen areas in one sweeping glance. You can even see the deck adjoining the breakfast room. The difference in this house lies in the layout of the bedrooms. Each is a private retreat, away from active areas. The master suite at the rear of the house features a full bath with double sinks. Two additional bedrooms, off in their own wing, share a full bath. This home is designed with basement, slab, and crawlspace foundation options.

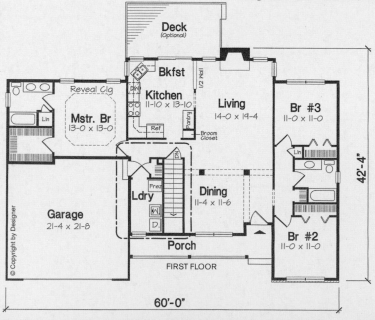

FIRST FLOOR

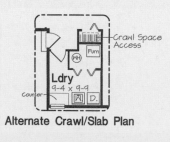

Alternate Crawl/Slab Plan

Clearing the Air

Several common products and practices reduce the quality of your indoor air. Here are some products you may want to consider to minimize indoor pollution.

■ Air fresheners, especially oil-based fresheners that plug into outlets, contain known or suspected neurotoxins. Asthmatics may suffer attacks in homes with air fresheners.

■ Candles, while good for a romantic atmosphere, produce black soot that accumulates on ceiling and carpet edges -- and on occupants' lungs.

■ Ask for low-VOC paints, coatings and carpets. The Carpet and Rug Institute's (CRI) "Green Label" testing and labeling program identifies carpet products that are truly low-VOC at www.carpet-rug.com.

■ Cars, gasoline, paint and other chemicals generate toxic gasses. When these are stored in garages, especially attached garages, they can leak into your home. Garages should be well ventilated, preferably with an exhaust fan. Store chemicals, fertilizers and gasoline in an outside shed as far away as possible from home entryways.

■ Pesticides and chemicals applied outside your home can be tracked into your home and can also come in through open windows. Use natural methods to control pests, fertilize lawns and gardens, and kill weeds. Learn about such organic and natural products on www.extremelygreen.com

Discover more ways to clear the air in your home at www.pathnet.org/homeowners.

Price Code B   **40028**

Total Sq. Ft.: 1,532
Width: 49'
Depth: 63'-6"
Bedrooms: 3
Baths: 2
Garage: 2-car

(For more plan info, visit www.familyhomeplans.com)

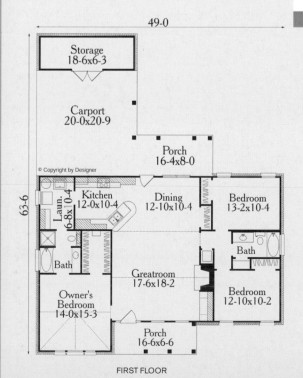

49-0

Storage
18-6x6-3

Carport
20-0x20-9

Porch
16-4x8-0

© Copyright by Designer

63-6

Kitchen
12-0x10-4

Laun.
6-8x10-4

Dining
12-10x10-4

Bedroom
13-2x10-4

Bath

Bath

Greatroom
17-6x18-2

Bedroom
12-10x10-2

Owner's
Bedroom
14-0x15-3

Porch
16-6x6-6

FIRST FLOOR

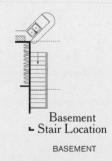

Basement
← Stair Location

BASEMENT

Price Code B 62036

Total Sq. Ft.: 1,538
Width: 50'
Depth: 56'
Bedrooms: 3
Baths: 2
Garage: 2-car

(For more plan info, visit www.familyhomeplans.com)

Welcome your friends and neighbors on the cozy front porch of this home. Leading your guests through the foyer, you'll enter the spacious great room which will prove to be a convenient gathering place with its inviting fireplace. Preparing meals is easy with ample counter space in the open kitchen with view to the dining room. As evening approaches and your guests depart, retreat to your master bath, complete with whirlpool tub, skylights, and 'his and her' walk-in closets. But don't worry about the children, they have their own bedrooms with shared bath.

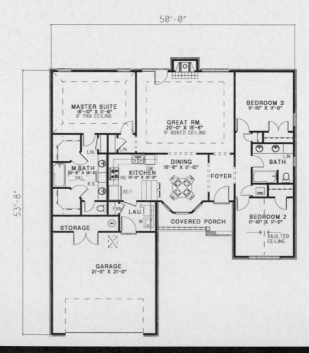

Price Code B 24721

Total Sq. Ft.: 1,539
Bedrooms: 3
Baths: 2
Garage: 2-car
Width: 50'
Depth: 45'-4"

(For more plan info, visit www.familyhomeplans.com)

It all adds up to comfort—1,539 sq. ft. A welcoming foyer glides straight ahead to the living room with built-ins and fireplace. Or, it follows a hallway where all three bedrooms are tucked in comfortably. The bright master suite is a treat with window seat, walk-in closet and ceiling treatment. The master bath is done up with a window over the tub and separate toilette. Bedrooms #2 and #3 share a bath and a front porch view. The U-shaped kitchen has it all—a recipe desk, peninsula counter to dining room, and a convenient laundry area.

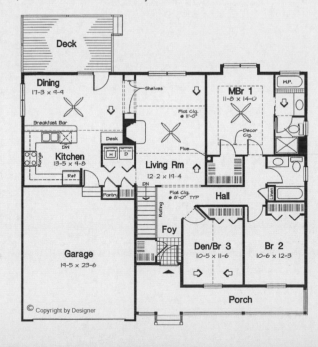

light, bright & airy

A towering, wide window with an arched top perfectly complements the dining room's stepped ceiling, which rises to 14 feet. Sliding glass doors brighten up a vast greatroom with its own fireplace and built-in television niche. A kitchen, with long counters and a range top, flows into the breakfast room, which connects to a back porch. A three-piece bath serves two front bedrooms, located across the hall from a master bedroom with a bay window, vaulted ceiling, and access to a walk-in closet and private bath.

Price Code B   99682

Total Sq. Ft.: 1,595
Width: 70'
Depth: 37'-4"
Bedrooms: 3
Baths: 2
Garage: 2-Car

(For more plan info, visit www.familyhomeplans.com)

Above: A soaring ceiling and round topped window enhance the formal dining room's sense of elegance. Right: Views from the dining room into the great room reveal a spacious area to relax with friends and family. This homeowner chose to relocate the fireplace to the rear wall.

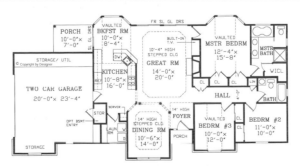

Price Code B 40006

Total Sq. Ft.: 1,539
Width: 51'-5"
Depth: 66'-6"
Bedrooms: 3
Baths: 2
Garage: 2-car

(For more plan info, visit www.familyhomeplans.com)

Editor's Choice

Twin gables and a palladian window setting introduce this design. The living spaces are open and spacious. A large island snack bar is enhanced by columns and connects the kitchen and great room. The convenient desk space is located near the carport entrance. Nine-foot ceilings cover all rooms, except the front bedroom presents a ten foot ceiling.

Storage
19-4x5-4

Carport
20-0x22-0

© Copyright by Designer

66-6

Patio

Owner's
Bedroom
17-9x13-8

Laun.
6-0x7-8

Kitchen
10-8x13-9

Greatroom
14-5x17-5

Bath

Bath

Dining
10-0x11-9

Foyer

Bedroom
11-2x12-0

Bedroom
10-7x11-4

Porch
18-0x6-0

51-5

Low-or-No VOC Paints

Paints that do not release significant pollutants and are virtually odor free.

Depending individuals' sensitivities to fumes, people can be driven from their homes during repainting. Not so long ago most conventional paints contained high levels of VOCs (volatile organic compounds) that produced a breathable gas when applied. The VOCs diminish air quality, and may be detrimental to your health. Today, alternative manufacturing techniques have allowed the development of low- and no-VOC paints that release no, or minimal VOC pollutants. Most major manufacturers now offer special no-VOC paints that are odorless and completely "VOC-free."

Application techniques for low- and no-VOC paints are the same as for conventional paints and coatings and typically cost about the same as a manufacturer's premium line of paints. Because low- or no-VOC paints have less odor and less impact on air quality than higher VOC-content paints, they are an excellent choice for anyone, since VOCs leach out of the paint over many years, posing a potential health hazard.

Courtesy of PATH

Price Code B 93161

Total Finished Sq. Ft.: 1,540
Bedrooms: 3
Full Baths: 2
Width: 60'-4"
Depth: 46'
Garage: 2-car

(For more plan info, visit www.familyhomeplans.com)

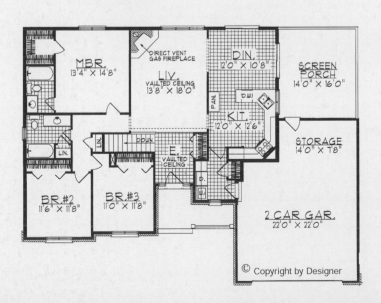

Price Code B 55011

Total Sq. Ft.: 1,543
Main Level: 1,061'
Upper Level: 482'
Width: 28'
Depth: 39'-9"
Bedrooms: 3
Baths: 2
Garage: none

(For more plan info, visit www.familyhomeplans.com)

An expansive window wall across the great room of this home adds a spectacular view and accentuates the high ceiling. The open kitchen shares an eating bar with the dining room and features a convenient "U" shape. Sliding glass doors in the dining room lead to the deck. Two family bedrooms sit to the back of the plan and share the use of a full bath. The master suite provides a walk-in closet and private bath. The loft on the upper level adds living or sleeping space.

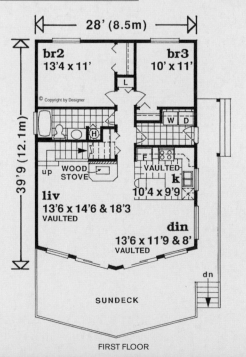

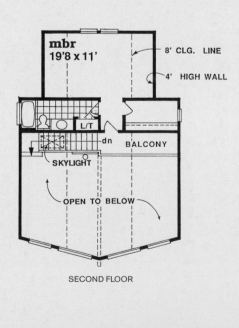

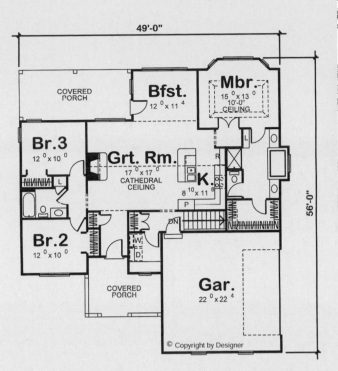

49'-0"

COVERED PORCH

Bfst. 12⁰ x 11⁴

Mbr. 15⁰ x 13⁰ 10'-0" CEILING

Br.3 12⁰ x 10⁰

Grt. Rm. 17' x 17' CATHEDRAL CEILING

K. 8¹⁰ x 11⁸

Br.2 12⁰ x 10⁰

COVERED PORCH

Gar. 22⁰ x 22⁴

56'-0"

© Copyright by Designer

Price Code B 44009

Total Finished Sq. Ft.: 1,547
Bedrooms: 3
Baths: 2
Garage: 2-car
Width: 49'
Depth: 56'

(For more plan info, visit www.familyhomeplans.com)

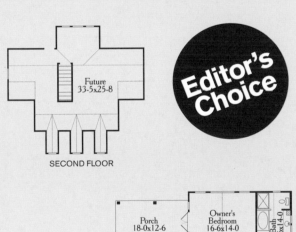

Future 33-5x25-8

SECOND FLOOR

Editor's Choice

Porch 18-0x12-6

Owner's Bedroom 16-6x14-0

Bath 8-6x14-0

Bedroom 12-0x10-4

Dining 10-0x15-4

Desk
Kitchen 11-0x15-4

Stor. 5-8x5-8

Bath

Greatroom 17-6x15-6

Garage 21-8x21-7

Bedroom 12-0x10-4

Porch 21-0x6-6

© Copyright by Designer

FIRST FLOOR

Price Code B 40029

Total Sq. Ft.: 1,551
Width: 56'
Depth: 52'-8"
Bedrooms: 3
Baths: 2
Garage: 2-car

(For more plan info, visit www.familyhomeplans.com)

ORDER NOW! Phone: **1-800-235-5700** Online: **www.FamilyHomePlans.com** Order Code: **H6SSM**

Price Code B 82026

Total Sq. Ft.: 1,525
Width: 51'-6"
Depth: 49'-10"
Bedrooms: 3
Baths: 2
Garage: 2-car

(For more plan info, visit www.familyhomeplans.com)

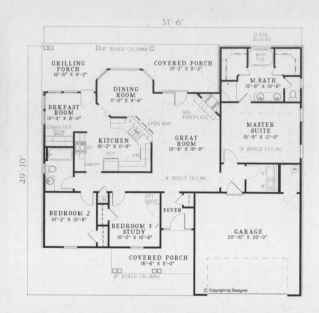

Price Code B 99654

Total Sq. Ft.: 1,554
Width: 64'-2"
Depth: 40'-8"
Bedrooms: 3
Baths: 2
Garage: 2-car

(For more plan info, visit www.familyhomeplans.com)

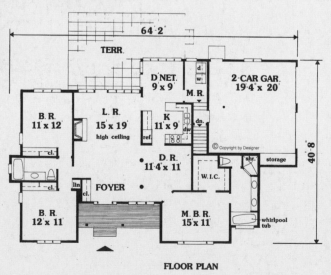

FLOOR PLAN

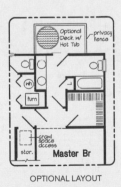

There's nothing like a big wrap porch and peaked dormers for charm. The interior is equally arresting with sloped roof and compelling fireplace. The kitchen features a far-reaching breakfast bar and a prep island, too. The dining room sidles up to the kitchen almost like its one big room. The main-floor master bedroom takes advantage of one of the bright dormers. Plus, there's a private master bath, walk-in closet and optional deck with hot tub. How's that for country living! Bedrooms #2 and #3 are tucked neatly upstairs, one on each side of the full bath. Plenty of windows, too.

Price Code B   34602

Total Sq. Ft.: 1,560
Main Level: 1,061'
Upper Level: 499'
Width: 44'
Depth: 34'
Bedrooms: 3
Baths: 2.5
Garage: none

(For more plan info, visit www.familyhomeplans.com)

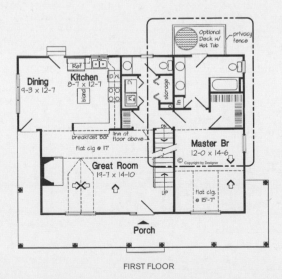

FIRST FLOOR

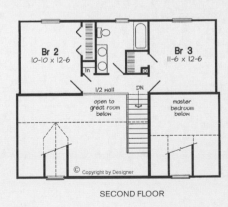

SECOND FLOOR

OPTIONAL LAYOUT

Price Code B 62277

Total Sq. Ft.: 1,560
Width: 52'-2"
Depth: 55'-8"
Bedrooms: 3
Baths: 2
Garage: 2-car

(For more plan info, visit www.familyhomeplans.com)

Cedar shake and brick are a wonderful combination for this home. The arched entry porch welcomes guests into an open great room viewing a formal dining room and accessing a large kitchen with breakfast room. The laundry room is located just steps from the kitchen for added convenience. Two bedrooms, one perfect for a home office, are located on the opposite side of the home and share a full bathroom. This split plan offers an elegant master suite with private access to the rear-grilling porch perfect for enjoying starlit evenings.

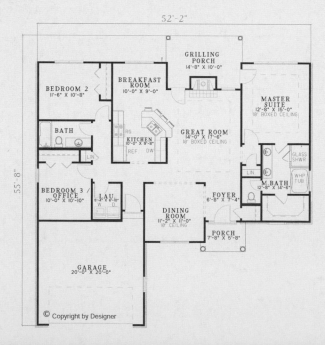

Work hard. Play hard. This 1,562 sq. ft. layout knows how to live. The great room partners with the dining room under cathedral ceilings. A fireplace and double French doors to the deck augment the space. The kitchen with breakfast counter has an eye for entertaining. Main-floor bedrooms #2 and #3 share equal access to the full bath and laundry area. The second-floor loft is dazzled by a bright overlook. The master suite has a private covered deck, and the master bath shows-off double vanities, and Whirlpool tub. Basement wet bar and optional game room anticipate guests.

Price Code B 24705

Total Sq. Ft.: 1,562
Main Level: 1,062'
Upper Level: 500'
Width: 45'-5"
Depth: 27'
Bedrooms: 3
Baths: 2

(For more plan info, visit www.familyhomeplans.com)

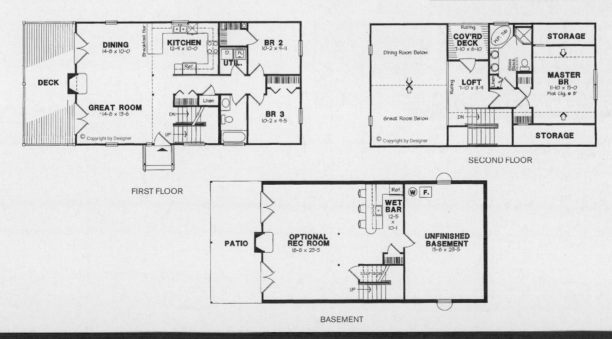

healthy homes

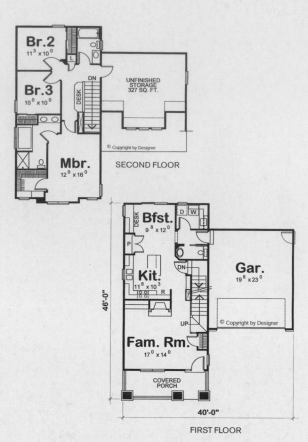

SECOND FLOOR

FIRST FLOOR

Price Code B   68234

Total Sq. Ft.: 1,568
Main Level: 787'
Upper Level: 781'
Width: 40'
Depth: 46'
Bedrooms: 3
Baths: 2.5
Garage: 2-car

(For more plan info, visit www.familyhomeplans.com)

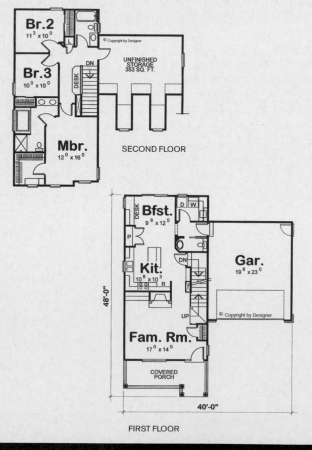

SECOND FLOOR

FIRST FLOOR

Price Code B   68188

Total Sq. Ft.: 1,575
Main Level: 787'
Upper Level: 788'
Width: 40'
Depth: 48'
Bedrooms: 3
Baths: 2.5
Garage: 2-car

(For more plan info, visit www.familyhomeplans.com)

Building a Radon-Free Home

Radon is an invisible, odorless, poisonous gas that comes from the soil. It results from the breakdown of uranium. Roughly 1 in every 15 homes has high radon levels, and 20,000 Americans die of radon-related lung cancer annually. In fact, radon is the second-leading cause of lung cancer in the United States behind smoking. The Surgeon General often reminds Americans to have their homes checked for radon.

The best way to protect a home from radon is to build the home with a mitigation system which will eliminate radon from the interior of your home from the beginning. This will cost around $500 for materials and labor (much less than the $1000 to $2500 it could cost to retrofit the house).

Find out more on avoiding the risks of radon at www.pathnet.org/homeowners

Courtesy of PATH

Price Code B 65085

Total Sq. Ft.: 1,572
Width: 54'
Depth: 52'
Bedrooms: 2
Baths: 1
Garage: 2-car

(For more plan info, visit www.familyhomeplans.com)

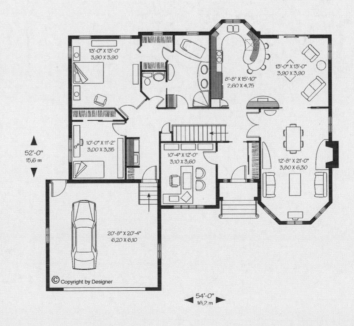

13'-0" X 13'-0"
3,90 X 3,90

8'-8" X 15'-10"
2,60 X 4,75

13'-0" X 13'-0"
3,90 X 3,90

10'-0" X 11'-2"
3,00 X 3,35

10'-4" X 12'-0"
3,10 X 3,60

12'-8" X 21'-0"
3,80 X 6,30

52'-0"
15,6 m

20'-8" X 20'-4"
6,20 X 6,10

© Copyright by Designer

54'-0"
16,2 m

Price Code B 10748

Total Sq. Ft.: 1,540
Width: 52'-4"
Depth: 45'
Bedrooms: 3
Baths: 2
Garage: none

(For more plan info, visit www.familyhomeplans.com)

Outdoor-Lovers' Delight. This one-level charmer packs a lot of convenience into a compact space. From the shelter of the front porch, the foyer leads three ways: right to the bedroom wing, left to the roomy kitchen and dining room, or straight ahead to the massive living room. You'll appreciate the quiet atmosphere in the sleeping wing, the elegant recessed ceilings and private bath in the master suite, and the laundry facilities that adjoin the bedrooms. You'll enjoy the convenience of a kitchen with a built-in pantry and adjacent dining room. And, you'll love the airy atmosphere in the sunny, fireplaced living room, which features a cooling fan, high ceilings, and double French doors to the huge, wrap-around porch.

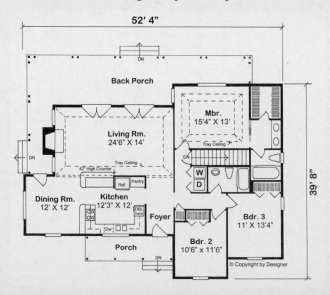

ORDER NOW! Phone: **1-800-235-5700** Online: **www.FamilyHomePlans.com** Order Code: **H6SSM**

Price Code B 24242

Total Sq. Ft.: 1,595
Main Level: 931'
Lower Level: 664'
Width: 32'-4"
Depth: 40'
Bedrooms: 4
Baths: 2.5
Garage: none

(For more plan info, visit www.familyhomeplans.com)

Charming Bungalow.
This attractive bungalow style home plan with an inviting covered porch can accommodate a large family. With not one square foot of wasted space, this four-bedroom home plan is the perfect habitation for the summer months. The efficient kitchen offers an eating booth, ample cabinet and counter space and all the modern conveniences to make meal preparation a snap. The master bedroom lets you have your privacy from the kids, it also boasts ample closet space and a private bath. The living room has a cozy fireplace and a bright, bay window. There is even a formal dining area. Upstairs the three secondary bedrooms share a full bath. Sip your cool drink, enjoy a summer breeze as you relax on your covered porch and savor the summer. This cottage makes a great vacation home plan.

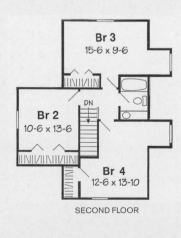

32'-4"
© Copyright by Designer

M Br 14-8 x 9-8
Kitchen 10-9 x 9-10
Dining 10-9 x 10
Living 11-6 x 18-0
Porch
FIRST FLOOR

Br 3 15-6 x 9-6
Br 2 10-6 x 13-6
Br 4 12-6 x 13-10
SECOND FLOOR

ORDER NOW! Phone: **1-800-235-5700** Online: **www.FamilyHomePlans.com** Order Code: **H6SSM**

Price Code B 24701

Total Sq. Ft.: 1,625
Width: 54'
Depth: 48'-4"
Bedrooms: 3
Baths: 2
Garage: 2-car

(For more plan info, visit www.familyhomeplans.com)

Pinch Yourself!

It's true—the dreamy charmer you've always wanted is here. The space is generous with 1,625 sq. ft. Features include an entry foyer, and smart home office (or bedroom #3) right at the front of the house. A double-sided fireplace in the large living room glows into the dining room. The kitchen is full of features: bright window, breakfast counter, openness to dining room, and close-at-hand laundry area. This home has a private side, too. The master suite with large walk-in has a lavish bath with shower and double sinks. An additional bedroom with shared bath overlooks a built-in garden planter.

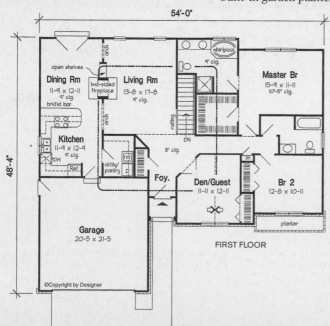

FIRST FLOOR

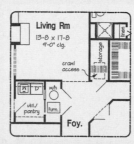

FIRST FLOOR ALTERNATE PLAN

HALF WALL

OPTIONAL LAYOUT

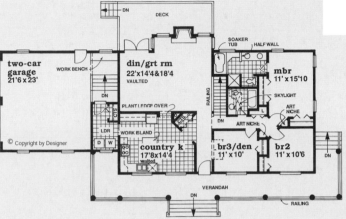

DN

DECK

two-car garage
21'6" x 23'

WORK BENCH

DN

SOAKER TUB

HALF WALL

din/grt rm
22'x14'4 & 18'4
VAULTED

mbr
11' x 15'10

RAILING

SKYLIGHT

PLANT LEDGE OVER

ART NICHE

DN

ART NICHE

© Copyright by Designer

LDR

D W

WORK ISLAND

country k
17'8 x14'4
vaulted

br3/den
11' x 10'

br2
11' x 10'6

DN

VERANDAH

DN

RAILING

FIRST FLOOR

Price Code B   55016

Total Sq. Ft.: 1,578
Width: 83'
Depth: 40'-6"
Bedrooms: 3
Baths: 2
Garage: 2-car

(For more plan info, visit www.familyhomeplans.com)

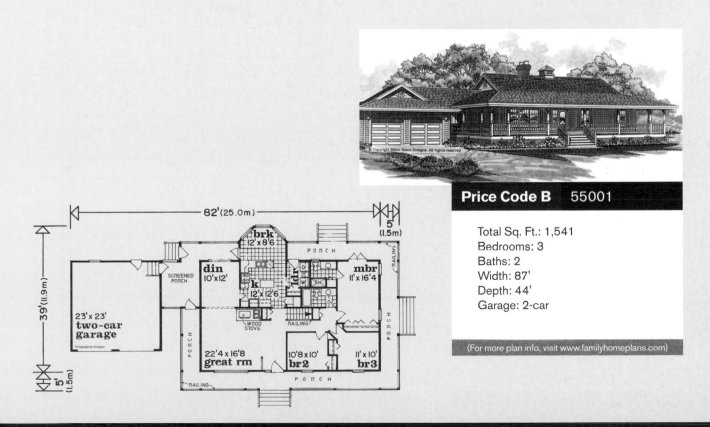

Price Code B   55001

Total Sq. Ft.: 1,541
Bedrooms: 3
Baths: 2
Width: 87'
Depth: 44'
Garage: 2-car

(For more plan info, visit www.familyhomeplans.com)

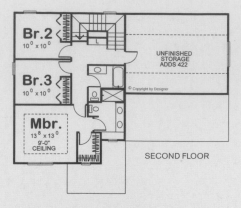

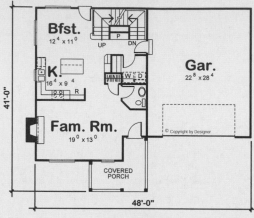

SECOND FLOOR

FIRST FLOOR

Price Code B 44016

Total Finished Sq. Ft.: 1,588'
Main Level: 830
Upper Level: 728
Bedrooms: 3
Baths: 2.25
Width: 48'
Depth: 41'
Garage: 2-car

(For more plan info, visit www.familyhomeplans.com)

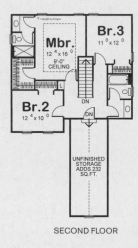

SECOND FLOOR

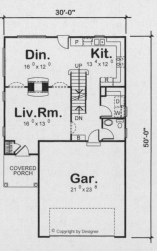

FIRST FLOOR

Price Code B 44011

Total Finished Sq. Ft.: 1,589
Main Level: 809'
Upper Level: 780'
Bedrooms: 3
Baths: 2.25
Width: 30'
Depth: 50'
Garage: 2-car

(For more plan info, visit www.familyhomeplans.com)

ORDER NOW! Phone: **1-800-235-5700** Online: **www.FamilyHomePlans.com** Order Code: **H6SSM**

Green Cleaning

Many everyday household cleaning products can be used that don't endanger your health, the health of your children, or the environment— and they're cheap. Here are 'green cleaning' recipes for any occasion.

All Purpose Cleaner: Add 1/2 cup ammonia and 1/3 cup washing soda to a gallon of warm water. Use to clean floors, tiles, and painted walls.

Window and Mirror Cleaner: Put ¼ cup white vinegar in a spray bottle, and fill to the top with water. Spray on desired surface, and rub with a newspaper or a rag. Squeegee dry.

Toilet, Tub and Tile Cleaner: Mix ½ cup borax and add enough lemon juice to make into a paste. Wet the sides of the surface and add the paste. Let stand for a few minutes, then scrub off and rinse.

Natural Pesticide: To naturally keep ants and other insects away, add a few teaspoons of orange oil to your green cleaning products. To kill ants that are already around, just spray them with diluted orange oil.

Discover many more green cleaning recipes at www.pathnet.org/home-owners.

Price Code B   63083

Total Sq. Ft.: 1,590
Bedrooms: 3
Full Baths: 2
Width: 43'
Depth: 59'
Garage: 2-car

(For more plan info, visit www.familyhomeplans.com)

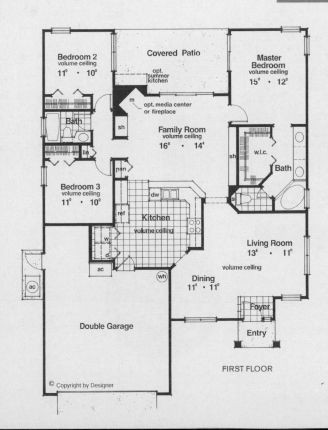

FIRST FLOOR

© Copyright by Designer

Price Code B 97178

Total Sq. Ft.: 1,591
Bedrooms: 3
Baths: 2
Width: 64'-8"
Depth: 57'
Garage: 3-car

(For more plan info, visit www.familyhomeplans.com)

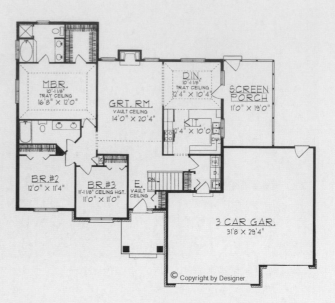

REAR EXTERIOR

Price Code B 92433

Total Sq. Ft.: 1,593
Width: 50'
Depth: 55'
Bedrooms: 3
Baths: 2
Garage: 2-car

(For more plan info, visit www.familyhomeplans.com)

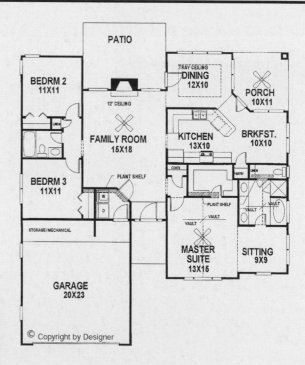

Editor's Choice

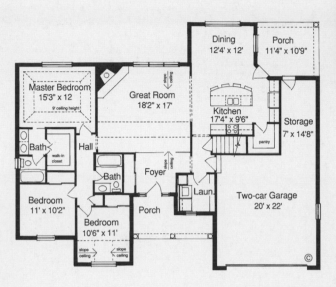

Price Code B   97740

Total Sq. Ft.: 1,593
Bedrooms: 3
Full Baths: 2
Garage: 3-car
Width: 60'
Depth: 48'-10"
Garage: 2-car

(For more plan info, visit www.familyhomeplans.com)

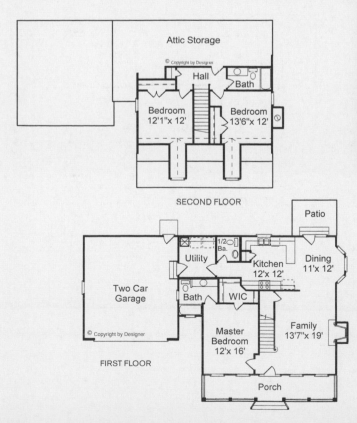

SECOND FLOOR

FIRST FLOOR

Price Code B   94682

Total Sq. Ft.: 1,609
Main Level: 1,072
Upper Level: 537
Bedrooms: 3
Baths: 2.5
Width: 62'
Depth: 46'
Garage: 2-Car

(For more plan info, visit www.familyhomeplans.com)

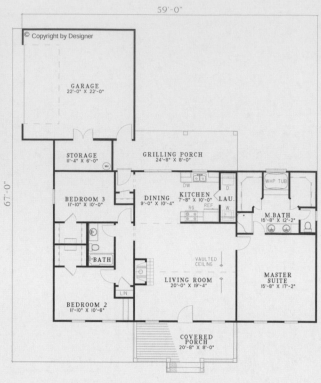

Price Code B 62086

Total Sq. Ft.: 1,597
Width: 59'
Depth: 67'
Bedrooms: 3
Baths: 2
Garage: 2-car

(For more plan info, visit www.familyhomeplans.com)

SECOND FLOOR

Price Code B 92424

Total Sq. Ft.: 1,598
Main Level: 812'
Upper Level: 786'
Width: 52'
Depth: 28'
Bedrooms: 3
Baths: 2.5
Garage: 2-car

(For more plan info, visit www.familyhomeplans.com)

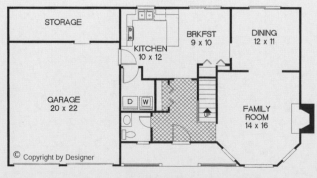

FIRST FLOOR

ORDER NOW! Phone: **1-800-235-5700** Online: **www.FamilyHomePlans.com** Order Code: **H6SSM**

STRG.
8'-2" X 5'-6"

D LAU.
7'-0" X 5'-6"
W

NOOK
9'-0" X 7'-0"

MASTER SUITE
10'-0" BOXED CEILING
12'-0" X 13'-8"

GARAGE
20'-0" X 20'-0"

KITCHEN
14'-8" X 12'-4"
REF. PANTRY
DW
RG

© Copyright by Designer

DINING RM.
10'-8" X 10'-0"

8" COLUMNS

LIN
M.B.
GLASS BLOCKS
SHWR
WHP TUB

BED RM. 3
12'-0" X 10'-8"

GREAT RM.
10'-0" BOXED CEILING
20'-0" X 14'-8"

LIN

SITTING AREA
9'-0" X 4'-0"

FOYER

PRCH.

BED RM. 2
12'-0" X 10'-4"

Price Code B   82008

Total Sq. Ft.: 1,598
Width: 48'
Depth: 60'-4"
Bedrooms: 3
Baths: 2
Garage: 2-car

(For more plan info, visit www.familyhomeplans.com)

Price Code B   65619

Total Sq. Ft.: 1,600
Main Level: 1,136'
Upper Level: 464'
Width: 58'
Depth: 42'
Bedrooms: 3
Baths: 2
Garage: 2-car

(For more plan info, visit www.familyhomeplans.com)

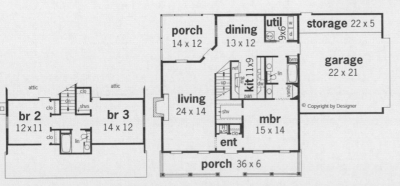

porch
14 x 12

dining
13 x 12

util
9x6

storage 22 x 5

garage
22 x 21

brm

attic

attic

br 2
12 x 11

clo
drn
shvs
clo

br 3
14 x 12

clo

lin

living
24 x 14

up
ref
kit 11x9
dw
pan

lin
vanity

shv

mbr
15 x 14

clo

ent

© Copyright by Designer

porch 36 x 6

rustic appeal

This economical country cottage features wide, angled spaces and 9'-4" high ceilings in both the great room and the master bedroom for roomy appeal and year-round comfort. The great room is designed with a cozy fireplace and raised hearth plus a built-in niche for a TV, making this room perfect for winter gatherings. On warm nights, a homey covered porch at the rear can be accessed through sliding glass doors.

Price Code B 69506

Total Sq. Ft.: 1,679
Main Level: 1,134'
Upper Level: 545'
Width: 42'
Depth: 45'
Bedrooms: 3
Baths: 2.5
Garage: none

(For more plan info, visit www.familyhomeplans.com)

SECOND FLOOR

FIRST FLOOR

An angled, stone fireplace warms the great room and provides a dramatic focal point for this part of the home which is open to the dining area and kitchen. The kitchen offers generous counter space and sunny views to the outdoors. Upstairs bedrooms are brightened by plenty of natural light.

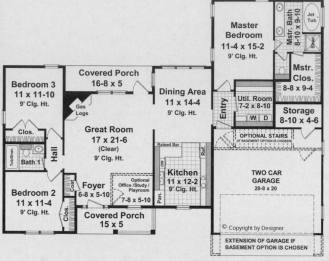

Bedroom 3
11 x 11-10
9' Clg. Ht.

Covered Porch
16-8 x 5

Dining Area
11 x 14-4
9' Clg. Ht.

Master
Bedroom
11-4 x 15-2
9' Clg. Ht.

Mstr. Bath
8-10 x 9-10

Jet Tub

Clos.

Gas Logs

Great Room
17 x 21-6
(Clear)
9' Clg. Ht.

Entry

Mstr. Clos.
8-8 x 9-4

Tub/Shwr

Bath 1

Hall

Raised Bar

Util. Room
7-2 x 8-10

W D

Storage
8-10 x 4-6

Foyer
6-8 x 5-10

Optional Office /Study / Playroom
7-8 x 5-10

Kitchen
11 x 12-2
9' Clg. Ht.

DW

Ref.

Pan.

OPTIONAL STAIRS
IF BASEMENT OPTION IS CHOSEN

Bedroom 2
11 x 11-4
9' Clg. Ht.

Clos.
Coat

Covered Porch
15 x 5

TWO CAR
GARAGE
20-8 x 20

© Copyright by Designer

EXTENSION OF GARAGE IF
BASEMENT OPTION IS CHOSEN

Price Code B   59057

Total Sq. Ft.: 1,600
Width: 61'-8"
Depth: 45'-8"
Bedrooms: 3
Baths: 2
Garage: 2-car

(For more plan info, visit www.familyhomeplans.com)

52'-6"

8" COLUMNS

GRILLING PORCH
15'-8" X 8'-0"

GLASS BLOCKS

BEDROOM 3
10'-8" X 10'-8"

BUILT-INS

BREAKFAST ROOM
12'-8" X 8'-6"
9' BOXED CEILING

WHP SHWR

M. BATH
12'-6" X 12'-0"

GREAT ROOM
15'-0" X 22'-8"
CATHEDRAL CEILING

ISLAND

KITCHEN
12'-8" X
10'-4" REF.

DW

58'-10"

BUILT-INS

VAULTED CEILING

MASTER SUITE
12'-6" X 14'-8"
9' BOXED CEILING

BEDROOM 2
10'-8" X 10'-8"

FOYER
6'-0" X
9'-0"

12" BOXED COLUMNS

DINING ROOM
9'-8" X 11'-8"
11' CEILING

LAU.
6'-6" X 4'-0"

W D

ENTRY

GARAGE
20'-0" X 22'-10"

© Copyright by Designer

VAULT

Price Code B   62399

Total Sq. Ft.: 1,600
Width: 52'-6"
Depth: 58'-10"
Bedrooms: 3
Baths: 2
Garage: 2-car

(For more plan info, visit www.familyhomeplans.com)

SECOND FLOOR

FIRST FLOOR

Price Code B   72018

Total Sq. Ft.: 1,605
Main Level: 790'
Upper Level: 815'
Width: 37'
Depth: 44'
Bedrooms: 3
Baths: 2.5
Garage: 2-car

(For more plan info, visit www.familyhomeplans.com)

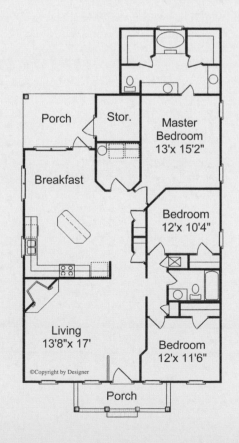

Porch

Stor.

Master Bedroom
13'x 15'2"

Breakfast

Bedroom
12'x 10'4"

Living
13'8"x 17'

Bedroom
12'x 11'6"

©Copyright by Designer

Porch

Price Code B   94522

Total Sq. Ft.: 1,606
Width: 33'
Depth: 64'
Bedrooms: 3
Baths: 2
Garage: no

(For more plan info, visit www.familyhomeplans.com)

ORDER NOW! Phone: **1-800-235-5700**   Online: **www.FamilyHomePlans.com**   Order Code: **H6SSM**

Price Code B 94624

Total Sq. Ft.: 1,615
Width: 38'
Depth: 63'
Bedrooms: 3
Baths: 2
Garage: 2-car

This home is great for a small family or as a first home. The exterior is made up of vinyl siding. A front entry garage accommodates two vehicles. As you enter the home, you'll discover a formal dining room to your right. The formal dining opens to the kitchen, which includes a snack bar. The kitchen also leads to a breakfast area. The family room has a raised ceiling, for added aesthetics, and a gas fireplace. Two of the bedrooms share a full bathroom. The master suite includes a standing shower, walk-in closet, dual vanity, and a garden tub.

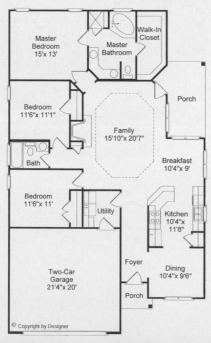

Price Code B 97760

Total Sq. Ft.: 1,611
Width: 66'-4"
Depth: 43'-10"
Bedrooms: 3
Bathrooms: 2

(For more plan info, visit www.familyhomeplans.com)

Steps to Reduce Exposure to Carbon Monoxide in Your Home

■ Keep gas appliances properly adjusted.

■ Consider purchasing a vented space heater when replacing an unvented one.

■ Use proper fuel in kerosene space heaters.

■ Over gas stoves, install and use an exhaust fan vented to the outdoors.

■ Open flues when fireplaces are in use.

■ Choose properly sized wood stoves that are certified to meet EPA emission standards. Make certain that doors on all wood stoves fit tightly.

■ Have a trained professional inspect, clean, and tune-up central heating system (furnaces, flues, and chimneys) annually. Repair any leaks promptly.

■ Do not idle the car inside garage.

Courtesy of Partnership for Advancing Housing Technology (PATH)
www.pathnet.org/homeowners

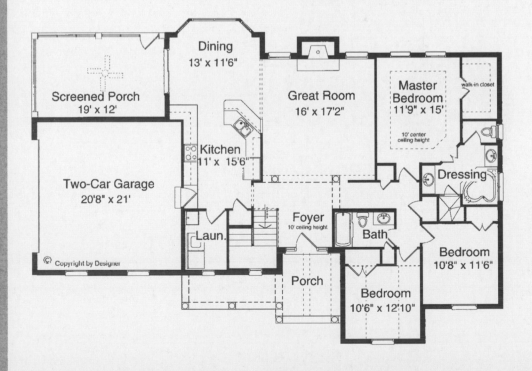

Price Code B 94683

Total Sq. Ft.: 1,618
Main Level: 1,046'
Upper Level: 572'
Width: 44'
Depth: 39'
Bedrooms: 3
Baths: 2.5
Garage: none

(For more plan info, visit www.familyhomeplans.com)

A wrapping porch provides a friendly welcome to friends and family. Once inside, views are drawn to the living room's fireplace and the bayed dining room beyond. The kitchen interacts openly with the dining area, which opens to a rear porch. The master suite features two walk-in closets. Upstairs, each of the two secondary bedrooms also boast walk-ins and are highlighted by deep dormers.

Editor's Choice

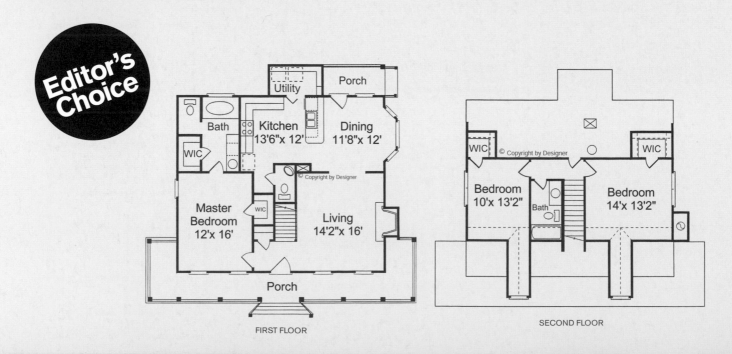

FIRST FLOOR

SECOND FLOOR

Price Code B 65246

Total Sq. Ft.: 1,625'
Main Level: 1,108'
Upper Level: 517'
Width: 36'
Depth: 36'
Bedrooms: 3
Baths: 2
Garage: none

(For more plan info, visit www.familyhomeplans.com)

A welcoming porch spans the front of this charming 1½-story home. A closed foyer buffers the inside from the outdoors, and leads guests into a spacious family room with fireplace and views to the expansive rear deck. The eat-in kitchen accesses the deck as well, and enjoys an open exchange with conversations in the family room. Interesting angles enhance the master bedroom which includes a sizeable walk-in closet and is just steps away from the main-floor bath. Upstairs, a balcony provides views to the lower level and bedrooms #2 and #3 share a corner bath.

36'-0"
10,8 m

13'-8" X 12'-8"
4,10 X 3,80

20'-0" X 14'-0"
6,00 X 4,20

13'-0" X 17'-0"
3,90 X 5,10

© Copyright by Designer

FIRST FLOOR

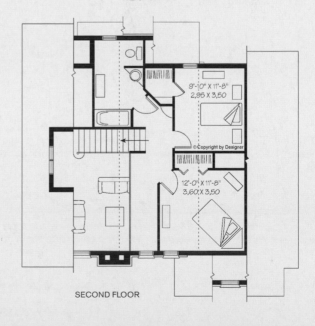

9'-10" X 11'-8"
2,95 X 3,50

12'-0" X 11'-8"
3,60 X 3,50

© Copyright by Designer

SECOND FLOOR

Price Code B 82012

Total Sq. Ft.: 1,627
Width: 52'-8"
Depth: 60'-6"
Bedrooms: 3
Baths: 2
Garage: 2-car

(For more plan info, visit www.familyhomeplans.com)

Entering through majestic columns into the traditional foyer, you instantly feel the grandeur of this home. Imagine an evening of exquisite cuisine as you entertain your close friends and colleagues in the elegant dining room enhanced by ten foot ceilings and beautifully crafted columns. A grilling porch, located off the spacious kitchen and breakfast room, provides the ease needed to serve your favorite recipes. Following the festivities, retreat to a private master suite and relax in your whirlpool tub.

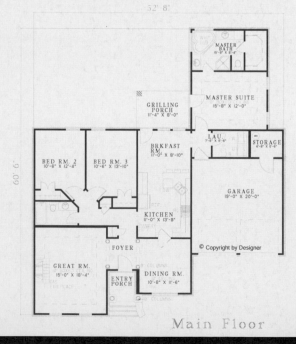

Main Floor

Price Code B 96561

Total Sq. Ft.: 1,628
Width: 73'
Depth: 50'
Bedrooms: 3
Baths: 2
Garage: Carport

(For more plan info, visit www.familyhomeplans.com)

Southern hospitality abounds in this easy living, compact design. A large, wrapping front porch invites guests inside to relax by the fireplace in the great room, enjoy a meal in the dining room, or gather along the kitchen's snack bar. A generous master suite includes his and her walk-in closets, and a luxurious corner tub. Secondary bedrooms share a central hall bath. A carport and breezeway provide airy shelter outside and access the home through a utility room adjoining the kitchen.

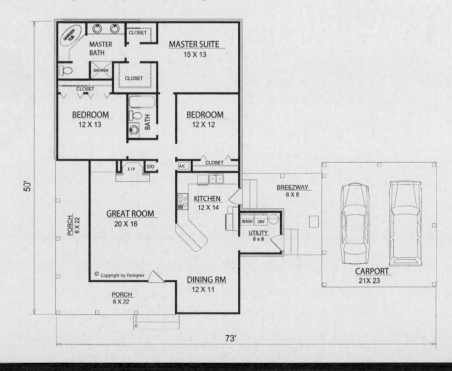

Price Code B   55027

Total Sq. Ft: 1,634'
Main Level: 1,099'
Upper Level: 535'
Width: 45'
Depth: 42'
Bedrooms: 3
Baths: 2
Garage: none

(For more plan info, visit www.familyhomeplans.com)

This design offers several different options to make the floor plan exactly as you like it. The exterior is graced by a wrapping veranda, round columns, stone facing with cedar-shingled accents and a trio of dormers. Inside, the open plan includes a vaulted great room with fireplace, a vaulted dining room, a vaulted kitchen and three bedrooms. The kitchen has a pass-through to the dining room and large pantry. The master suite is found on the first floor for privacy and contains a walk-in closet with dressing room, a sitting area and full skylit bath. Family bedrooms are on the second floor.

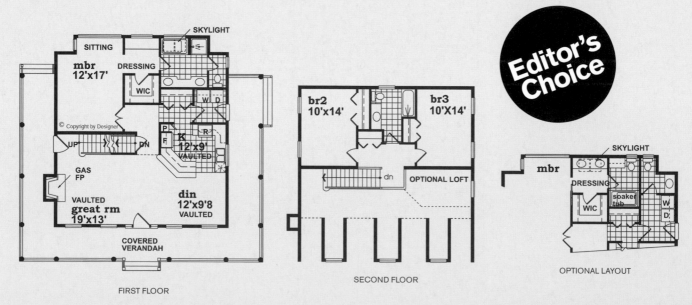

Editor's Choice

FIRST FLOOR
SITTING
SKYLIGHT
mbr 12'x17'
DRESSING
WIC
W D
UP   DN
GAS FP
© Copyright by Designer
K 12'x9' VAULTED
P F R
VAULTED great rm 19'x13'
din 12'x9'8 VAULTED
COVERED VERANDAH

SECOND FLOOR
br2 10'x14'
br3 10'X14'
dn
OPTIONAL LOFT

OPTIONAL LAYOUT
SKYLIGHT
mbr
DRESSING
WIC
soaker tub
W D

Price Code B   62219

Total Sq. Ft.: 1,636'
Width: 53'
Depth: 59'-10"
Bedrooms: 3
Baths: 2
Garage: 2-car

(For more plan info, visit www.familyhomeplans.com)

This home features all the amenities you've come to expect in your future home. Enjoy hours of quality time in front of the fireplace in the great room with access to the formal dining room with eight inch columns. The kitchen features a snack bar open to the breakfast room with easy access to the rear grilling porch for summer barbecues. The master bath affords the convenience of an expansive walk-in closet and double vanities. The whirlpool tub offers solace from the day's worries as the steam envelops you. The children have the privacy of bedrooms located on the opposite side of the home with a full bath between.

Price Code B 44010

Total Sq. Ft.: 1,641
Main Level: 854'
Upper Level: 787'
Width: 44'
Depth: 42'
Bedrooms: 3
Baths: 2.25
Garage: 2-car

(For more plan info, visit www.familyhomeplans.com)

A smart choice for growing families, this 1,641 sq. ft. home offers plenty of amenities, plus room to expand. On the main level, the living room, kitchen and dining area flow together, their boundaries subtly defined by tasteful columns and corners. A sensibly located half bath, bench and closet provide functionality to an area just inside from the garage. Upstairs, the master suite and secondary bedrooms are situated for privacy, yet close enough for attending to the needs of younger children. A generously sized unfinished storage area helps keep things in order and offers the opportunity to become a playroom, office, or homework/computer center.

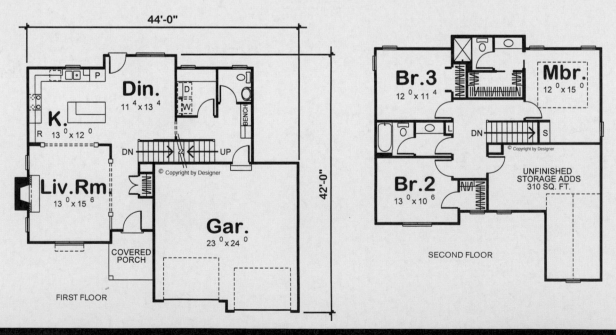

A classic pillared porch and pediment detailing define the exterior. The spacious interior across 1,642 sq. ft. is bright and airy. The graceful parlor and dining room with ceiling treatments and built-in cabinetry-live close together for added formality. The great room with corner fireplace opens to the breakfast room. The wide-open kitchen stirs up appetites with prep island and peninsula lunch bar. One side of the house sleeps bedrooms 2 and 3, and their well-planned bathroom with double sinks. The lavish master suite has special ceiling treatments, windowing, a wide walk-in and elaborate bath with tub window.

Price Code B   24717

Total Sq. Ft.: 1,642
Width: 59'
Depth: 44'
Bedrooms: 3
Baths: 2
Garage: 2-car

(For more plan info, visit www.familyhomeplans.com)

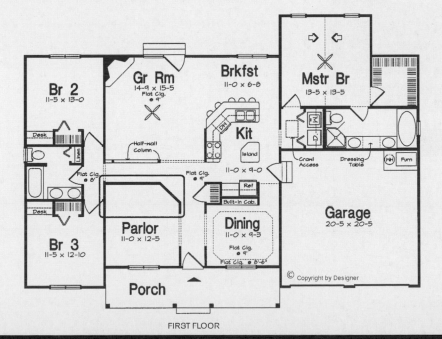

FIRST FLOOR

Optional Basement Stairs

OPTIONAL LAYOUT

Editor's Choice

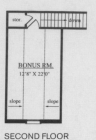

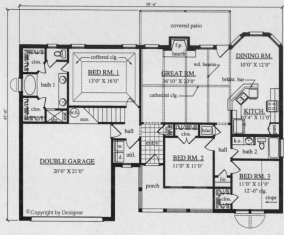

SECOND FLOOR

FIRST FLOOR

Price Code B 75000

Total Sq. Ft.: 1,636
Width: 59'-6"
Depth: 47'-6"
Bedrooms: 3
Baths: 2
Garage: 2-car

(For more plan info, visit www.familyhomeplans.com)

MAIN FLOOR

Price Code B 93100

Total Finished Sq. Ft.: 1,642'
Width: 57'
Depth: 66'
Bedrooms: 3
Baths: 2.25
Garage: 2-car

(For more plan info, visit www.familyhomeplans.com)

SECOND FLOOR

BONUS ROOM
15'-3" x 21'-0"

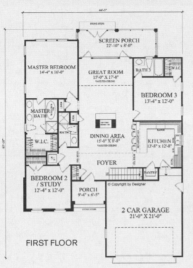

FIRST FLOOR

SCREEN PORCH
22'-10" x 8'-0"

MASTER BEDROOM
14'-4" x 16'-0"

GREAT ROOM
15'-0" X 17'-8"
VAULTED CEILING

BATH 3

W.I.C.

BEDROOM 3
13'-4" x 12'-0"

MASTER BATH

DINING AREA
15'-0" X 9'-8"
VAULTED CEILING

KITCHEN
13'-8" x 12'-8"

W.I.C.

FOYER

BEDROOM 2 / STUDY
12'-4" x 12'-0"

PORCH
9'-6" x 6'-5"

2 CAR GARAGE
21'-0" X 21'-0"

© Copyright by Designer

Price Code B — 86100

Total Sq. Ft.: 1,684
Bonus Area: 332'
Width: 44'-5"
Depth: 63'-10"
Bedrooms: 3
Baths: 3
Garage: 2-car

(For more plan info, visit www.familyhomeplans.com)

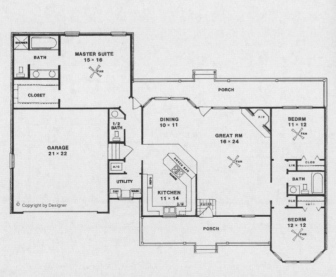

SHOWER

BATH

MASTER SUITE
15 × 16

FAN

CLOSET

1/2 BATH

GARAGE
21 × 22

A/C

UTILITY

DRY WASH

KITCHEN
11 × 14

DINING
10 × 11

GREAT RM
16 × 24

FAN

PORCH

F/P

BEDRM
11 × 12

FAN

LIN

CLOS

BATH

CLO

BEDRM
12 × 12

FAN

PORCH

© Copyright by Designer

Price Code B — 96513

Total Sq. Ft.: 1,648
Width: 68'
Depth: 50'
Bedrooms: 3
Baths: 2.5
Garage: 2-car

(For more plan info, visit www.familyhomeplans.com)

ORDER NOW! Phone: **1-800-235-5700** Online: **www.FamilyHomePlans.com** Order Code: **H6SSM**

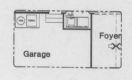

ALTERNATE SLAB /
CRAWLSPACE PLAN

Price Code B 24725

Total Sq. Ft.: 1,661
Width: 56'
Depth: 46'
Bedrooms: 3
Baths: 2.5
Garage: 2-car

(For more plan info, visit www.familyhomeplans.com)

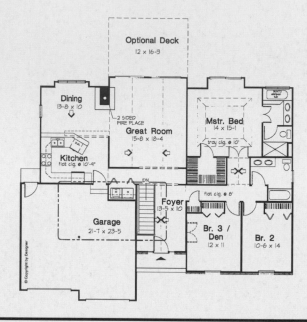

Price Code B 96824

Total Sq. Ft.: 1,698
Width: 59'
Depth: 61'
Bedrooms: 3
Baths: 2.5
Garage: 2-car

(For more plan info, visit www.familyhomeplans.com)

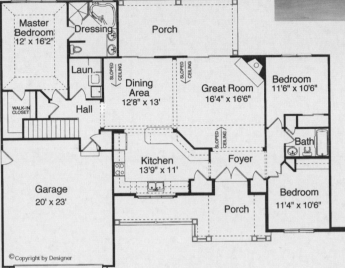

Master Bedroom 12' x 16'2"

Dressing

Porch

Laun.

Dining Area 12'8" x 13'

Great Room 16'4" x 16'6"

Bedroom 11'6" x 10'6"

WALK-IN CLOSET

Hall

Bath

Kitchen 13'9" x 11'

Foyer

Garage 20' x 23'

Bedroom 11'4" x 10'6"

Porch

© Copyright by Designer

Price Code B   50021

Total Sq. Ft.: 1,651
Width: 60'-9"
Depth: 49'
Bedrooms: 3
Baths: 2
Garage: 2-car

(For more plan info, visit www.familyhomeplans.com)

BONUS RM.

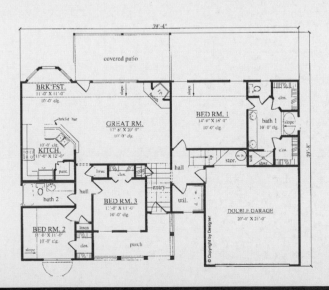

covered patio

BRK'FST. 11'-0" X 11'-0" 10'-0" clg.

GREAT RM. 17'-6" X 20'-0" 10'-0" clg.

KITCH. 11'-0" X 12'-0"

BED RM. 1 14'-0" X 16'-0" 10'-0" clg.

bath 1

BED RM. 3 11'-0" X 11'-0" 10'-0" clg.

entry

hall

util.

DOUBLE GARAGE 20'-0" X 21'-0"

bath 2

BED RM. 2 10'-0" X 11'-0" 10'-0" clg.

porch

© Copyright by Designer

Price Code B   79007

Total Sq. Ft.: 1,688'
Width: 60'
Depth: 50'
Bedrooms: 3
Baths: 2
Garage: 2-car

(For more plan info, visit www.familyhomeplans.com)

Price Code B 79005

Total Sq. Ft.: 1,643
Width: 51'
Depth: 59'
Bedrooms: 3
Baths: 2
Garage: 2-car

(For more plan info, visit www.familyhomeplans.com)

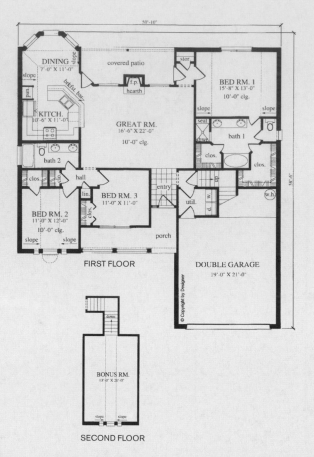

FIRST FLOOR

DINING
7'-0" X 11'-0"

covered patio

stor

f.p.
hearth

BED RM. 1
15'-8" X 13'-0"
10'-0" clg.

KITCH.
10'-6" X 11'-0"

GREAT RM.
16'-6" X 22'-0"
10'-0" clg.

bath 1

bath 2

BED RM. 3
11'-0" X 11'-0"

entry

hall

BED RM. 2
11'-0" X 12'-0"
10'-0" clg.

porch

DOUBLE GARAGE
19'-0" X 21'-0"

BONUS RM.
13'-0" X 21'-0"

SECOND FLOOR

Price Code B 10674

Total Sq. Ft.: 1,600
Width: 58'
Depth: 51'
Bedrooms: 3
Baths: 2
Garage: 2-car

(For more plan info, visit www.familyhomeplans.com)

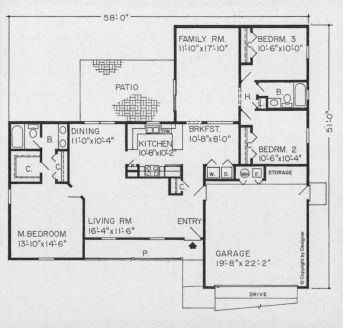

FAMILY RM.
11'-10"x17'-10"

BEDRM. 3
10'-6"x10'-0"

PATIO

DINING
11'-0"x10'-4"

BRKFST.
10'-8"x8'-0"

KITCHEN
10'-8"x10'-2"

BEDRM. 2
10'-6"x10'-4"

STORAGE

LIVING RM
16'-4"x11'-6"

ENTRY

M.BEDROOM
13'-10"x14'-6"

GARAGE
19'-8" x 22'-2"

DRIVE

Keeping Your Home Safe from Fires

Smoke Alarms

The majority of home fire deaths happen at night, most often from smoke and poisonous gases, not the fire itself. Install smoke alarms on every level of your home, including the basement and workshop, and outside all sleeping areas. For extra protection, consider installing a smoke alarm in every bedroom.

Home Escape Plan

Most people underestimate how fast a fire spreads. You may have as little as two minutes to get your family to safety. Plan and practice exactly what to do in advance. Have at least two exits from every room and a meeting place outside the home. Conduct a home fire drill with everyone in your household at least twice a year.

Fire Extinguishers

A multipurpose dry chemical Class ABC fire extinguisher is the best choice for general home use. Mount the extinguisher on a bracket on the wall near an exit so that anyone using it can escape from the room if a fire spreads.

Courtesy of PATH
www.pathnet.org/homeowners

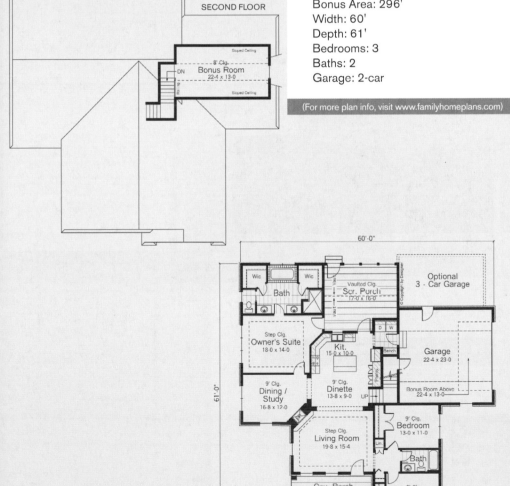

Price Code C	42503

Total Sq. Ft.: 1,792
Bonus Area: 296'
Width: 60'
Depth: 61'
Bedrooms: 3
Baths: 2
Garage: 2-car

(For more plan info, visit www.familyhomeplans.com)

Price Code B   24729

Total Sq. Ft.: 1,663
Main Level: 850'
Upper Level: 813'
Width: 31'
Depth: 43'
Bedrooms: 3
Baths: 2.5
Garage: none

(For more plan info, visit www.familyhomeplans.com)

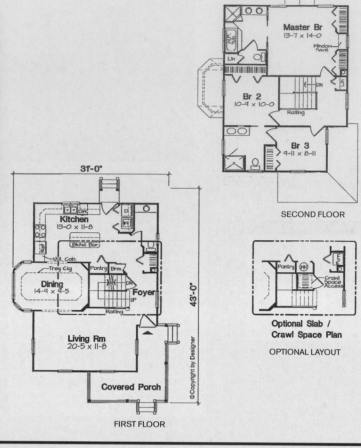

Master Br
13-7 x 14-0

Br 2
10-9 x 10-0

Br 3
9-11 x 8-11

SECOND FLOOR

31'-0"

Kitchen
13-0 x 11-8

Dining
14-9 x 4-5

Foyer

Living Rm
20-5 x 11-8

Covered Porch

FIRST FLOOR

43'-0"

©Copyright by Designer

Optional Slab /
Crawl Space Plan

OPTIONAL LAYOUT

Price Code B   65682

Total Sq. Ft.: 1,672'
Width: 68'
Depth: 60'
Bedrooms: 3
Baths: 2
Garage: 2-car

(For more plan info, visit www.familyhomeplans.com)

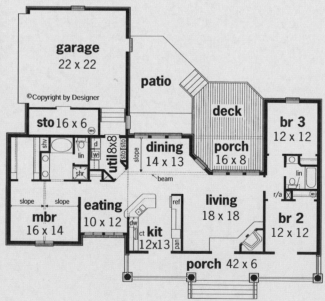

garage
22 x 22

patio

deck

porch
16 x 8

br 3
12 x 12

©Copyright by Designer

sto 16 x 6

util 8x8

dining
14 x 13

br 2
12 x 12

eating
10 x 12

mbr
16 x 14

kit
12x13

living
18 x 18

porch 42 x 6

Price Code B 68172

Total Sq. Ft.: 1,675
Main Level: 1,241'
Upper Level: 434'
Width: 80'
Depth: 51'
Bedrooms: 3
Baths: 2.5
Garage: 2-car

(For more plan info, visit www.familyhomeplans.com)

A screened porch and extensive wrap-around porches make this home an outdoor lover's dream. The living spaces are very open, with a centrally located island/eating bar. Behind the kitchen, a large walk-in pantry eases food preperation. The master suite enjoys a double vanity, whirlpool, shower and walk-in closet. The upper level includes two secondary bedrooms, a full bath and an optional game room.

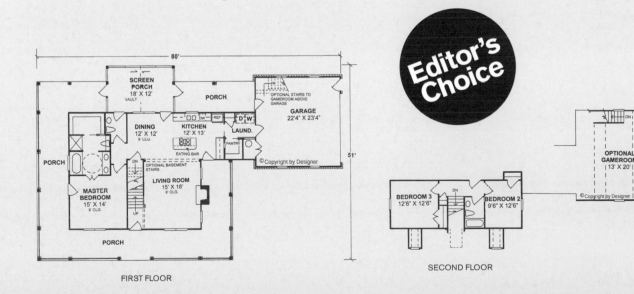

Price Code B 24738

Total Sq. Ft.: 1,554'
Width: 60'-3"
Depth: 55'-6"
Bedrooms: 3
Baths: 2
Garage: 2-car

(For more plan info, visit www.familyhomeplans.com)

Affordably Upscale. The concept behind this house was simple; design an affordable house with as many upscale features as possible. We wanted to cater to the first time home buyer, or the growing family needing more space, without sacrificing budget. We believe we hit a home run with this design. Square footage was maximized by using an open floor plan concept. Notice the size of the dining room, a generous 11'4 x 14'3. The only elements separating the dining room from the vaulted great room and kitchen/breakfast areas are strategically placed, elegant columns (see interior illustration). Another feature that adds to the family-friendly floor plan is the back foyer/laundry room off the garage. The cabinet area can be used for storing coats, shoes, etc. We also decided to split the bedrooms to give mom and dad a little privacy. The master bedroom has its own foyer and access to the covered rear porch.

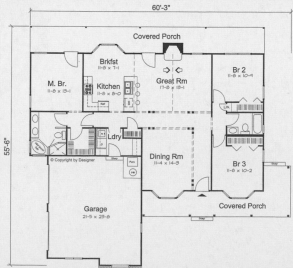

Built-ins surround the fireplace in the vaulted great room
of this design. A wrap around snack bar connects the kitchen to the great room
and dining area. The large walk-in pantry presents great storage for the kitchen.

Price Code B 40005

Total Sq. Ft.: 1,680
Width: 56'-4"
Depth: 68'-6"
Bedrooms: 3
Baths: 2
Garage: 2-car carport

(For more plan info, visit www.familyhomeplans.com)

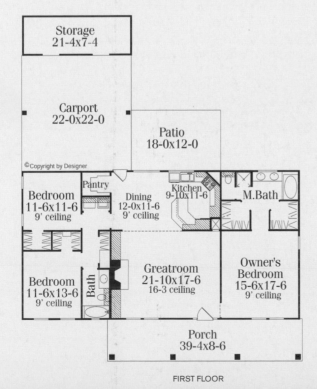

Storage
21-4x7-4

Carport
22-0x22-0

© Copyright by Designer

Patio
18-0x12-0

Bedroom
11-6x11-6
9' ceiling

Pantry

Dining
12-0x11-6
9' ceiling

Kitchen
9-10x11-6

M. Bath

Bedroom
11-6x13-6
9' ceiling

Bath

Greatroom
21-10x17-6
16-3 ceiling

Owner's
Bedroom
15-6x17-6
9' ceiling

Porch
39-4x8-6

FIRST FLOOR

Optional
Basement
Option

Basement Stair Location

Greatroom
16-8x17-6
16-3 ceiling

SECOND FLOOR

Price Code B   82010

Total Sq. Ft.: 1,684
Main Level: 1,155'
Upper Level: 529'
Width: 47'
Depth: 50'
Bedrooms: 3
Baths: 2.5
Garage: 2-car

(For more plan info, visit www.familyhomeplans.com)

Become enchanted by European beauty as you enter this home. Nine foot ceilings create a marvelous openness throughout the entire plan especially in the great room. Spend hours entertaining friends and family, before journeying to the elegant dining room for a spectacular meal followed by conversation over coffee. A clever grilling porch just off the kitchen area provides ample room and convenience to prepare the cuisine. After the party ends, retreat to your private master suite or relax in the whirlpool tub of your master bath. A large bonus room and two bedrooms, with adjoining bath on the upper level, make an excellent children's suite.

Editor's Choice

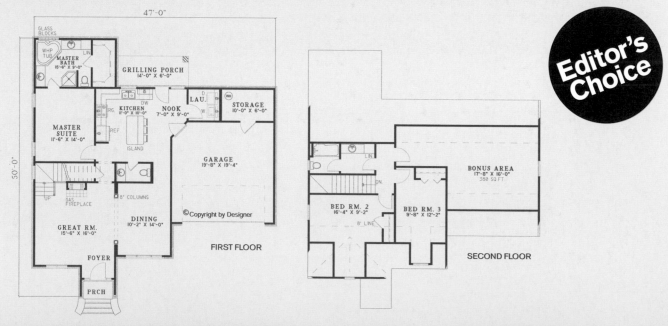

ORDER NOW! Phone: **1-800-235-5700**   Online: **www.FamilyHomePlans.com**   Order Code: **H6SSM**

Keeping Your Home Safe From Poisonings

Poison Centers

Every Poison Control Center in the country can be reached by calling the AAPCC* nationwide hotline, 1-800-222-1222. Post this number, along with your other emergency numbers, by every phone on your home. If you think someone is poisoned, call the poison center immediately. Experts will answer your call, 24 hours a day, seven days a week.

Medicines and Household Cleaners

Make sure all medications, caustic cleaning products (example: drain openers, toilet and oven cleaners, rust removers, etc.), automotive fluids (example: windshield washing solution and antifreeze), pesticides, fertilizer and other household chemicals are in their original containers and in a locked cabinet.

Carbon Monoxide Alarms

Carbon monoxide gas is poisonous, but you can't see, smell or taste it. Check all fuel-burning appliances to be sure they work properly: furnace, hot water heater, stove, oven, fireplace, wood stove, and space heater. Put a carbon monoxide alarm near where people sleep. Be sure your alarm has the Underwriters Laboratories (UL 2034) label.

*American Association of Poison Control Centers

Courtesy of PATH
www.pathnet.org/homeowners

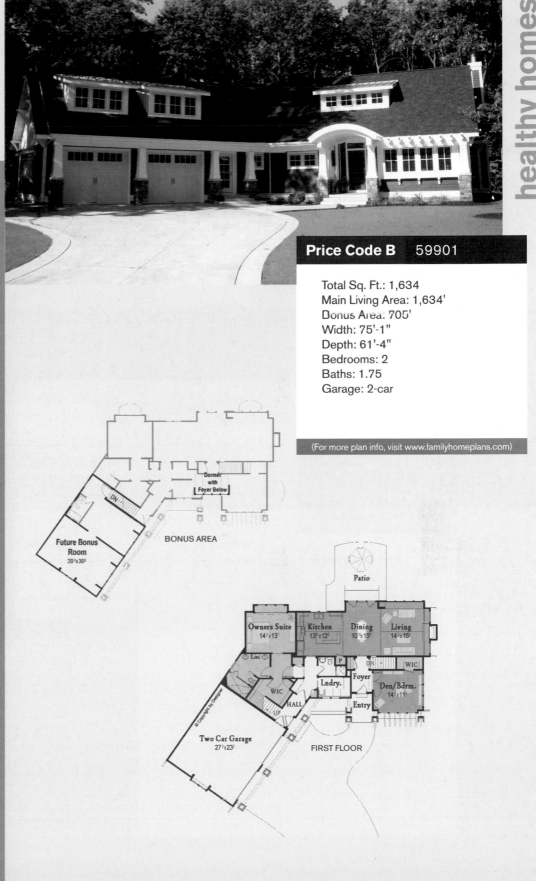

Price Code B 59901

Total Sq. Ft.: 1,634
Main Living Area: 1,634'
Bonus Area: 705'
Width: 75'-1"
Depth: 61'-4"
Bedrooms: 2
Baths: 1.75
Garage: 2-car

(For more plan info, visit www.familyhomeplans.com)

european charm

It's irresistible the way this design makes big promises and keeps them. It all begins with exterior charm, from towering pavilion affects, and pitched roofs to wonderfully elongated windows. A formal foyer gives guests plenty of time to prepare for the wonderland of charm. Main floor ceilings soar to 9' (13' in the family room) while the entry hall sweeps smoothly to the family room and fireplace, or directly to the kitchen with island. Tucked politely to the side of the kitchen, the dining room has access to the outdoors. Hugging close to the kitchen's opposite side is a laundry and shower room (ideal when the kids or grandkids come in from rough and muddy play). A spectacular second level begins on the mezzanine, overlooking the downstairs family room. The master bedroom has a private passage through a great walk-in closet and into a luxurious full-sized bathroom. One of the secondary bedrooms, also with a walk-in closet, gets cozy with a loft-style sitting area. Bedroom #3 prizes a walk-in closet and a special window seat.

Above: A generous island snack bar provides ample workspace, plus a convenient spot for casual dining. Top Right: Natural light brightens the view from the kitchen to the dining area and living room. Middle and Bottom Right: The charming master bath exudes a sense of luxury usually found in larger homes.

Price Code D 65409

Total Sq. Ft.: 1,727
Main Level: 837'
Upper Level: 890'
Width 36'
Depth 39'-8"
Bedrooms: 3
Baths: 1.75
Garage: 1-car

(For more plan info, visit www.familyhomeplans.com)

FIRST FLOOR

SECOND FLOOR

Price Code B 34029

Total Sq. Ft.: 1,686'
Width: 61'
Depth: 54'
Bedrooms: 3
Full Baths: 2
Garage: 2-car

(For more plan info, visit www.familyhomeplans.com)

Keep dry during the rainy season under this home's covered porch. A foyer separates the dining room with a decorative ceiling from the breakfast area and the kitchen. Off the kitchen is the laundry room, conveniently located. The living room features a vaulted beamed ceiling and a fireplace. A full bath is located between the living room and two bedrooms, both with a large closet. On the other side of the living room is the master bedroom with a decorative ceiling and a skylight above the entrance to its private bath. For those who enjoy outdoor living, an optional deck is offered, accessible through sliding glass doors off of the master bedroom. This home is designed with basement, slab, and crawlspace foundation options.

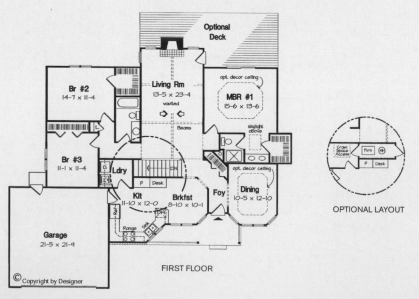

FIRST FLOOR

OPTIONAL LAYOUT

Stamped concrete, tinted to take on the hue of wood, provides a beautiful, maintenance-free alternative for the flooring on this comfortable front porch.
Plan #19422

smarter building materials

IT'S TRUE... THEY DON'T BUILD 'EM LIKE THEY USED TO

From start to finish, building a home requires careful attention to a myriad of choices and decisions. Making decisions has always been a part of new home construction, but due to advancements in the development of today's building materials, your wise choices can be rewarded in a home with unprecedented qualities and characteristics.

In recent years, a progression of new techniques and technologies have changed the face of practically every component of a home, from the foundation on up. For example, today's fiber-cement siding and composite lumber materials provide the look of wood with far more durability. They are impervious to termites and fire, and require little or no maintenance. High impact shingles ward off high winds and hail, and carry their warranties for half a century. Insulated concrete forms (ICFs) create super-insulated, incredibly strong exterior walls. And environmentally friendly materials such as bamboo flooring and recycled content carpet (made from recycled soda bottles) add beauty to the inside of our homes.

With these and other new building materials, you can expect to build a truly smarter home that is easier to maintain, incredibly durable, far more energy efficient and respectable in its use of resources from our environment.

Price Code B   40010

Total Sq. Ft.: 1,688'
Width: 70'-1"
Depth: 48'
Bedrooms: 3
Baths: 2
Garage: 2-car

(For more plan info, visit www.familyhomeplans.com)

Large porches offering full views will be the focal point of outdoor entertaining and enjoyment. In the great room, built-in cabinets flank the fireplace. Plenty of storage is available with an abundance of walk-in closets, a pantry and large utility room with sink.

Porch
31-4x8-0

Bath

Master Bedroom
13-6x15-6

Bath

Shlvs.   Shlvs.

Greatroom
15-4x19-5

Breakfast
9-10x10-6

Shelves   Sink

Laundry
8-6x9-4

Storage
8-6x9-4

Kitchen
9-6x11-6

Bedroom
13-6x11-6

Shlvs.

Bedroom
10-11x11-6

Foyer

Dining
12-0x11-6

Garage
21-6x21-6

©Copyright by Designer

Porch
31-4x8-0

FIRST FLOOR

REAR EXTERIOR

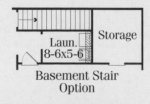

Laun.
8-6x5-6

Storage

Basement Stair Option

FIRST FLOOR OPTION

Price Code B 65866

Total Sq. Ft.: 1,698
Main Level: 1,290'
Bonus Area: 1,153'
Width: 58'
Depth: 58'-2"
Bedrooms: 3
Baths: 2.5
Garage: 2-car

(For more plan info, visit www.familyhomeplans.com)

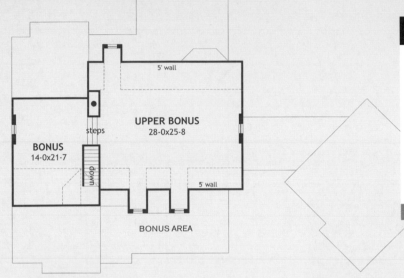

BONUS
14-0x21-7

steps

down

UPPER BONUS
28-0x25-8

5' wall

5' wall

BONUS AREA

Editor's Choice

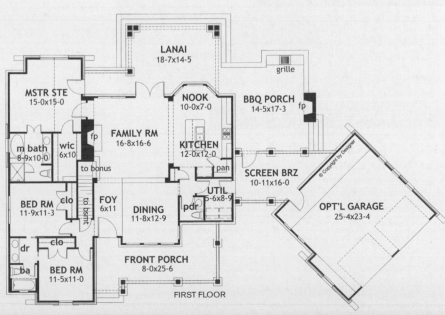

LANAI
18-7x14-5

grille

MSTR STE
15-0x15-0

NOOK
10-0x7-0

BBQ PORCH
14-5x17-3

fp

m bath
8-9x10-0

wic
6x10

fp

FAMILY RM
16-8x16-6

KITCHEN
12-0x12-0

pan

SCREEN BRZ
10-11x16-0

© Copyright by Designer

to bonus

BED RM
11-9x11-3

clo

to bsmt

FOY
6x11

DINING
11-8x12-9

pdr

UTIL
6-6x8-9

OPT'L GARAGE
25-4x23-4

dr

clo

BED RM
11-5x11-0

ba

FRONT PORCH
8-0x25-6

FIRST FLOOR

Price Code B   72023

Total Sq. Ft.: 1,694
Main Level: 1,235'
Upper Level: 459'
Width: 48'
Depth: 42'
Bedrooms: 3
Baths: 2.5
Garage: 2-car

(For more plan info, visit www.familyhomeplans.com)

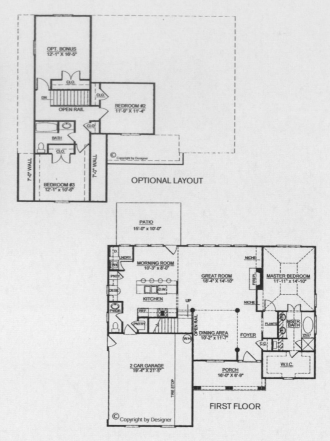

OPTIONAL LAYOUT

FIRST FLOOR

Price Code B   92460

Total Sq. Ft.: 1,695
Main Level: 880'
Upper Level: 815'
Width: 50'
Depth: 48'-8"
Bedrooms: 3
Baths: 2.5
Garage: 2-car

(For more plan info, visit www.familyhomeplans.com)

SECOND FLOOR

FIRST FLOOR

Editor's Choice

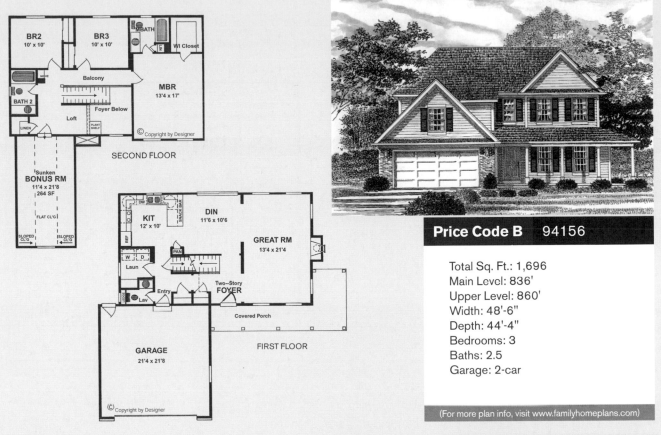

BR2 10' x 10'

BR3 10' x 10'

MBATH

WI Closet

Balcony

BATH 2

MBR 13'4 x 17'

Foyer Below

LINEN

Loft

PLANT SHELF

© Copyright by Designer

SECOND FLOOR

Sunken
BONUS RM
11'4 x 21'8
264 SF

FLAT CL'G

SLOPED CL'G

SLOPED CL'G

KIT 12' x 10'

DIN 11'6 x 10'6

SNACK BAR

REF

DW

PAN

W D

Laun

GREAT RM 13'4 x 21'4

Two--Story **FOYER**

Entry

Lav

Covered Porch

GARAGE 21'4 x 21'8

FIRST FLOOR

© Copyright by Designer

Price Code B 94156

Total Sq. Ft.: 1,696
Main Level: 836'
Upper Level: 860'
Width: 48'-6"
Depth: 44'-4"
Bedrooms: 3
Baths: 2.5
Garage: 2-car

(For more plan info, visit www.familyhomeplans.com)

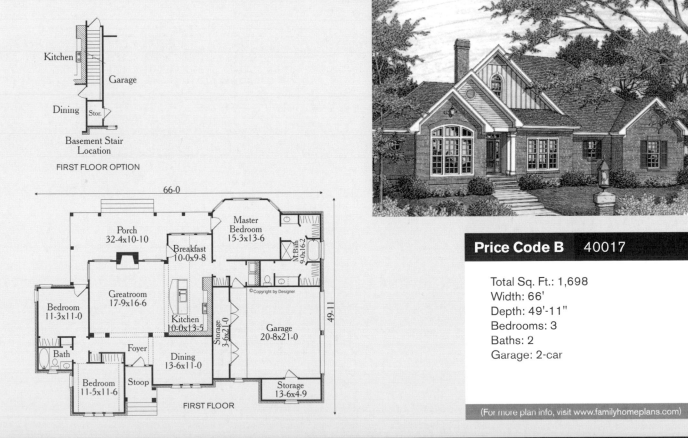

Kitchen

Garage

Dining

Stor.

Basement Stair Location

FIRST FLOOR OPTION

66-0

Porch 32-4x10-10

Master Bedroom 15-3x13-6

Breakfast 10-0x9-8

M. Bath 9-0x16-2

Greatroom 17-9x16-6

Bedroom 11-3x11-0

Kitchen 10-0x13-5

Storage 3-6x21-0

Garage 20-8x21-0

© Copyright by Designer

49-11

Bath

Foyer

Dining 13-6x11-0

Bedroom 11-5x11-6

Stoop

Storage 13-6x4-9

FIRST FLOOR

Price Code B 40017

Total Sq. Ft.: 1,698
Width: 66'
Depth: 49'-11"
Bedrooms: 3
Baths: 2
Garage: 2-car

(For more plan info, visit www.familyhomeplans.com)

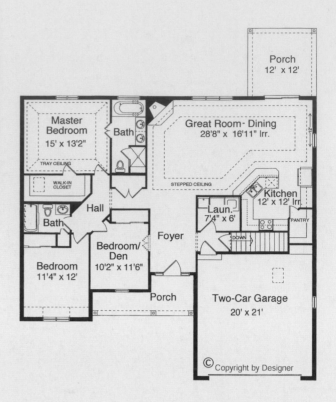

Price Code B 50042

Total Sq. Ft.: 1,698
Width: 51'-8"
Depth: 49'-8"
Bedrooms: 3
Baths: 2
Garage: 2-car

(For more plan info, visit www.familyhomeplans.com)

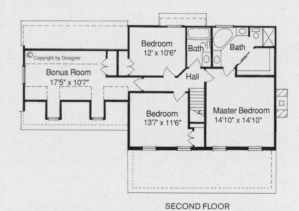

Price Code B 92690

Total Sq. Ft.: 1,698
Main Level: 868'
Upper Level: 830'
Width: 54'-4"
Depth: 28'-4"
Bedrooms: 3
Full Baths: 2.5
Garage: 2-car

(For more plan info, visit www.familyhomeplans.com)

ORDER NOW! Phone: **1-800-235-5700** Online: **www.FamilyHomePlans.com** Order Code: **H6SSM**

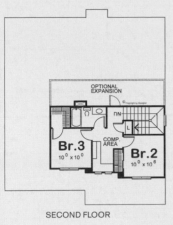
OPTIONAL EXPANSION

© Copyright by Designer

Br.3
10⁰ x 10⁰

COMP. AREA

Br.2
10⁰ x 10⁶

SECOND FLOOR

Mbr.
15⁰ x 13⁰
10'-0" CEIL.

Fam. Rm.
14⁶ x 15⁴

Bfst.
9⁴ x 11⁰

Kit.
13³ x 11²

Gar.
19⁸ x 20⁴

Den
10⁰ x 10⁶

47'-8"

© Copyright by Designer

COVERED PORCH

FIRST FLOOR

Price Code B 68235

Total Sq. Ft.: 1,699
Main Level: 1,268'
Upper Level: 431'
Width: 40'
Depth: 47'-8"
Bedrooms: 3
Baths: 2.5
Garage: 2-car

(For more plan info, visit www.familyhomeplans.com)

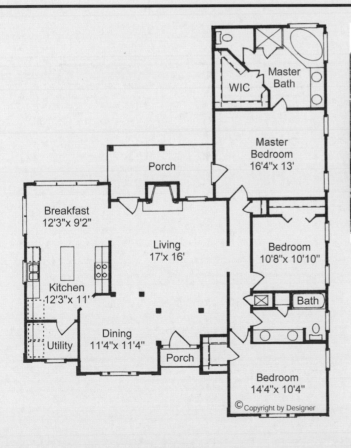

Breakfast
12'3"x 9'2"

Porch

WIC

Master Bath

Master Bedroom
16'4"x 13'

Living
17'x 16'

Kitchen
12'3"x 11'

Bedroom
10'8"x 10'10"

Bath

Utility

Dining
11'4"x 11'4"

Porch

Bedroom
14'4"x 10'4"

© Copyright by Designer

Price Code B 94602

Total Sq. Ft.: 1,704
Width: 45'
Depth: 58'-4"
Bedrooms: 3
Full Baths: 2
Garage: none

(For more plan info, visit www.familyhomeplans.com)

Price Code B 63093

Total Sq. Ft.: 1,704
Width: 50'
Depth: 50'-8"
Bedrooms: 3
Baths: 2
Garage: 2-car

(For more plan info, visit www.familyhomeplans.com)

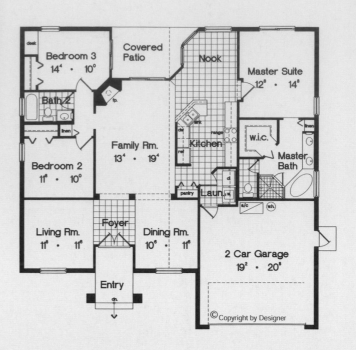

Price Code B 50006

Total Sq. Ft.: 1,707
Main Level: 908'
Upper Level: 799'
Width: 53'-8"
Depth: 45'-10"
Bedrooms: 4
Baths: 2.5
Garage: 2-car

(For more plan info, visit www.familyhomeplans.com)

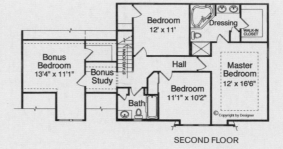

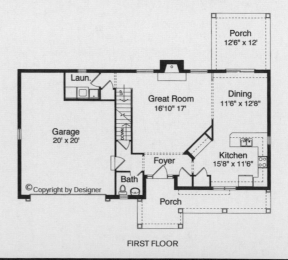

ORDER NOW! Phone: **1-800-235-5700** Online: **www.FamilyHomePlans.com** Order Code: **H6SSM**

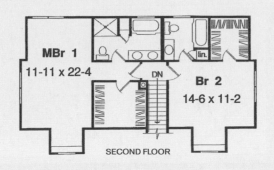

MBr 1
11-11 x 22-4

Br 2
14-6 x 11-2

DN

SECOND FLOOR

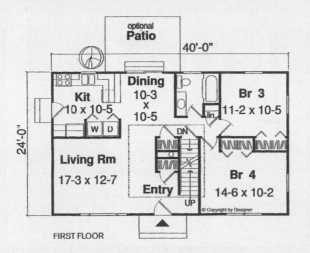

optional **Patio**

40'-0"

24'-0"

Kit
10 x 10-5

Dining
10-3 x 10-5

Br 3
11-2 x 10-5

lin.

DN

Living Rm
17-3 x 12-7

Entry

UP

Br 4
14-6 x 10-2

© Copyright by Designer

FIRST FLOOR

Entry

UP

Slab/crawlspace option

OPTIONAL LAYOUT

Price Code B   34077

Total Sq. Ft.: 1,757
Main Level: 957'
Upper Level: 800'
Width: 40'
Depth: 24'
Bedrooms: 4
Baths: 3
Garage: none

(For more plan info, visit www.familyhomeplans.com)

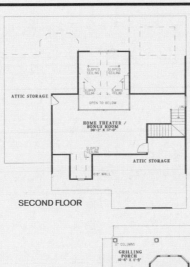

ATTIC STORAGE

SLOPED CEILING   SLOPED CEILING

SLOPED CEILING

OPEN TO BELOW

HOME THEATER / BONUS ROOM

SLOPED CEILING

ATTIC STORAGE

SECOND FLOOR

52'-6"

GRILLING PORCH

COVERED PORCH

MASTER SUITE

DINING ROOM

BREAKFAST ROOM

55'-6"

KITCHEN

GREAT ROOM
OPEN TO ABOVE

M. BATH

BALCONY LINE ABOVE

BEDROOM 2

FOYER

BEDROOM 3 / STUDY

GARAGE

COVERED PORCH

© Copyright by Designer

FIRST FLOOR

Price Code B   62208

Total Sq. Ft.: 1,723
Width: 52'-6"
Depth: 55'-6"
Bedrooms: 3
Baths: 2
Garage: 2-car

(For more plan info, visit www.familyhomeplans.com)

Price Code B   86101

Total Sq. Ft.: 1,738
Main Level: 1,138'
Upper Level: 600'
Width: 34'-10"
Depth: 50'-8"
Bedrooms: 3
Baths: 2.5
Garage: none

(For more plan info, visit www.familyhomeplans.com)

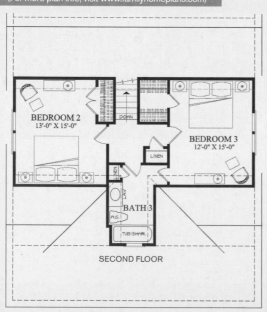

BEDROOM 2
13'-0" X 15'-0"

BEDROOM 3
12'-0" X 15'-0"

LINEN

BATH 3

SECOND FLOOR

PORCH
34'-10" X 10'-0"

© Copyright by Designer

MASTER BEDROOM
14'-0" X 16'-0"

GREAT ROOM
16'-4" X 14'-0"

BATH

P'DR
ROOM

DINING
AREA
13'-4" X 8'-0"

PANTRY

BREAKFAST BAR

WARDROBE

FOYER

KITCHEN
14'-4" X 10'-0"

UTILITY

PORCH
34'-10" X 8'-0"

FIRST FLOOR

This home's open floor plan seems to expand beyond its actual square footage. The great room, enhanced by a tray ceiling, flows freely with the kitchen and dining room. A private study off the foyer adjoins a second bedroom. The master suite shares a rear covered porch with the dining room, for sheltered gatherings or a private space to relax.

Price Code B   94151

Total Sq. Ft.: 1,716
Bedrooms: 2
Baths: 2
Width: 48'
Depth: 58'
Garage: 2-car

(For more plan info, visit www.familyhomeplans.com)

DIN RM
13'4 x 13'

Covered Porch

MBR
14'4 x 14'

GREAT RM
tray cl'g
16'2 x 13'6

step cl'g

WIC

MBATH

KITCHEN
13'4 x 13'6

DW

SNACK BAR

REF

PANT | SHELV | **WIC**

FOYER

LINEN

BATH2

D W

Laun

STUDY
10' x 10'1

Covered Porch

BR2
12'2 x 12'

TWO-CAR GARAGE
19'4 x 21'8

© Copyright by Designer

Editor's Choice

Price Code B 72020

Total Sq. Ft.: 1,725
Main Level: 842'
Upper Level: 883'
Width: 45'
Depth: 36'
Bedrooms: 3
Baths: 2.5
Garage: 2-car

(For more plan info, visit www.familyhomeplans.com)

An appealing covered entry greets guests to an interior that offers both formal and family areas. Fireplaces in the living and family rooms invite cozy, relaxed conversations. The breakfast area with windows on all sides allows meals and nature to be enjoyed at the same time.

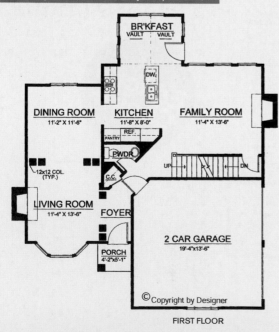

FIRST FLOOR

SECOND FLOOR

ORDER NOW! Phone: **1-800-235-5700** Online: **www.FamilyHomePlans.com** Order Code: **H6SSM**

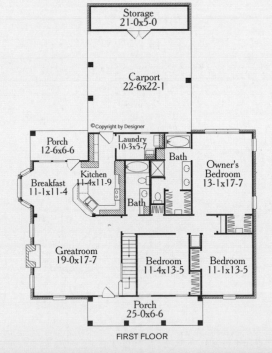

This home's large great room opens to the kitchen and the bayed dining area, providing a wonderful space for family gatherings. An angled bar provides an additional sitting area for the kitchen. The rear porch allows outdoor access. A working desk is located across from the laundry room. The master suite features dual lavatories, a tub and separate shower, linen closet and two walk-in closets. If future space is needed, an additional 1,035 square feet can be added upstairs.

Price Code B 40034

Total Sq. Ft.: 1,726
Width: 51'-8"
Depth: 70'-6"
Bedrooms: 3
Baths: 2
Garage: 2-car

(For more plan info, visit www.familyhomeplans.com)

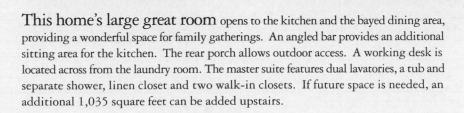

Storage
21-0x5-0

Carport
22-6x22-1

©Copyright by Designer

Porch
12-6x6-6

Laundry
10-3x5-7

Bath

Owner's
Bedroom
13-1x17-7

Kitchen
11-4x11-9

Breakfast
11-1x11-4

Bath

Greatroom
19-0x17-7

Bedroom
11-4x13-5

Bedroom
11-1x13-5

Porch
25-0x6-6

FIRST FLOOR

Future
47-6x20-9

SECOND FLOOR

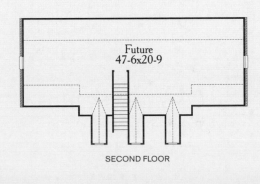

Price Code B 50040

Total Sq. Ft.: 1,727
Main Level: 941'
Upper Level: 786'
Bedrooms: 3
Baths: 2.5
Width: 57'-10"
Depth: 42'-4"
Garage: 2-car

(For more plan info, visit www.familyhomeplans.com)

A stone and siding exterior brings dimension and color to the exterior of this charming home. A two-story foyer greets you upon arrival and the great room, with views to the rear and sides yard, offers a 12' ceiling height. The breakfast bay with entry to a covered porch creates a bright and cheery place to start the day. Additional storage and a convenient writing desk are provided with the extended counter space. A furniture alcove adds space to the formal dining room, and a rear entry hall offers storage closets and a large laundry room. A second floor master bedroom, with a ceiling that slopes to 9', keeps the parents close at hand to the younger family members. This home has a full basement that can be accessed for additional square footage.

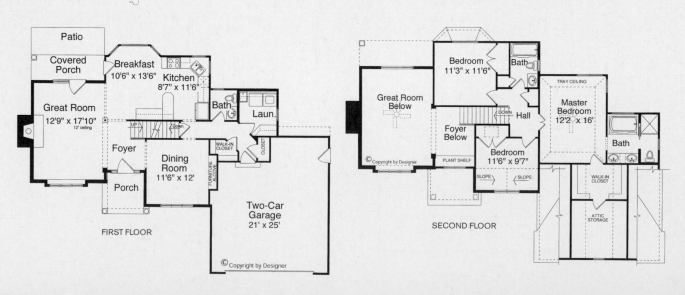

Price Code B 40030

Total Sq. Ft.: 1,730
Width: 61'
Depth: 62'
Bedrooms: 3
Baths: 2
Garage: 2-car

(For more plan info, visit www.familyhomeplans.com)

Triple pairs of French doors lead into the great room from the raised, brick porch. The great room enjoys a front and rear view, and displays a fireplace with built-in cabinets. Nine foot ceilings add spaciousness to the first level of the home. The kitchen joins a large breakfast room with a snack bar and serves a pantry, microwave cabinet, and plenty of cabinets and work space. The private master bedroom accommodates an enormous walk-in closet, whirlpool tub, dual lavatories, stall shower, and linen closets. Two additional bedrooms with ample closet space share a full bath. Future upstairs space can provide an additional 520 square feet when needed.

Editor's Choice

Price Code C 62177

Total Sq. Ft.: 1,760
Bedrooms: 4
Baths: 2
Garage: 2-car
Width: 53' 2"
Depth: 64' 4"

(For more plan info, visit www.familyhomeplans.com)

A quaint porched cape with gabled front facade adds charm to this drive under garage design. Inside, the angled kitchen wall expands the sense of space into the dining room and makes the kitchen part of the living area without sacrificing formality. The cathedraled breakfast nook is a nice surprise in this story and one half design. The first floor master suite provides maximum privacy for a growing family while eliminating stairs all together for the empty nester. Upstairs, a cozy sitting area is nestled in the front gable, allowing light from its radius window to flow into the foyer through the staircase's open railing. Two spacious bedrooms share a hall bath on the second floor. This plan is only available as a basement due to drive under garage design.

High Wind and Impact Resistant Asphalt Roofing Shingles

Designed to resist damage from impact and high winds

In areas where storms and high winds can damage many roofs, high wind- and impact-resistant shingles offer additional protection to the home and its occupants. These shingles meet the most stringent standards for impact resistance (Class 4) set by Underwriters Laboratories (UL), and wind resistance set by UL and the American Society for Testing and Materials (ASTM International).

The sturdy construction of these shingles lets them last for years without having to be replaced. Most come with a 30- to 50-year limited product warranty, and 10-year coverage against algae growth. Wind resistance limited warranties are generally for winds of between 100 and 130 mph.

The material cost for wind- and impact-resistant shingles is about 50 percent higher than for conventional shingles. Installation labor cost may be slightly higher than for conventional shingles. However, depending on location and frequency of storms, the costs for this type of roofing could be less than the costs of replacing roofing due to impact or wind. Additionally, insurance companies may offer a discount to homeowners on their homeowner's insurance policy for shingles meeting Class 4 rating.

Courtesy of PATH
www.pathnet.org/homeowners

Price Code B 99123

Total Sq. Ft.: 1,732
Main Level: 1,289'
Lower Level: 443'
Bedrooms: 3
Baths: 2.25
Width: 43'
Depth: 40'
Garage: 2-car

(For more plan info, visit www.familyhomeplans.com)

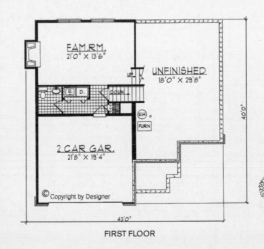

FIRST FLOOR

SECOND FLOOR

Price Code B 94603

Total Sq. Ft.: 1,737
Main Level: 1,238'
Upper Level: 499'
Bedrooms: 3
Baths: 2.5
Width: 38'-4"
Depth: 49'
Garage: 2-car

(For more plan info, visit www.familyhomeplans.com)

Twin dormers perch above a long front porch, providing this 1-story home a comfortable sense of welcome. Upon entering, guests are greeted by a formal dining room. Farther inside, the living room is positioned for privacy and lies open to the kitchen's breakfast area. The main floor master suite looks out onto the front porch. Upstairs, secondary bedrooms share a central bath, and a balcony overlooks the living room below. Ample space for storage is available in the attic area.

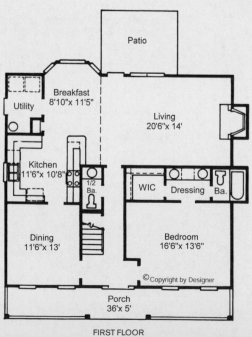

FIRST FLOOR

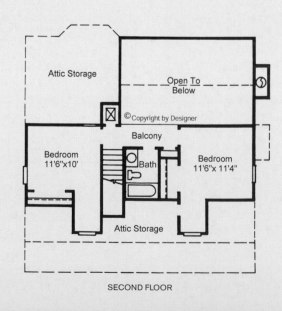

SECOND FLOOR

Price Code B   62321

Total Sq. Ft.: 1,732
Bonus Area: 243'
Width: 52'
Depth: 63'-10"
Bedrooms: 3
Baths: 2
Garage: 2-car

(For more plan info, visit www.familyhomeplans.com)

Form and Function combine in this home. A covered porch protects visitors from the elements. Walking into the foyer, they are greeted with a stunning view of the great room that includes a ten-foot ceiling, inviting fireplace, entry to the screened porch and a smooth transition into the dining room and kitchen. A sitting room adjoins the master suite for late-night reading after a relaxing bath in the whirlpool tub.t

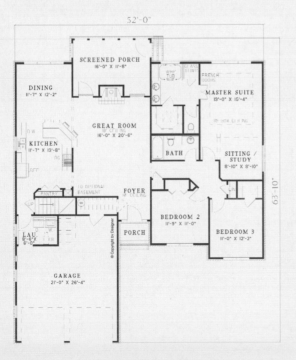

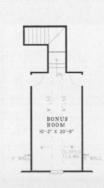

Price Code B 10839

Total Sq. Ft.: 1,738
Width: 66'
Depth: 52'
Bedrooms: 2
Baths: 2
Garage: 3-car

(For more plan info, visit www.familyhomeplans.com)

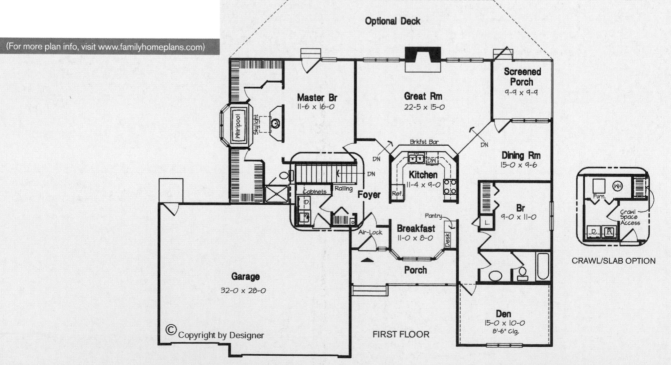

Optional Deck

Master Br
11-6 x 16-0

Great Rm
22-5 x 15-0

Screened
Porch
9-9 x 9-9

Brkfst Bar

Dining Rm
15-0 x 9-6

Kitchen
11-4 x 9-0

Foyer

Cabinets   Railing

Ref

Pantry

Br
9-0 x 11-0

Air-Lock

Breakfast
11-0 x 8-0

Desk

Porch

Garage
32-0 x 28-0

© Copyright by Designer

FIRST FLOOR

Den
15-0 x 10-0
8'-6" Clg.

Furn.

Crawl
Space
Access

CRAWL/SLAB OPTION

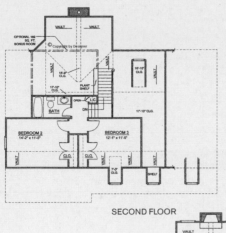

SECOND FLOOR

FIRST FLOOR

Price Code C   98240

Total Sq. Ft.: 1,764
Main Level: 1,296'
Upper Level: 468'
Width: 49'
Depth: 46'
Bedrooms: 3
Baths: 2.5
Garage: 2-car

(For more plan info, visit www.familyhomeplans.com)

SECOND FLOOR

Editor's Choice

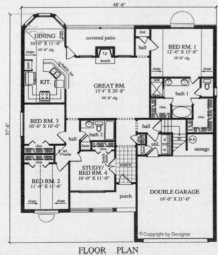

FLOOR PLAN

BP25-1749-NE

FIRST FLOOR

BP25-1749-NE

Price Code B   75004

Total Sq. Ft.: 1,749
Width: 48'-6"
Depth: 57'-6"
Bedrooms: 4
Baths: 2
Garage: 2-car

(For more plan info, visit www.familyhomeplans.com)

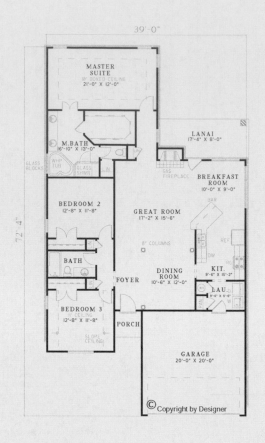

Price Code B   62035

Total Sq. Ft.: 1,750
Width: 39'
Depth: 72'-4"
Bedrooms: 3
Baths: 2
Garage: 2-car

(For more plan info, visit www.familyhomeplans.com)

Price Code C   98224

Total Sq. Ft.: 1,751
Width: 64'
Depth: 40'-6"
Bedrooms: 3
Baths: 2.5
Garage: 2-car

(For more plan info, visit www.familyhomeplans.com)

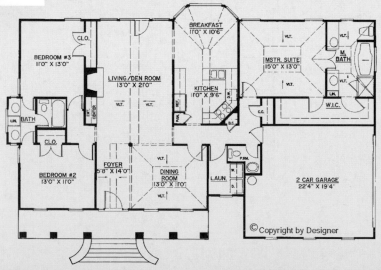

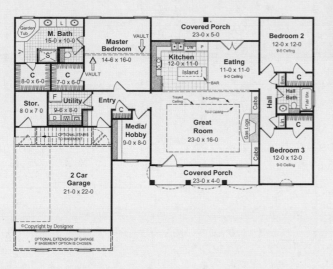

Price Code C   59010

Total Sq. Ft.: 1,751
Width: 64'
Depth: 45'-10"
Bedrooms: 3
Baths: 2
Garage: 2-car

(For more plan info, visit www.familyhomeplans.com)

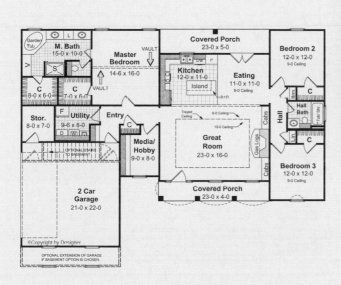

Price Code C   59011

Total Sq. Ft.: 1,751
Width: 64'
Depth: 45'-10"
Bedrooms: 3
Baths: 2
Garage: 2-car

(For more plan info, visit www.familyhomeplans.com)

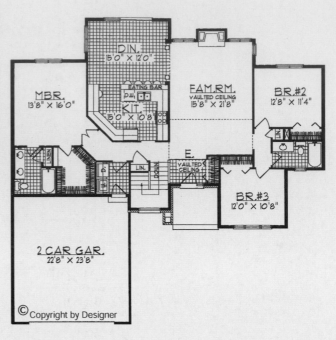

Price Code C 93191

Total Sq. Ft.: 1,756
Width: 59'
Depth: 58'
Bedrooms: 3
Baths: 2
Garage: 2-car

(For more plan info, visit www.familyhomeplans.com)

© Copyright by Designer

Price Code C 63090

Total Sq. Ft.: 1,758
Width: 60'
Depth: 45'
Bedrooms: 3
Baths: 2
Garage: 2-car

(For more plan info, visit www.familyhomeplans.com)

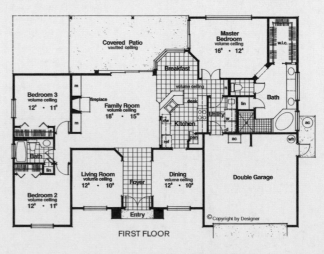

ORDER NOW! Phone: **1-800-235-5700** Online: **www.FamilyHomePlans.com** Order Code: **H6SSM**

Bamboo Flooring

The look of wood flooring from a fast growing, renewable plant source

A flooring material which resembles wood but grows like grass? Bamboo flooring is an attractive alternative to wood or laminate flooring. Botanically classified as a grass, bamboo matures into a merchantable size in three to five years compared with 50 to 100 years for most hardwood species. The appearance of bamboo is very similar to wood flooring. It comes in vertical and flat-grain patterns and generally is offered in a light, honey or natural color and a darker, amber "carbonized" color.

Bamboo flooring can be nailed or floated and its strength and dimensional stability compare very well with traditional wood flooring. Some bamboo flooring products are highly dent resistant. Other bamboo flooring products are softer, so be sure to check with the manufacturer for product warranty information. The cost for prefinished bamboo flooring typically ranges from $4 to $8 per square foot plus installation. Common thicknesses for bamboo flooring products are 1/2, 5/8, and 3/4 inches. Widths range from 3 to 4 inches and lengths range from 2 to 6 feet.

Besides the environmental benefits of this sustainable, fast-growing resource, bamboo makes an attractive, stable, dent-resistant alternative to wood flooring.

Courtesy of PATH
www.pathnet.org/homeowners

Price Code C 50104

Total Sq. Ft.: 1,751
Width: 62'-8"
Depth: 42'-2"
Bedrooms: 3
Baths: 2
Garage: 2-car

(For more plan info, visit www.familyhomeplans.com)

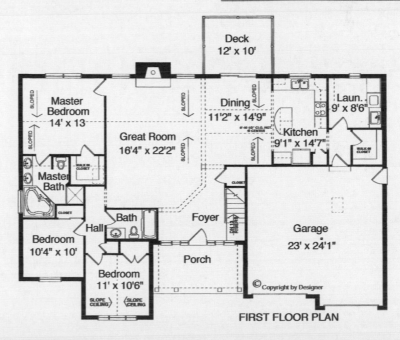

FIRST FLOOR PLAN

wrap-around comfort

This popular 1,936 sq. ft. design has been winning favor among homeowners and builders for easy adaptability to diverse types of terrains, especially steep and narrow lots. Winsome on the outside this classic Victorian with trademark great porch, turret effects and complementary windowing also delivers a family-loving open-style interior. A free-flowing living and dining room, 9' ceilings, fireplace, spacious kitchen, breakfast area, powder room, and library with built-ins deliver contemporary appeal and comfortable flexibility. The second level features a master suite with its own fireplace and master bath while two additional and beautifully proportioned bedrooms share a full bath. Plus, a bonus room over the garage awaits creative transformation

Comfortable free-flowing spaces are brightened by plenty of natural light. This particular home was modified to reflect the preferences of its owner. Left: In the family room, an angled wall draws attention to the fireplace and widescreen TV. Top Left: In the kitchen, angles reposition the island with its breakfast/lunch counter. Top Right: The dining room enjoys expansive vistas to the outdoors through a generous bay of windows and garden doors.

Price Code C   65177

Total Sq. Ft.: 1,936
Main Level: 1,044'
Upper Level: 892'
Width 58'
Depth 43'-6"
Bedrooms: 3
Baths: 2.5
Garage: 2-car

(For more plan info, visit www.familyhomeplans.com)

FIRST FLOOR

SECOND FLOOR

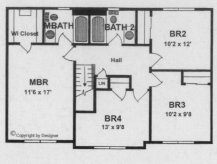

SECOND FLOOR

Price Code C 94160

Total Sq. Ft.: 1,760
Main Level: 972'
Upper Level: 788'
Width: 64'-4"
Depth: 24'
Bedrooms: 3
Baths: 2.5
Garage: 2-car

(For more plan info, visit www.familyhomeplans.com)

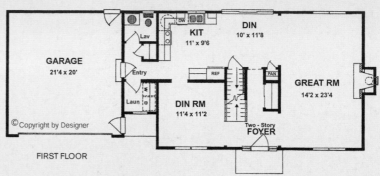

FIRST FLOOR

Price Code C 74000

Total Sq. Ft.: 1,760
Main Level: 884'
Upper Level: 876'
Width: 24'
Depth: 39'
Bedrooms: 3
Baths: 2.5
Garage: none

(For more plan info, visit www.familyhomeplans.com)

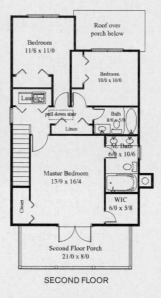

SECOND FLOOR

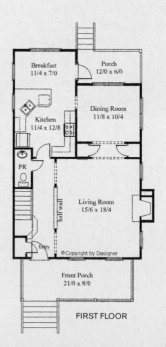

FIRST FLOOR

ORDER NOW! Phone: **1-800-235-5700** Online: **www.FamilyHomePlans.com** Order Code: **H6SSM**

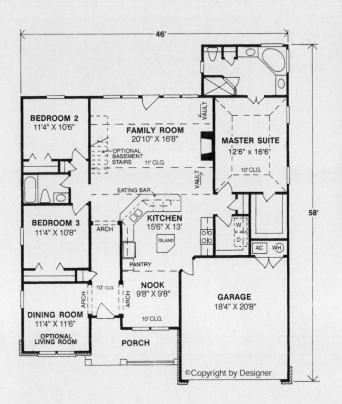

46'

58'

BEDROOM 2
11'4" X 10'6"

FAMILY ROOM
20'10" X 16'8"

OPTIONAL
BASEMENT
STAIRS 11' CLG.

VAULT

MASTER SUITE
12'6" x 16'6"

10' CLG.

EATING BAR

VAULT

BEDROOM 3
11'4" X 10'8"

ARCH

KITCHEN
15'6" X 13'

ISLAND

W D

AC WH

PANTRY

10' CLG.

ARCH

ARCH

NOOK
9'8" X 9'8"

GARAGE
18'4" X 20'8"

DINING ROOM
11'4" X 11'6"

ARCH

10' CLG.

OPTIONAL
LIVING ROOM

PORCH

©Copyright by Designer

Price Code C   68139

Total Sq. Ft.: 1,762
Width: 46'
Depth: 58'
Bedrooms: 3
Baths: 2.75
Garage: 2-car

(For more plan info, visit www.familyhomeplans.com)

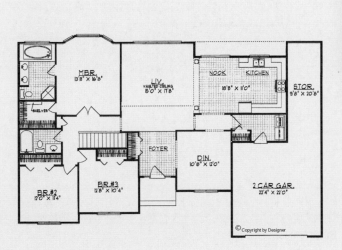

MBR.
13'8" X 16'8"

LIV.
VAULTED CEILING
15'0" X 17'8"

NOOK

KITCHEN
18'8" X 11'0"

STOR.
9'8" X 20'8"

SHELVES

FOYER

DIN.
10'8" X 12'0"

2 CAR GAR.
22'4" X 22'0"

BR #2
12'0" X 11'4"

BR #3
12'8" X 10'4"

©Copyright by Designer

Price Code C   93133

Total Sq. Ft.: 1,763
Width: 67'-8"
Depth: 43'
Bedrooms: 3
Baths: 2
Garage: 3-car

(For more plan info, visit www.familyhomeplans.com)

ORDER NOW!   Phone: **1-800-235-5700**   Online: **www.FamilyHomePlans.com**   Order Code: **H6SSM**

Price Code D 59114

Total Sq. Ft.: 2,000
Bonus Area: 359'
Width: 69'
Depth: 60'
Bedrooms: 3
Baths: 2.5
Garage: 2-car

(For more plan info, visit www.familyhomeplans.com)

European Country. This inviting home has European Country styling with upscale features. The front and rear covered porches add plenty of usable outdoor living space, and include that much-requested outdoor kitchen. Expansive great room includes a beautiful trayed ceiling and features built-in cabinets and a gas fireplace. The spacious kitchen features an oversized island with a large eating bar and breakfast area. The hall bath is equipped with dual lavatories for convenience. The master bedroom has a raised ceiling and opens into the well-equipped bath with dual lavatories, oversized corner jet tub, and large his and her walk-in closets. There is a storage area off the garage for projects and storage. The media/hobby space could be used as a home office, dining room, or playroom. This is a very flexible home with plenty of options to choose from. Make this your family's next home!

OPTIONAL LAYOUT

Recycled Wood/Plastic Composite Lumber

Mix of wood fibers and waste plastics turns into durable material

Recycled wood/plastic composite lumber is one of the prime uses for recycled plastic trash bags and waste wood fibers. The composite material is used to produce building products such as decking, door and window frames, and exterior moldings. Recycled wood/plastic composite lumber typically consists of a 50/50 mix of wood fibers from recovered saw dust and waste plastics that include high-density polyethylene, PVC, and others.

Manufacturers claim that products produced with recycled wood/plastic lumber are more durable than conventional preservative-treated lumber. The plastic encapsulates and binds the wood together to resist moisture penetration and degradation from fungal rot. As there is no need for painting or sealing, and given the material's durability, composite lumber products cost less to maintain than wood decks, railings, and fences. Also, these products contain no toxic chemicals such as those used in conventional treated lumber.

In general, recycled wood/plastic composites are cost-competitive with high-end decking materials such as finger jointed pine and redwood, but are significantly more expensive than standard treated products. Retail costs for 2 x 6-inch material are approximately $2.00 per linear foot.

Courtesy of PATH
www.pathnet.org/homeowners

Price Code C · 94518

Total Sq. Ft.: 1,765
Main Level: 1,400'
Upper Level: 365'
Width: 42'
Depth: 58'
Bedrooms: 3
Baths: 3
Garage: 2-car

(For more plan info, visit www.familyhomeplans.com)

FIRST FLOOR

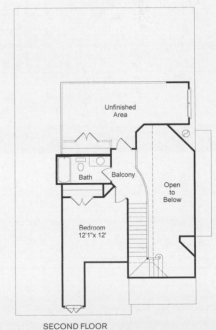

SECOND FLOOR

Price Code C   68204

Total Sq. Ft.: 1,765
Main Level: 1,218'
Upper Level: 547'
Width: 42'
Depth: 52'
Bedrooms: 3
Baths: 2.5
Garage: 2-car

(For more plan info, visit www.familyhomeplans.com)

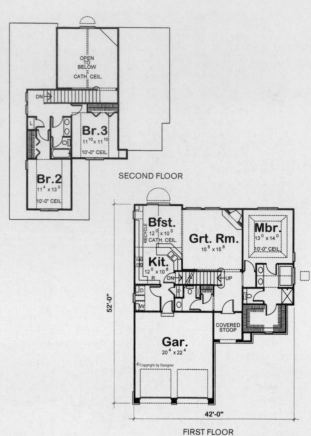

SECOND FLOOR

FIRST FLOOR

Price Code C   94159

Total Sq. Ft.: 1,765
Width: 57'
Depth: 70'
Bedrooms: 2
Baths: 2
Garage: 2-car

(For more plan info, visit www.familyhomeplans.com)

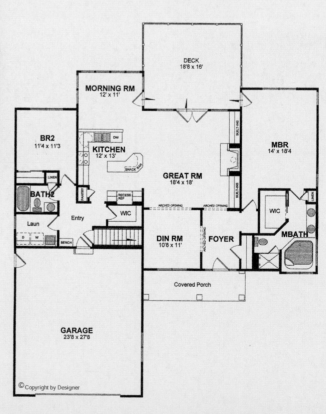

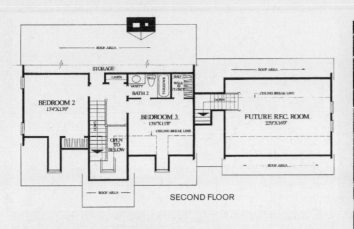

SECOND FLOOR

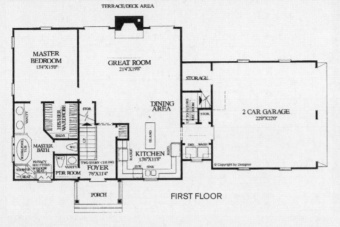

FIRST FLOOR

Price Code C   86102

Total Sq. Ft.: 1,762
Main Level: 1,211'
Upper Level: 551'
Width: 64'-4"
Depth: 39'-4"
Bedrooms: 3
Baths: 2.5
Garage: 2-car

(For more plan info, visit www.familyhomeplans.com)

SECOND FLOOR

FIRST FLOOR

Price Code C   94519

Total Sq. Ft.: 1,768
Main Level: 1,247'
Upper Level: 521'
Width: 35'-6"
Depth: 57'
Bedrooms: 3
Baths: 2.5
Garage: none

(For more plan info, visit www.familyhomeplans.com)

ORDER NOW! Phone: **1-800-235-5700** Online: **www.FamilyHomePlans.com** Order Code: **H6SSM**

Price Code C 50015

Total Sq. Ft.: 1,770
Main Level: 924'
Upper Level: 846'
Width: 50'
Depth: 36'-8"
Bedrooms: 3
Baths: 2.5
Garage: 2-car

(For more plan info, visit www.familyhomeplans.com)

The garage and covered front stoop are tastefully paired

with this home's brick facade. Inside, the foyer offers options of visiting the great room, the utility and kitchen area, or the upper level. Storage needs are addressed by a long closet in the hall, along with the utility room's hanging space. The kitchen has a pantry and abundant, wrapping counter space. All three bedrooms share the upper level and each has plenty of closet space.

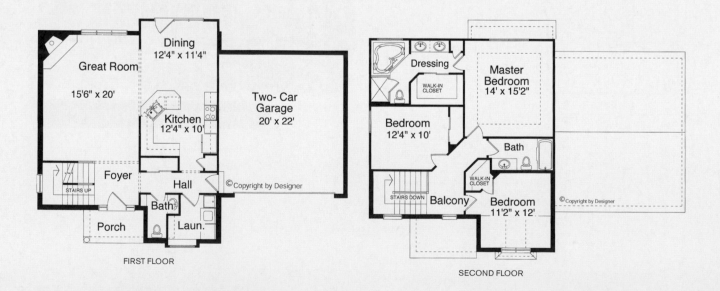

FIRST FLOOR

Great Room
15'6" x 20'

Dining
12'4" x 11'4"

Kitchen
12'4" x 10'

Two-Car Garage
20' x 22'

Foyer

STAIRS UP

Hall

Bath

Porch

Laun.

©Copyright by Designer

SECOND FLOOR

Dressing

WALK-IN CLOSET

Master Bedroom
14' x 15'2"

Bedroom
12'4" x 10'

Bath

STAIRS DOWN

Balcony

WALK-IN CLOSET

Bedroom
11'2" x 12'

©Copyright by Designer

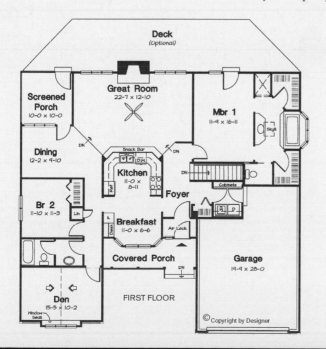

Price Code C 24714

Total Sq. Ft.: 1,771
Width: 54'
Depth: 50'
Bedrooms: 2
Baths: 2
Garage: 2-car

(For more plan info, visit www.familyhomeplans.com)

With double peaked roofs, dormers, covered front porch,

and Palladian windows, this home is truly breathtaking. The u-shaped kitchen with snack bar is located at the heart of the home and opens to the great room where the fireplace and the screened porch draw attention. A bright bayed breakfast area enjoys views beyond the front porch. A den (or bedroom #2) and #3 border a shared bath. The master bedroom with his and her walk-in closets is located on the opposite side of the house and features its own deck entry and a pampering bath.

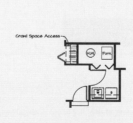
Editor's Choice

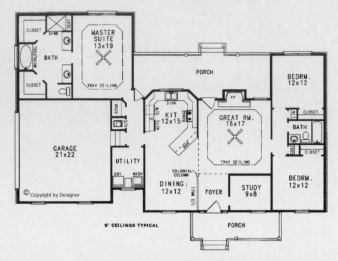

Price Code C   96525

Total Sq. Ft.: 1,771
Width: 68'
Depth: 50'
Bedrooms: 3
Baths: 2
Garage: 2-car

(For more plan info, visit www.familyhomeplans.com)

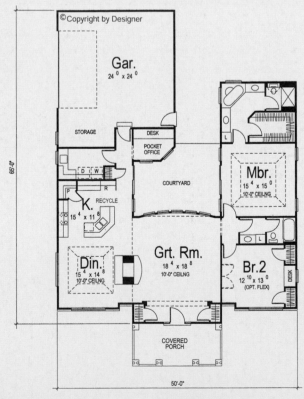

Price Code C   44000

Total Sq. Ft.: 1,772
Width: 50'
Depth: 65'
Bedrooms: 2
Baths: 2
Garage: 2-car

(For more plan info, visit www.familyhomeplans.com)

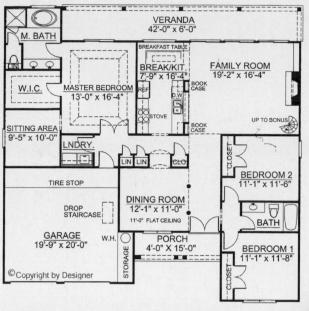

VERANDA
42'-0" x 6'-0"

M. BATH

BREAKFAST TABLE

BREAK/KIT.
7'-9" x 16'-4"

FAMILY ROOM
19'-2" x 16'-4"

W.I.C.

MASTER BEDROOM
13'-0" x 16'-4"

REF

BOOK CASE

D.W.

STOVE

BOOK CASE

SITTING AREA
9'-5" x 10'-0"

UP TO BONUS

LNDRY.

LIN LIN CLO

CLOSET

BEDROOM 2
11'-1" x 11'-6"

TIRE STOP

DROP STAIRCASE

DINING ROOM
12'-1" x 11'-0"
11'-0" FLAT CEILING

BATH

GARAGE
19'-9" x 20'-0"

W.H.

STORAGE

PORCH
4'-0" X 15'-0"

BEDROOM 1
11'-1" x 11'-8"

CLOSET

©Copyright by Designer

Editor's Choice

Price Code C   72024

Total Sq. Ft.: 1,775
Width: 52'
Depth: 52'
Bedrooms: 3
Baths: 2
Garage: 2-car

(For more plan info, visit www.familyhomeplans.com)

Price Code C   50105

Total Sq. Ft.: 1,775
Width: 70'
Depth: 44'-2"
Bedrooms: 3
Baths: 2
Garage: 2-car

(For more plan info, visit www.familyhomeplans.com)

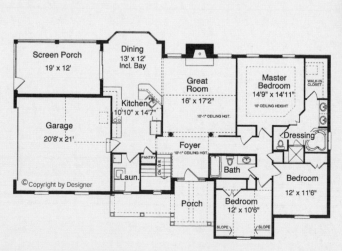

Screen Porch
19' x 12'

Dining
13' x 12'
Incl. Bay

Great Room
16' x 17'2"
10'-1" CEILING HGT.

Master Bedroom
14'9" x 14'11"
10' CEILING HEIGHT

WALK-IN CLOSET

Kitchen
10'10" x 14'7"

Garage
20'8" x 21'

Dressing

Foyer
10'-1" CEILING HGT.

PANTRY

Laun.

Bath

Bedroom
12' x 11'6"

©Copyright by Designer

Porch

Bedroom
12' x 10'6"

SLOPE   SLOPE

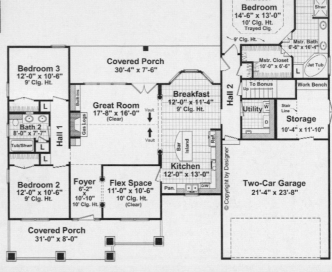

BONUS AREA

Unfinished
Bonus Room
11'-4" x 23'-8"
8' Clg. Ht.

Attic Access

Sloped Clg.   Sloped Clg.

Price Code C   59148

Total Sq. Ft.: 1,800
Bonus Area: 326'
Width: 65'
Depth: 56'-8"
Bedrooms: 3
Baths: 2
Garage: 2-car

(For more plan info, visit www.familyhomeplans.com)

Master
Bedroom
14'-6" x 13'-0"
10' Clg. Ht.
Trayed Clg.

Mstr. Bath
6'-6" x 16'-4"

Mstr. Closet
10'-0" x 6'-6"

Work Bench

Bedroom 3
12'-0" x 10'-6"
9' Clg. Ht.

Covered Porch
30'-4" x 7'-6"

Great Room
17'-8" x 16'-0"
(Clear)

Breakfast
12'-0" x 11'-4"
9' Clg. Ht.

To Bonus

Utility

Storage
10'-4" x 11'-10"

Bath 2
8'-0" x 7'-7"

Tub/Shwr

Kitchen
12'-0" x 13'-0"

Bar Island

Two-Car Garage
21'-4" x 23'-8"

Bedroom 2
12'-0" x 10'-6"
9' Clg. Ht.

Foyer
6'-2" x 10'-10"

Flex Space
11'-0" x 10'-6"
10' Clg. Ht.
(Clear)

© Copyright by Designer

Covered Porch
31'-0" x 8'-0"

Optional Loft
12⁰ · 20⁰

window seat

SECOND FLOOR

Price Code C   63111

Total Sq. Ft.: 1,782
Width: 40'
Depth: 61'
Bedrooms: 3
Baths: 2
Garage: 2-car

(For more plan info, visit www.familyhomeplans.com)

Family Rm.
14⁰ · 17²

Master Suite
12⁴ · 14⁸

Master
Bath

w.i.c.

Kitchen

Living Rm.
13⁰ · 9²

Bedroom 2
11⁸ · 11⁴

Nook

Dining Rm.
10² · 12⁸

Bath 2

Laun.

Foyer

2 Car Garage
19⁰ · 18⁰

Entry

Bedroom 3
11⁴ · 11⁰

FIRST FLOOR

Concrete Floor Finishes

Maintenance-free floors that are healthy, decorative and durable

Concrete is one of the most durable and versatile floor surfaces available. Stained concrete surfaces are a hot design trend in restaurants and stores, and are seen increasingly in residential settings. Treatments can impart the look and luster of granite, marble, or other scarce natural materials at a fraction of the cost.

Unlike carpet or vinyl, concrete is not subject to damage from tears, stains, wear, or flooding. There are no fibers or crevices that can trap dirt or allergens. Concrete can easily be swept or washed and requires little other maintenance.

A wide range of effects is possible. Decorative concrete surfaces are usually installed by skilled applicators or artisans. Methods and procedures vary greatly with different products, for instance some chemical stains may only be applied to slabs that have been fully cured for sixty days, while others work best if applied within a few days of casting.

Courtesy of PATH
www.pathnet.org/homeowners

Price Code C   44001

Total Sq. Ft.: 1,780
Width: 66'-8"
Depth: 55'
Bedrooms: 3
Baths: 2
Garage: 3-car

(For more plan info, visit www.familyhomeplans.com)

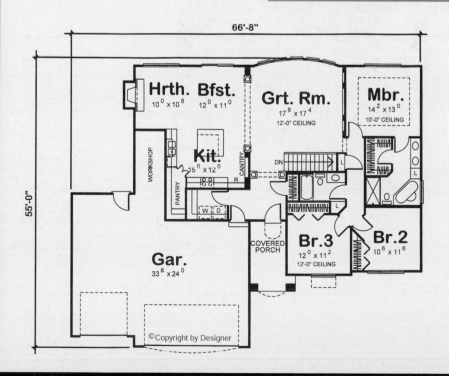

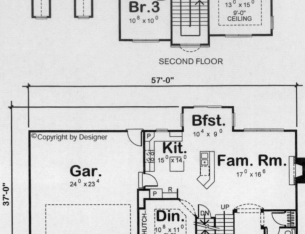

Br.2
10⁴ x 10⁰

Br.3
10⁸ x 10⁰

Mbr.
13⁰ x 15⁰
9'-0" CEILING

UNFINISHED STORAGE
ADDS 432 SQ.FT.

DN

SECOND FLOOR

57'-0"

Bfst.
10⁴ x 9⁰

Kit.
15⁰ x 14⁰

Fam. Rm.
17⁰ x 16⁶

Gar.
24⁰ x 23⁴

©Copyright by Designer

37'-0"

Din.
10⁸ x 11⁰
8'-0" CEILING

UP
DN

COVERED PORCH

FIRST FLOOR

Price Code C 44004

Total Finished Sq. Ft.: 1,783
Main Level: 931'
Upper Level: 852'
Width: 57'
Depth: 37'
Bedrooms: 3
Baths: 2.5
Garage: 2-car

(For more plan info, visit www.familyhomeplans.com)

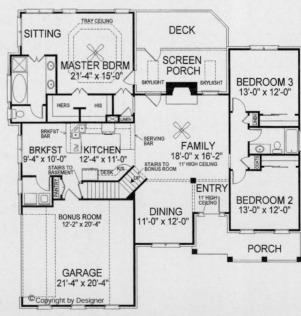

SITTING

TRAY CEILING

DECK

SCREEN PORCH

SKYLIGHT   SKYLIGHT

MASTER BDRM
21'-4" x 15'-0"

HERS   HIS

LINEN

BEDROOM 3
13'-0" x 12'-0"

BRKFST BAR

SERVING BAR

FAMILY
18'-0" x 16'-2"
11' HIGH CEILING

BRKFST
9'-4" x 10'-0"

KITCHEN
12'-4" x 11'-0"

STAIRS TO BASEMENT

PANTRY

DESK

STAIRS TO BONUS ROOM

UP

ENTRY
11' HIGH CEILING

BEDROOM 2
13'-0" x 12'-0"

BONUS ROOM
12'-2" x 20'-4"

DINING
11'-0" x 12'-0"

PORCH

GARAGE
21'-4" x 20'-4"

©Copyright by Designer

Price Code C 92420

Total Sq. Ft.: 1,787
Width: 55'-8"
Depth: 56'-6"
Bedrooms: 3
Baths: 2
Garage: 2-car

(For more plan info, visit www.familyhomeplans.com)

ORDER NOW! Phone: **1-800-235-5700** Online: **www.FamilyHomePlans.com** Order Code: **H6SSM**

Price Code C 24610

Total Sq. Ft.: 1,785
Main Level: 891'
Upper Level: 894'
Width: 46'-8"
Depth: 35'-8"
Bedrooms: 3
Baths: 2.25
Garage: 2-car

(For more plan info, visit www.familyhomeplans.com)

Peaked roofs and double dormers attract the eye while a smart 1,785 sq. ft. layout steals the heart. The great room with enormous Palladian window and cozy fireplace gets the lion's share of attention. The kitchen with wide lunch counter and plenty of cabinets is a welcoming place. The open kitchen and dining areas invite family and guests to munch and mingle comfortably. A half bath, laundry room and pantry reside behind the kitchen, near the garage entry. The upstairs master bedroom with bath and roomy walk-in closet is tucked away for added privacy. Two additional bedrooms with bright windowing border a shared bath.

Dining 12-1 x 11-4 **Kitchen** 13 x 11-4
pantry
DN
W D

Great Rm 14 x 21-8
open to above
UP

Garage 22 x 23-4

©Copyright by Designer

FIRST FLOOR

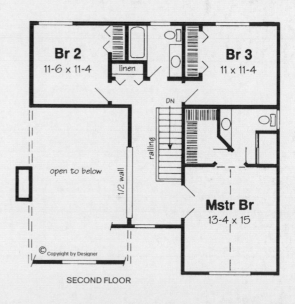

Br 2 11-6 x 11-4   linen   **Br 3** 11 x 11-4
open to below
1/2 wall
railing
DN

Mstr Br 13-4 x 15

©Copyright by Designer

SECOND FLOOR

Price Code C 20198

Total Sq. Ft.: 1,792
Width: 56'
Depth: 32'
Bedrooms: 3
Baths: 2
Garage: 2-car

(For more plan info, visit www.familyhomeplans.com)

This economical home-sweet-home can live happily along the coast or curbside in your favorite town. Beautiful decorative beams and sloped ceilings enhance the interior. The 1,792 sq. ft. layout makes the most of available space and light. The large, open-style living room hosts a great stone fireplace which shares its warmth with both the corner kitchen and dining areas. A huge deck draws guests outside. The far side of the house embraces the master suite, its roomy walk-in closet and windowed bath. Bedrooms #2 and #3 border a shared bath while each enjoys their own view of the country-style front porch.

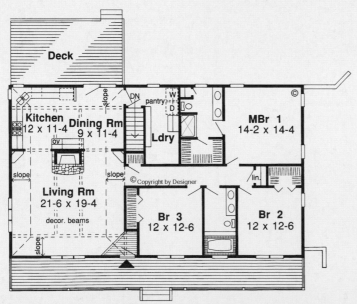

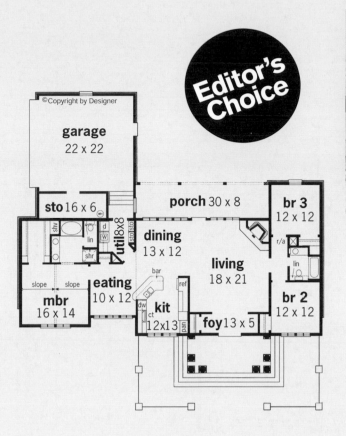

Editor's Choice

garage
22 x 22

sto 16 x 6

util 8x8

porch 30 x 8

dining
13 x 12

br 3
12 x 12

living
18 x 21

eating
10 x 12

mbr
16 x 14

kit
12 x 13

foy 13 x 5

br 2
12 x 12

©Copyright by Designer

Price Code C   65683

Total Sq. Ft.: 1,792
Width: 68'
Depth: 62'
Bedrooms: 3
Baths: 2
Garage: 2-car

(For more plan info, visit www.familyhomeplans.com)

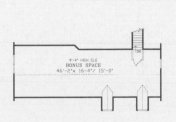

9'-4" HIGH CLG
BONUS SPACE
46'-2" x 16-4'/ 15'-0"

SECOND FLOOR

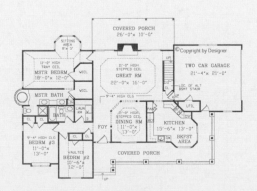

FIRST FLOOR

Price Code C   99680

Total Sq. Ft.: 1,793
Width: 69'-10"
Depth: 51'-8"
Bedrooms: 3
Baths: 2
Garage: 2-car

(For more plan info, visit www.familyhomeplans.com)

smarter building materials

ORDER NOW! Phone: **1-800-235-5700** Online: **www.FamilyHomePlans.com** Order Code: **H6SSM**

REAR EXTERIOR

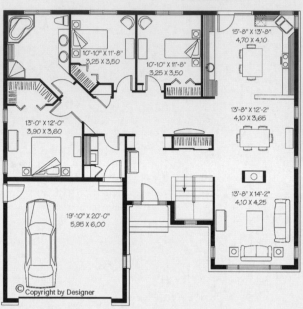

Price Code C 65491

Total Sq. Ft.: 1,795
Width: 50'-8"
Depth: 50'
Bedrooms: 3
Baths: 1
Garage: 2-car

(For more plan info, visit www.familyhomeplans.com)

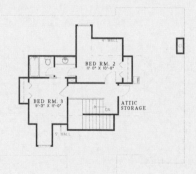

SECOND FLOOR

Price Code C 82013

Total Sq. Ft.: 1,797
Main Level: 1,356'
Upper Level: 441'
Width: 48'
Depth: 43'
Bedrooms: 3
Baths: 2.5
Garage: 2-car

(For more plan info, visit www.familyhomeplans.com)

FIRST FLOOR

Fiber-Cement Siding

A durable exterior cladding material

For homeowners that want the look of wood but don't want the hassles and costs associated with it, fiber-cement siding may be a satisfactory alternative. This product is available from several manufacturers in a variety of textures that are said to provide the appearance of wood. Fiber-cement siding should be more durable than wood – it is termite-resistant, water-resistant, non-combustible, and warranted to last 50 years.

Fiber-cement siding is composed of cement, sand, and cellulose fiber that has been autoclaved (cured with pressurized steam) to increase its strength and dimensional stability. The fiber is added as reinforcement to prevent cracking. The planks come in 5¼" to 12" widths and ⁵⁄₁₆" and ⁷⁄₁₆" thickness. The cost of fiber cement siding is more than vinyl and less than stucco and wood siding, making it an affordable and durable product.

Courtesy of PATH
www.pathnet.org/homeowners

Price Code C 93176

Total Sq. Ft.: 1,795
Width: 68'
Depth: 59'
Bedrooms: 3
Baths: 2
Garage: 3-car

(For more plan info, visit www.familyhomeplans.com)

SCREEN PORCH
12'8" X 12'8"

BR #2
12'4" X 11'8"

LIV.
10'-1 1⁄8" CEILING
14'0" X 19'0"

DIN.
10'0" X 14'0"

KIT.
9'6" X 14'0"

MBR.
13'0" X 14'10"

PANTRY

DEN/
BR #3
12'0" X 11'4"

3 CAR GAR.
29'8" X 24'4"

© Copyright by Designer

Price Code C 59012

Total Sq. Ft.: 1,799
Main Living: 1,799'
Width: 78'
Depth: 46'
Bedrooms: 3
Baths: 2.5
Garage: 2-car

(For more plan info, visit www.familyhomeplans.com)

SECOND FLOOR

FIRST FLOOR

REAR EXTERIOR

Price Code C 65622

Total Sq. Ft.: 1,800
Width: 66'
Depth: 60'
Bedrooms: 3
Baths: 2
Garage: 2-car

(For more plan info, visit www.familyhomeplans.com)

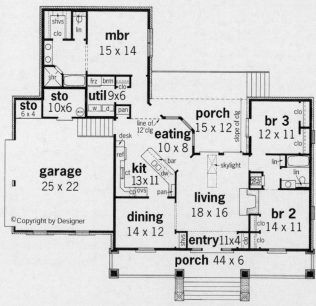

ORDER NOW! Phone: **1-800-235-5700** Online: **www.FamilyHomePlans.com** Order Code: **H6SSM**

Price Code C   65625

Total Sq. Ft.: 1,800
Width: 66'
Depth: 60'
Bedrooms: 3
Baths: 2
Garage: 2-car

(For more plan info, visit www.familyhomeplans.com)

Many of us seek a floor plan that locates the master suite near the kitchen and utility area, with the secondary bedrooms on the opposite side of the home. This plan accomplishes the task in a space saving manner that affords larger than usual room sizes. The kitchen has two pantries and a desk while the adjacent eating area sports a sloped ceiling. The living room has 12' ceilings with skylights, a brick fireplace and French door access to front and rear porches.

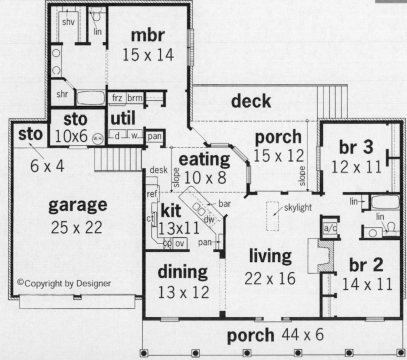

©Copyright by Designer

the smaller the better

You know the adage, "Good things come in small packages." Here's proof! This design with 1,980 sq. ft. is a gem of a home. Its multi-faceted living spaces begin with a stunning great room that plays a pivotal role in the main floor layout as it flows openly from the dining room to the kitchen and breakfast area while allowing related but individual rooms to maintain separate identities. A half-bath and laundry area make good neighbors as they are modestly private, yet conveniently nearby. Upstairs, two large bedrooms maintain unique personalities, one with an enormous double-door walk-in closet and its own sitting area. Each enjoys plentiful windowing and natural light. A shared bath features separate areas for bath and shower, and a big bright window of its own.

Bottom: The family room is warmed by handsome fireplace and brightened by generous windows to the rear of the home. Left: The dinings area enjoys plenty of natural light and opens freely to the family room. Below: The kitchen's island provides abundant space for food preperation, plus a practical breakfast/lunch counter.

Price Code C 65431

Total Sq. Ft.: 1,980
Width: 43'
Depth: 53'-4"
Bedrooms: 2
Baths: 2
Garage: 1-car

(For more plan info, visit www.familyhomeplans.com)

14'-0" X 18'-0"
4,20 X 5,40

14'-4" X 17'-4"
4,30 X 5,20

13'-4" X 12'-0"
4,00 X 3,60

16'-8" X 20'-4"
5,00 X 6,10

FIRST FLOOR

© Copyright by Designer

14'-4" X 11'-0"
4,30 X 3,30

16'-0" X 14'-0"
4,80 X 4,20

SECOND FLOOR

Price Code C   59015

Total Sq. Ft.: 1,800
Main Level: 1,639'
Upper Level: 161'
Width: 64'
Depth: 39'
Bedrooms: 3
Baths: 2
Garage: 2-car

(For more plan info, visit www.familyhomeplans.com)

Upon entry, this home feels larger that it actually is, with its trayed ceiling in the great room. The design's open floor plan features a split-bedroom layout for added privacy. An expansive and well appointed master suite includes large his and her walk-in closets, an oversized jet tub, separate shower, compartmentalized toilet and dual vanities. The large front and rear covered porches provide a quiet place for family conversations. In the laundry area there is plenty of room for that freezer.

Editor's Choice

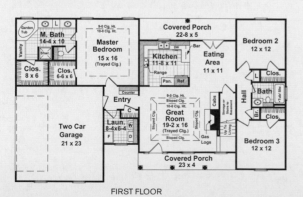

FIRST FLOOR

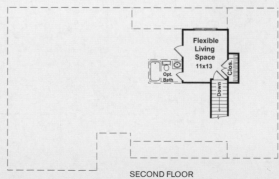

SECOND FLOOR

This is a great open plan with split-bedroom layout. The master suite has a trayed ceiling, large closet for him and her, jet tub, over-sized shower, and large vanity next to her closet. Enjoy the vaulted ceiling, gas logs, and built-ins in the great room. All bedrooms feature walk-in closets with their own private bath. Note that Bedroom 2 could be used as an "In-law suite". A "Flex Space" is provided for uses such as an office/media center/half bath/hobby room/or winter-wear closet. The kitchen is large with an over-sized bar. The plan has a covered front porch, screen porch, and patio for small groups to gather. Garage is nearly 26 feet deep to provide more space than is normal for parking and open storage. This house is sized right to fulfill the needs of new couples, families with children, and empty-nesters that may need to take care of an elderly family member.

Price Code C   59068

Total Sq. Ft: 1,800
Width: 63'-4"
Depth: 53'
Bedrooms: 3
Baths: 3
Garage: 2-car

(For more plan info, visit www.familyhomeplans.com)

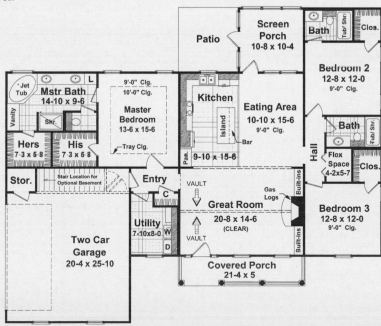

Price Code C 93143

Total Sq. Ft: 1,802
Width: 69'
Depth: 51'-4"
Bedrooms: 3
Baths: 2
Garage: 2-car

(For more plan info, visit www.familyhomeplans.com)

This hip-roofed ranch has an exterior that tastefully mixes brick and siding. The cozy front porch invites your guests into the recessed entrance with transoms and sidelights, filling the formal entry with glowing light. The foyer is centrally located, dividing the bedrooms from the living area. A large Great room with cathedral ceilings and a large fireplace is the perfect spot for family gatherings. There is a large kitchen with ample cupboard space, and a spacious nook that leads to the back yard. The large two stall garage has plenty of storage or work shop space. The spacious master bedroom has a large walk-in closet. Double doors open into the master bath with a whirlpool tub, a double vanity and a large corner shower. Two additional bedrooms share a full bath and each have large closets, with the second having cathedral ceilings.

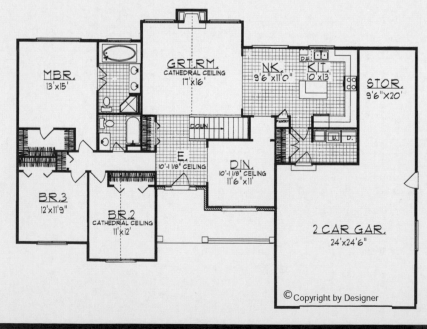

Recycled Content Carpet

Said to be more resilient and colorfast than virgin fiber carpet

Approximately five billion pounds of carpet are replaced each year in the U.S. Much of the old carpet, along with plastic soda bottles and other textiles, can be woven into new carpet fibers. Recycled content carpet has a similar look, feel, and price as virgin fiber (typically polyester, nylon, and olefin) carpet, but takes advantage of post-consumer recycled materials.

Recycled carpet can be made from recycled polyethelene terephthalate (PET) or from recovered textile fibers. PET plastic is usually found in plastic soda bottles. About 40 two-liter soda bottles are recycled per square yard of carpeting.

Recycled content carpet fiber is said to be more resilient and colorfast than virgin fiber carpet and usually comes with the same warranties for colorfastness, static control, and resistance to stain, crushing, and matting as virgin synthetic fiber carpets.

Courtesy of PATH
www.pathnet.org/homeowners

Price Code C   44005

Total Sq. Ft: 1,800
Bedrooms: 3
Baths: 2.5
Garage: 2-car
Width: 59'-8"
Depth: 60'

(For more plan info, visit www.familyhomeplans.com)

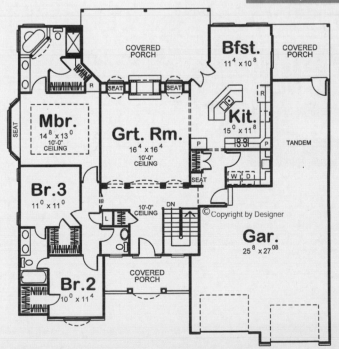

Editor's Choice

Price Code C 93193

Total Sq. Ft: 1,802
Width: 71'
Depth: 51'-4"
Bedrooms: 3
Baths: 2.5
Garage: 3-car

(For more plan info, visit www.familyhomeplans.com)

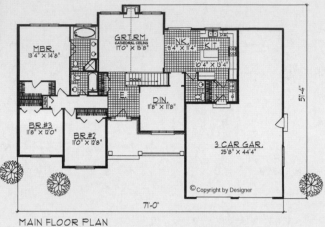

MAIN FLOOR PLAN

Price Code C 94642

Total Sq. Ft: 1,802
Main Level: 1,185'
Upper Level: 617'
Width: 42'-10"
Depth: 70'
Bedrooms: 3
Baths: 2
Garage: 2-car

(For more plan info, visit www.familyhomeplans.com)

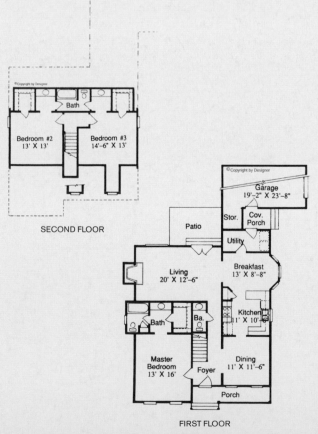

SECOND FLOOR

FIRST FLOOR

Price Code x   59017

Total Sq. Ft: 1,802
Width: 65'
Depth: 50'-10"
Bedrooms: 3
Baths: 2
Garage: 2-car

(For more plan info, visit www.familyhomeplans.com)

This is a wonderful split-bedroom design with open living spaces. The master suite includes pampering amenities such as generously sized his and her walk-in closets, an oversized jet tub, separate shower, compartmentalized toilet and dual vanities. Spacious front and rear covered porches provide a quiet location for those lazy afternoons with the family.

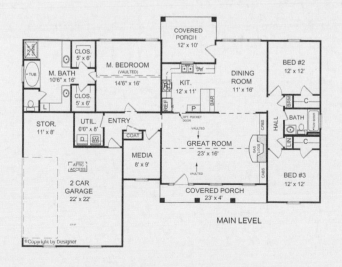

MAIN LEVEL

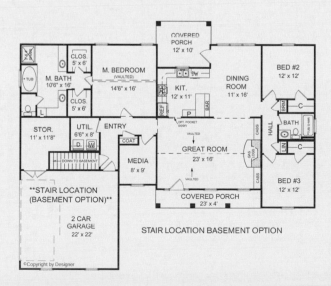

STAIR LOCATION BASEMENT OPTION

Price Code C   94155

Total Sq. Ft: 1,802
Width: 61'
Depth: 49'-4"
Bedrooms: 3
Baths: 2
Garage: 2-car

(For more plan info, visit www.familyhomeplans.com)

This well-planned one story has plenty of features to love. It's large open floor plan allows the great room, dining area and kitchen to flow together without interruption beneath an airy vaulted ceiling. Privacy is enjoyed by all bedrooms, with the master suite entirely seperate from the secondary quarters, which are split by a shared bath.

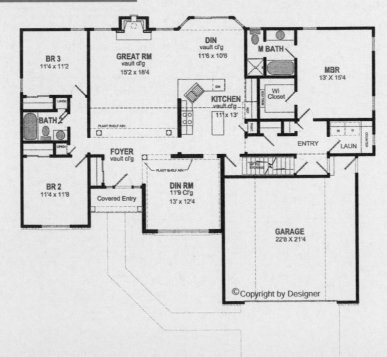

Price Code C   96541

Total Sq. Ft: 1,815
Main Level: 1,257
Upper Level: 558
Width: 47'
Depth: 52'
Bedrooms: 3
Baths: 2.5
Garage: 2-car

(For more plan info, visit www.familyhomeplans.com)

Decorative arches and windows give a metropolitan feel to this unique floor plan. Two floors and a bonus room offer more space for buyers with smaller lots. The awesome great room with grand ceilings and fireplace opens to a distinctively styled kitchen with a corner sink and a great view. The spacious master suite, dual closets and vanities, and large tub are icing on the cake for this wonderfully designed home.

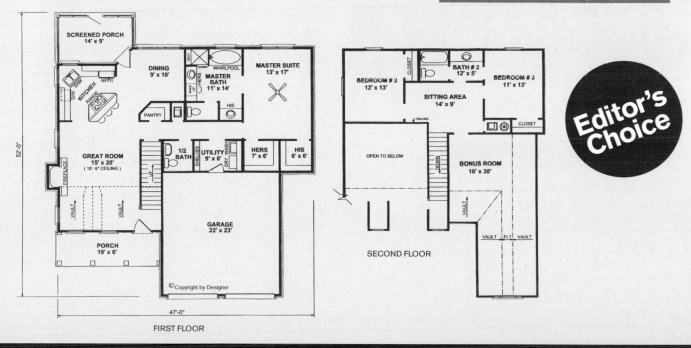

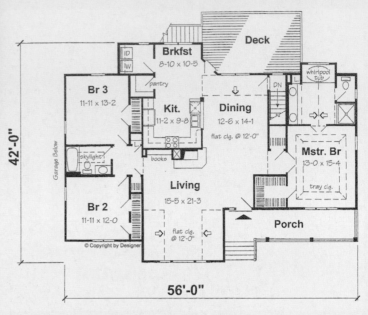

42'-0"

Deck

Brkfst
8-10 x 10-5

whirlpool tub

Br 3
11-11 x 13-2

pantry

Kit.
11-2 x 9-8

Dining
12-6 x 14-1
flat clg. @ 12'-0"

Mstr. Br
13-0 x 15-4
tray clg.

Garage Below

skylight

books

Living
15-5 x 21-3

Br 2
11-11 x 12-0

flat clg. @ 12'-0"

Porch

© Copyright by Designer

56'-0"

Price Code C   24651

Total Sq. Ft: 1,821
Width: 56'
Depth: 42'
Bedrooms: 3
Baths: 2
Garage: 2-car

(For more plan info, visit www.familyhomeplans.com)

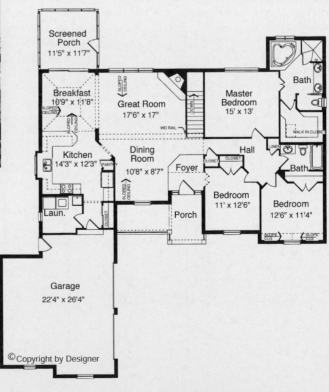

Screened Porch
11'5" x 11'7"

Breakfast
10'9" x 11'8"

Great Room
17'6" x 17'

Master Bedroom
15' x 13'

Bath

WD RAIL

WALK IN CLOSET

Kitchen
14'3" x 12'3"

pantry

Dining Room
10'8" x 8'7"

Foyer

Hall

LINEN

CLOSET

CLOSET

Bath

Laun.

CLOSET

Porch

Bedroom
11' x 12'6"

Bedroom
12'6" x 11'4"

SLOPE CLG.

Garage
22'4" x 26'4"

© Copyright by Designer

Price Code C   50100

Total Sq. Ft: 1,824
Width: 66'
Depth: 74'
Bedrooms: 3
Baths: 2
Garage: 2-car

(For more plan info, visit www.familyhomeplans.com)

Insulating Concrete Forms

Foam forms that are filled with reinforced concrete and reinforcement bar to create insulated structural walls

Concrete forms have taken a new shape—and purpose. Insulating concrete forms (ICFs) are rigid plastic foam forms that hold concrete in place during curing and remain in place afterwards to serve as thermal insulation for concrete walls. The foam blocks, or planks are lightweight and result in energy-efficient, durable construction.

Insulation values of ICF walls vary depending on the material and its thickness. Typical insulation values range from R-17 to R-26, compared to between R-13 and R-19 for most wood-framed walls. Additionally, ICFs are more resistant to moisture, termites and other pests, and can dramatically increase the strength of the home while reducing noise from the outside.

Courtesy of PATH
www.pathnet.org/homeowners

Price Code C   94654

Total Sq. Ft.: 1,819
Width: 43'
Depth: 47'
Bedrooms: 3
Baths: 2.5
Garage: 2-car

(For more plan info, visit www.familyhomeplans.com)

FIRST FLOOR

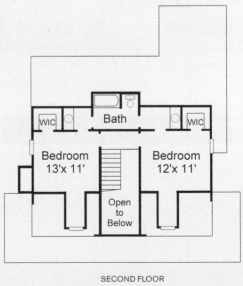

SECOND FLOOR

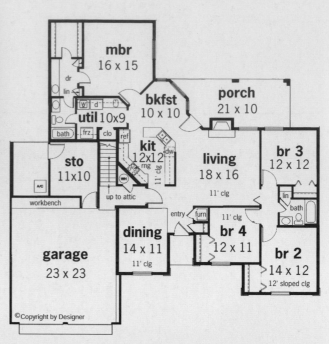

Price Code C   65684

Total Sq. Ft.: 1,828
Width: 64'
Depth: 62'
Bedrooms: 4
Baths: 2
Garage: 2-car

(For more plan info, visit www.familyhomeplans.com)

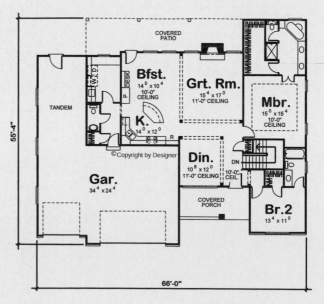

Price Code C   44019

Total Sq. Ft.: 1,830
Width: 66'
Depth: 55'-4"
Bedrooms: 2
Bathrooms: 1.5
Garage: 4-car

(For more plan info, visit www.familyhomeplans.com)

Price Code C 34031

Total Sq. Ft.: 1,831
Width: 60'
Depth: 52'
Bedrooms: 3
Baths: 2.5
Garage: 2-car

(For more plan info, visit www.familyhomeplans.com)

Progress is pretty when a traditional ranch style grows up to look like this. A porch and tiled foyer glide into the family room with fireplace. The flow moves to the kitchen and lunch island. The windowed breakfast area is outfitted with planning desk. Powder room resides close by. The master bedroom owns one side of the house. Special ceiling details a sense of drama. Double sinks and window add master bath luxury. Bedroom #2 and #3 get A-plus for equal size and style. While they share a bathroom, each gets its own sink with wall detail for enhanced privacy.

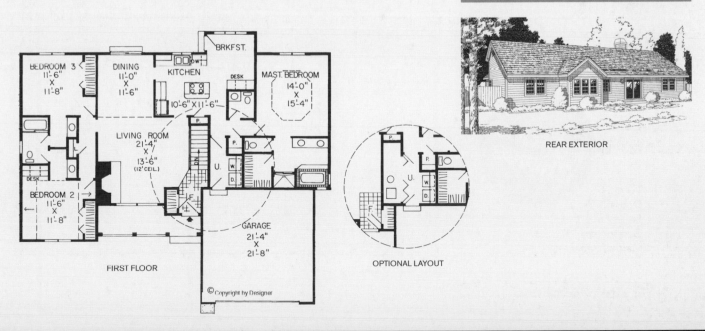

REAR EXTERIOR

FIRST FLOOR

OPTIONAL LAYOUT

Price Code C 63113

Total Sq. Ft.: 1,831
Width: 59'
Depth: 55'-4"
Bedrooms: 3
Baths: 2
Garage: 2-car

(For more plan info, visit www.familyhomeplans.com)

Editor's Choice

This plan offers the best of the traditional and the contemporary.

The traditional split living and dining room, as you enter the foyer, invites formal entertaining without compromising the extended view a see through plan offers. The family room is perfect for those large gatherings and daily living. It borders the patio and outdoor living area. The master suite with its view of the rear yard also has a bath fit for the masters of the house.

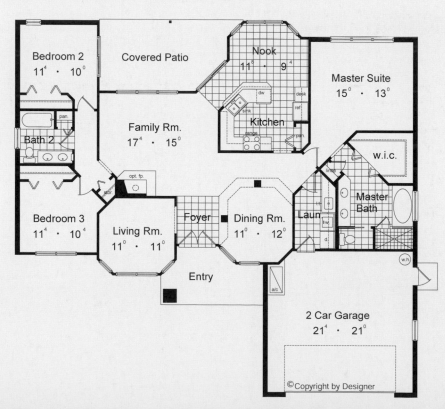

Bedroom 2
$11^4 \cdot 10^0$

Covered Patio

Nook
$11^0 \cdot 9^4$

Master Suite
$15^0 \cdot 13^0$

Bath 2

Family Rm.
$17^4 \cdot 15^0$

Kitchen

w.i.c.

Bedroom 3
$11^4 \cdot 10^4$

opt. fp.

stor.

Living Rm.
$11^0 \cdot 11^0$

Foyer

Dining Rm.
$11^0 \cdot 12^0$

Laun

Master Bath

Entry

2 Car Garage
$21^4 \cdot 21^0$

©Copyright by Designer

ORDER NOW! Phone: **1-800-235-5700** Online: **www.FamilyHomePlans.com** Order Code: **H6SSM**

This charming two-story lives surprisingly large on the inside. Guests are greeted by a soaring foyer, open to a sunny bayed dining room. A few more steps reveal the great room, breakfast area and kitchen, which interact openly with one another. Upstairs, the master suite includes a sizeable walk-in closet. Two secondary bedrooms share a hall bath.

Price Code C   94152

Total Sq. Ft.: 1,832
Main Level: 972'
Upper Level: 860'
Width: 38'
Depth: 53'
Bedrooms: 3
Baths: 2.5
Garage: 2-car

(For more plan info, visit www.familyhomeplans.com)

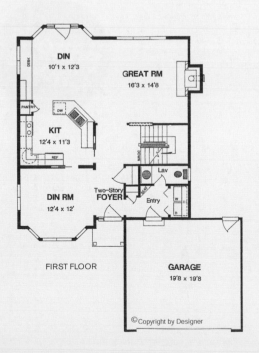

FIRST FLOOR

SECOND FLOOR

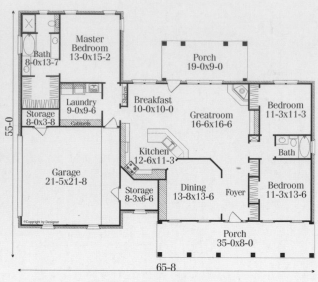

FIRST FLOOR

Price Code C 40016

Total Sq. Ft.: 1,836
Width: 65'-8"
Depth: 55'
Bedrooms: 3
Baths: 2
Garage: 2-car

(For more plan info, visit www.familyhomeplans.com)

FIRST FLOOR OPTION

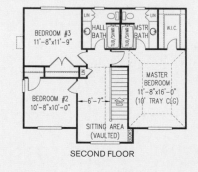

SECOND FLOOR

Editor's Choice

Price Code C 96819

Total Sq. Ft.: 1,840
Main Level: 1,014'
Upper Level: 826'
Width: 62'-7"
Depth: 45'
Bedrooms: 3
Baths: 2.5
Garage: 2-car

(For more plan info, visit www.familyhomeplans.com)

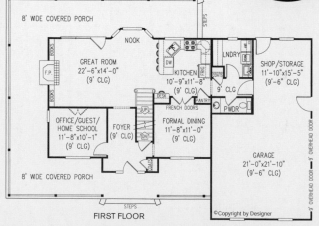

FIRST FLOOR

SECOND FLOOR

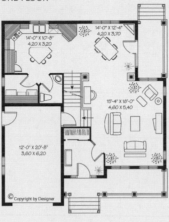

FIRST FLOOR

Price Code C   65411

Total Sq. Ft.: 1,844
Main Level: 896'
Upper Level: 948'
Width: 35'-4"
Depth: 39'-8"
Bedrooms: 3
Baths: 1.5
Garage: 1-car

(For more plan info, visit www.familyhomeplans.com)

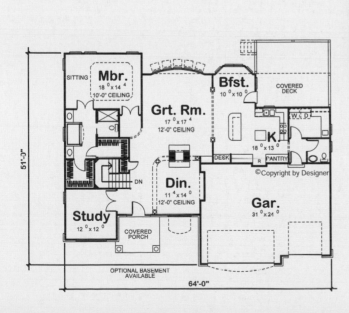

Price Code C   44006

Total Sq. Ft.: 1,850
Width: 64'
Depth: 51'
Bedrooms: 1
Baths: 2
Garage: 3-car

(For more plan info, visit www.familyhomeplans.com)

Price Code C 59019

Total Sq. Ft.: 1,855
Width: 72'-8"
Depth: 51'
Bedrooms: 3
Baths: 2.5
Garage: 2-car

(For more plan info, visit www.familyhomeplans.com)

Great atrium windows beautiful split bedroom plan house. 3 bedrooms can be built with 2, 2.5, 3, or 3.5 baths. Great room features 12-foot ceilings, and fireplace with gas logs and transoms above the windows. Great views of great room and back yard from kitchen. Large master bedroom which features jet tub in master bath. Other key features include walk-in pantry, large utility room, wet wear closet, and large garage.

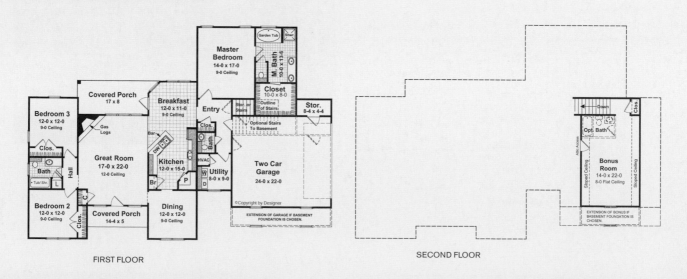

FIRST FLOOR

SECOND FLOOR

Insulative Vinyl Siding

Foam insulated vinyl siding systems that provide thermal insulation benefits

Two new products give vinyl siding a competitive edge by increasing its energy efficiency and enhancing its impact resistance. One product is an insulative foam underlayment, custom contoured to fit snugly behind hundreds of different brands and styles of vinyl siding. The other is line of vinyl siding products fused to a foam backing material, to create an all-in-one siding and insulation system.

Progressive Foam Technologies, Inc. makes contoured foam underlayment under the brand name "Thermowall". The material is shaped to precisely fit behind nearly any manufacturer's siding profile sold in the United States. Installed over exterior walls just before placement of the siding, the underlayment provides a continuous solid backing that helps vinyl siding resist impacts that might otherwise cause cracks or dents. By adding an additional foam insulation layer, the R-values of exterior walls are increased by R-2.8 to 3.3, depending on the profile, not including the vinyl siding.

Crane Performance Siding uses a similar concept to create lines of solid-core siding products including Craneboard and Techwall Plus. These products fuse a contoured polystyrene backing material to a vinyl exterior facing for a solid insulated wall system with an overall R-rating of 4 to 4.5, depending on the product selected.

Both the foam underlayer and the solid core siding are made to fit most exteriors. Unlike conventional siding, the foam offers protection against dents and other impact damage, allowing the siding to remain aesthetically pleasing, functional, and lasting.

Courtesy of PATH
www.pathnet.org/homeowners

smarter building materials

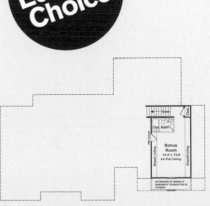

REAR EXTERIOR

Price Code C 59018

Total Sq. Ft.: 1,852
Width: 78'
Depth: 49'-6"
Bedrooms: 3
Baths: 2.5
Garage: 2-car

(For more plan info, visit www.familyhomeplans.com)

Editor's Choice

FIRST FLOOR

OPTIONAL LAYOUT

smarter building materials

Price Code C 71031

Total Sq. Ft.: 1,855
Main Level: 874'
Upper Level: 981'
Width: 54'-4"
Depth: 30'
Bedrooms: 3
Baths: 2.5
Garage: 2-car

(For more plan info, visit www.familyhomeplans.com)

This simple design features all the amenities. A grand room with fireplace dominates one side of the house, while the kitchen and dining areas fill the rest of the first floor. Three large bedrooms and a bonus room above the garage make use of every inch of this modestly sized home.

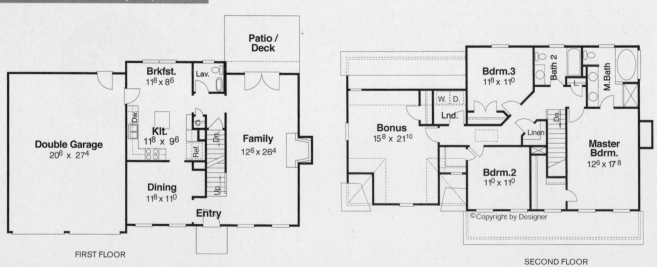

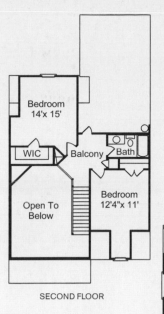

Bedroom
14'x 15'

WIC | Balcony | Bath

Open To Below

Bedroom
12'4"x 11'

SECOND FLOOR

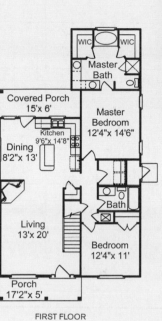

WIC | WIC

Master Bath

Covered Porch
15'x 6'

Kitchen
9'6"x 14'8"

Dining
8'2"x 13'

Master Bedroom
12'4"x 14'6"

Bath

Living
13'x 20'

Bedroom
12'4"x 11'

Porch
17'2"x 5'

FIRST FLOOR

Price Code C   94623

Total Sq. Ft: 1,857
Width: 30'
Depth: 58'-6"
Bedrooms: 4
Baths: 4

(For more plan info, visit www.familyhomeplans.com)

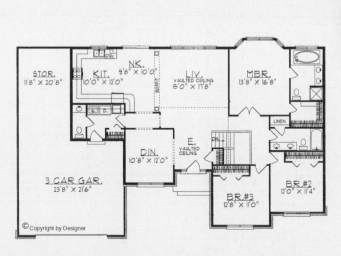

STOR.
11'8" x 20'8"

KIT.
10'0" x 12'0"

NK.
9'8" x 10'0"

LIV.
VAULTED CEILING
15'0" x 11'8"

M.B.R.
13'8" x 16'8"

LINEN

DIN.
10'8" x 12'0"

E.
VAULTED CEILING

DN

3 CAR GAR.
23'8" x 21'6"

BR.#3
12'8" x 11'0"

BR.#2
12'0" x 11'4"

© Copyright by Designer

Price Code C   99174

Total Sq. Ft.: 1,859
Width: 69'-8"
Depth: 43'
Bedrooms: 3
Baths: 2.5
Garage: 3-car

(For more plan info, visit www.familyhomeplans.com)

ORDER NOW! Phone: **1-800-235-5700**   Online: **www.FamilyHomePlans.com**   Order Code: **H6SSM**

Price Code C 68170

Total Sq. Ft.: 1,867
Main Level: 1,375'
Upper Level: 492'
Width: 49'
Depth: 60'
Bedrooms: 3
Baths: 2.5
Garage: 2-car

(For more plan info, visit www.familyhomeplans.com)

A great partial wrap-around porch on the front of this home is a welcome sight at the end of any busy day. A small formal entry way leads to a great room that is a combination living and dining area. Off the great room are two more porches at the rear of the home. One is screened for three season living. The large kitchen offers an eating bar, pantry, and nook for eating or working. There is also a powder bath off the kitchen, along with a separate laundry room. The second floor features two bedrooms with walk in closets, and a bath. A game room is also an option on the upper level.

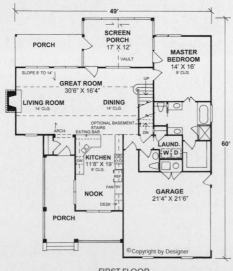

FIRST FLOOR

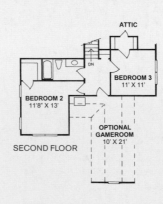

SECOND FLOOR

Right: Radiant floor heating warms a bathroom from your toes on up by circulating hot water through tubes beneath the flooring material.

smarter homebuilding technologies

THE SUPER-HOMES OF TOMORROW ARE HERE TODAY

Just as technology has changed our world for the better, so it has improved the quality of our homes inside and out. For the most part, advancements in new home technology have made homes increasingly energy efficient, while at the same time, more comfortable than ever before. Many of these technologies play their roles behind the scenes — or more literally, behind the walls — where we rarely, if ever, see them. Their effects, however, are profound, especially in long-term cost savings.

Take radiant barriers for instance. They help keep our homes cooler in the summer by blocking the downward transfer of heat from hot attics. Conversely, radiant heating systems, installed beneath the floor, provide soft, silent warmth from our toes on up. Frost Protected Shallow Foundations (FPSFs) utilize a home's warmth to allow footings to be placed only 12 to 16 inches deep. Tankless water heaters reduce the cost of heating water by 10% - 20% and devices known as plumbing manifolds save in the expense of installing rigid pipe by feeding flexible water supply lines to individual fixtures.

These are just a few examples of how burgeoning technologies can work in your favor by making your new home smarter, while saving you money. Find out more about the latest innovations in new home technology at www.pathnet.org/homeowners.

Price Code C   94521

Total Sq. Ft.: 1,865
Width: 46'-10"
Depth: 77'-11"
Bedrooms: 4
Baths: 2
Garage: 2-car

(For more plan info, visit www.familyhomeplans.com)

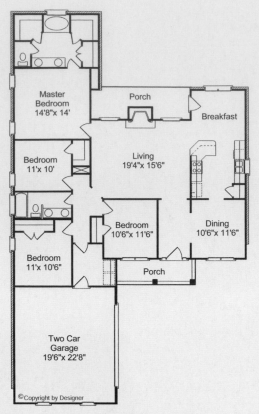

Price Code C   93107

Total Sq. Ft.: 1,868
Width: 72'
Depth: 42'-4"
Bedrooms: 3
Baths: 2
Garage: 2-car

(For more plan info, visit www.familyhomeplans.com)

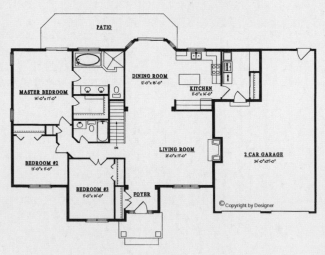

ORDER NOW! Phone: **1-800-235-5700**   Online: **www.FamilyHomePlans.com**   Order Code: **H6SSM**

Price Code C   65634

Total Sq. Ft.: 1,868
Width: 62'
Depth: 64'
Bedrooms: 3
Baths: 2
Garage: 2-car

(For more plan info, visit www.familyhomeplans.com)

This home's U-shaped kitchen services the dining room and its own eating area. It also boasts a built-in desk, a handy pantry closet and access to the nearby laundry room and carport. The wide master bedroom hosts a lavish master bath with a spa tub, a separate shower and his-and-her dressing areas. Across the home, the two secondary bedrooms share another bath.

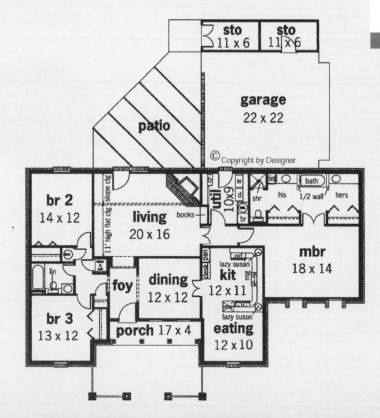

Price Code C 63114

Total Sq. Ft.: 1,868
Width: 45'
Depth: 66'
Bedrooms: 3
Baths: 2
Garage: 2-car

(For more plan info, visit www.familyhomeplans.com)

This innovative plan takes advantage of an angled entry into the home, maximizing visual impact upon entering, and makes it possible to have four bedrooms. The joining of the family and dining space makes it possible for creative interior decoration. The master suite also takes advantage of the angled entry to create long vistas into the space.

Editor's Choice

FIRST FLOOR

OPTIONAL LAYOUT

Price Code D   10515

Total Sq. Ft.: 2,044
Main Living Area: 1,299'
Upper Living Area: 745'
Width: 40'
Depth: 40'
Bedrooms: 3
Baths: 2.5
Garage: none

(For more plan info, visit www.familyhomeplans.com)

Great Getaway This vacation style floor plan makes a great lake house plan. All 2,015 sq. ft. are surrounded with a scenic deck and the A-frame front showcases bold windowing (on two levels) and natural lighting. These features also make this a great mountain home plan.

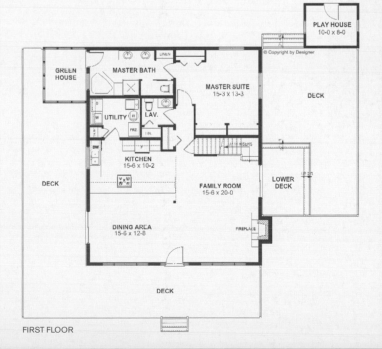

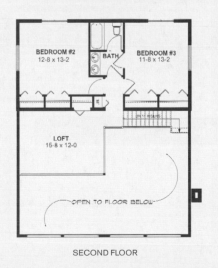

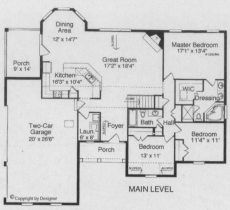

MAIN LEVEL

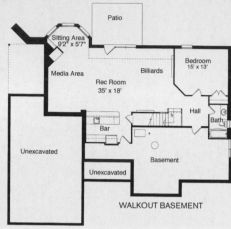

WALKOUT BASEMENT

Price Code C   50056

Total Sq. Ft.: 1,874
Width: 62'-8"
Depth: 56'-7"
Bedrooms: 3
Baths: 2
Garage: 3-car

(For more plan info, visit www.familyhomeplans.com)

Price Code C   40031

Total Sq. Ft.: 1,875
Width: 62'-2"
Depth: 69'-10"
Bedrooms: 3
Baths: 2.5
Garage: 2-car

(For more plan info, visit www.familyhomeplans.com)

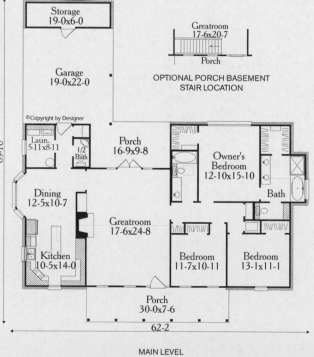

MAIN LEVEL

xDICK

Tankless Water Heaters

Hot water on-demand with 10-20% water heating savings

Throw away your water heater tank and shave ten to twenty percent off your water heating bill. Tankless water heaters have an electric, gas, or propane heating device that is activated by the flow of water. Once activated, the heater provides a constant supply of hot water. Large units intended for whole house water heating are located centrally in the house while, in point-of-use applications, the water heater usually sits in a closet or under a sink. Residential gas models are available that can heat more than five gallons per minute by 60°F, generally more than enough for two showers to be run simultaneously. Whole house electric units typically have a capacity closer to three gallons per minute.

Courtesy of PATH
www.pathnet.org/homeowners

Price Code C   75006

Total Sq. Ft.: 1,876
Width: 60'
Depth: 54'
Bedrooms: 4
Baths: 2.5
Garage: 2-car

(For more plan info, visit www.familyhomeplans.com)

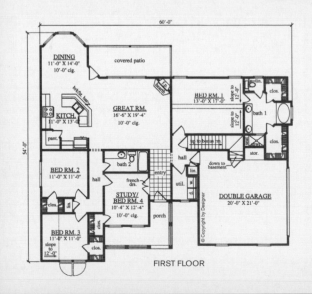

FIRST FLOOR

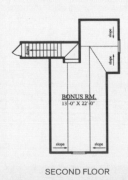

SECOND FLOOR

an intimate cottage
with spectacular spaces

Quaint brick and stone, and deeply pitched rooflines create the storybook aura of this serenely versatile 2,012 sq. ft. home. Inside, with four spacious bedrooms, two baths, a family room with fireplace, a dining room, casual kitchen and a two-car garage, this design deserves its place in the sun. Speaking of sun, the plan is configured to bring a panoramic view to nearly every room, beginning with the family room with fireplace and cathedral ceiling, and also in the dining area. Even the kitchen, with its crowd-pleasing island, has an eye on the outdoors. A main-level master bedroom accesses the adjoining master bath through a large walk-in closet. Upstairs, three uniquely shaped bedrooms, styled with clever nooks and windows to dream by, easily share a large bathroom. A sweeping mezzanine overlooks the open living and dining room. With so many features and enormous potential for majestic views, this design has an ongoing reputation as a residence and resort all in one.

PHOTOS COURTESY OF DESIGNER

Left: The family room offers an engaging environment to enjoy the company of friends and family. A soaring cathedral ceiling allows views to this area from a second story mezzanine. Below: This homeowner chose to reconfigure the master suite's bath to accommodate a vintage tub and make-up vanity.

Price Code D 65125

Total Sq. Ft.: 2,012
Main Level: 1,324'
Upper Level: 688'
Width: 56'
Depth: 41'
Bedrooms: 4
Baths: 2
Garage: 2-car

(For more plan info, visit www.familyhomeplans.com)

© Copyright by Designer

19'-0" X 20'-0"
5,70 X 6,00

12'-0" X 14'-8"
3,60 X 4,40

13'-0" X 19'-0"
3,90 X 5,70

16'-0" X 15'-0"
4,80 X 4,50

11'-8" X 12'-8"
3,50 X 3,80

56'-0"
16,5 m

FIRST FLOOR

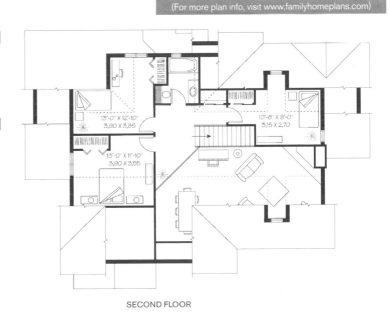

13'-0" X 12'-10"
3,90 X 3,85

10'-8" X 9'-0"
3,15 X 2,70

13'-0" X 11'-10"
3,90 X 3,55

SECOND FLOOR

Price Code C 96560

Total Sq. Ft.: 1,878
Width: 68'
Depth: 60'
Bedrooms: 3
Baths: 2
Garage: 2-car

(For more plan info, visit www.familyhomeplans.com)

Beautiful columns, French styled windows and stucco accents make his classy home a great choice for those with attention to detail. This spacious open floor plan takes your breath away upon entering. Six decorative columns adorn the arched entryway and extend into the foyer, dining and living area. The master suite opens to a luxurious master bath with separate dual vanities, large tub, and spacious closet area.

Radiant Barriers

Block the effects of radiant heat gain in homes by reflecting radiant heat rather than absorbing it

A roof exposed to the sun for a prolonged period will absorb a great deal of heat, sometimes reaching temperatures in excess of 170° Fahrenheit. Radiant barriers can help prevent overheated attics from warming the interior of a home. Conventional thermal insulation can slow down radiant heat transfer, but will not stop it.

All radiant barriers have at least one reflective (or low emissivity) surface, usually a sheet or coating of aluminum. Radiant barriers come in various forms, including: reflective foil, reflective paint coatings, and reflective chips and can be combined with thermal insulation for increased energy efficiency.

Radiant barriers are fairly simple to use, and installation in new or existing homes is relatively easy. Once installed, it is virtually maintenance-free.

Some studies have shown that radiant barriers can reduce cooling costs by between 5 and 10 percent. The material cost of radiant barriers is between 15 and 75 cents per square foot.

Courtesy of PATH
www.pathnet.org/homeowners

Price Code C   62190

Total Sq. Ft.: 1,875
Main Level: 1,588'
Upper Level: 287'
Width: 42'
Depth: 68'-6"
Bedrooms: 4
Baths: 3
Garage: 2-car

(For more plan info, visit www.familyhomeplans.com)

Editor's Choice

FIRST FLOOR

SECOND FLOOR

Price Code C   63224

Total Sq. Ft.: 1,879
Main Level: 946'
Upper Level: 933'
Width: 57'
Depth: 35'
Bedrooms: 4
Baths: 2.5
Garage: 2-car

(For more plan info, visit www.familyhomeplans.com)

Guests are greeted by a foyer that opens onto a living/dining space beneath soaring ceilings and a stair case which opens a dramatic space. The kitchen is family oriented with an oversized breakfast area and a view to the front yard. The master suite enjoys views to the rear, and the master bath pampers with a corner soaking tub, dual sink vanity and private toilet room. The second floor offers the option of three bedrooms, or two bedrooms with a loft overlooking the living space below.

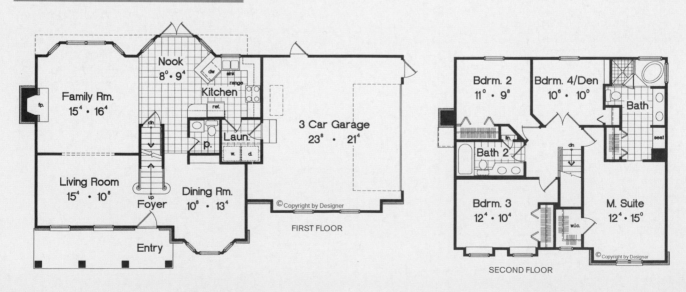

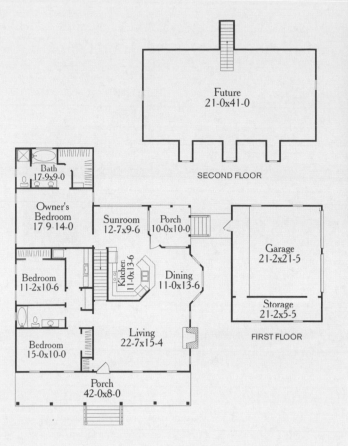

Future
21-0x41-0

SECOND FLOOR

Bath
17-9x9-0

Owner's
Bedroom
17 9 14-0

Sunroom
12-7x9-6

Porch
10-0x10-0

Kitchen
11-0x13-6

Dining
11-0x13-6

Garage
21-2x21-5

Storage
21-2x5-5

FIRST FLOOR

Bedroom
11-2x10-6

Bedroom
15-0x10-0

Living
22-7x15-4

Porch
42-0x8-0

Price Code C   40032

Total Sq. Ft.: 1,879
Width: 45'
Depth: 62'
Bedrooms: 3
Baths: 2
Garage: 2-car

(For more plan info, visit www.familyhomeplans.com)

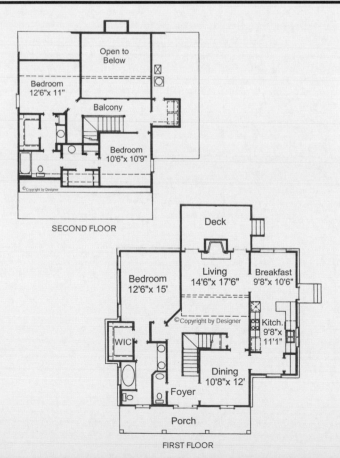

Open to
Below

Bedroom
12'6"x 11"

Balcony

Bedroom
10'6"x 10'9"

©Copyright by Designer

SECOND FLOOR

Deck

Living
14'6"x 17'6"

Breakfast
9'8"x 10'6"

Bedroom
12'6"x 15'

©Copyright by Designer

Kitch.
9'8"x
11'1"

WIC

Dining
10'8"x 12'

Foyer

Porch

FIRST FLOOR

Price Code C   94607

Total Sq. Ft.: 1,880
Main Level: 1,244'
Upper Level: 636'
Width: 40'-6"
Depth: 50'
Bedrooms: 3
Baths: 2.5
Garage: none

(For more plan info, visit www.familyhomeplans.com)

Price Code C   65624

Total Sq. Ft.: 1,891
Width: 49'
Depth: 64'
Bedrooms: 2
Baths: 2
Garage: 2-car

(For more plan info, visit www.familyhomeplans.com)

This clever design proves that privacy doesn't have to be compromised even in high-density urban neighborhoods. From within, views are oriented to a beautiful, lush entry courtyard and a covered rear porch. The exterior appearance is sheltered, but warm and welcoming. The innovative interior design centers on a unique kitchen, which directs traffic away from the working areas while still serving the entire home. The sunken family room features a 14-ft. vaulted ceiling and a warm fireplace. The master suite is highlighted by a sumptuous master bath with an oversized shower and a whirlpool tub, plus a large walk-in closet. The formal living room is designed and placed in such a way that it can become a third bedroom, a den, or an office or study room, depending on family needs and lifestyles.

Editor's Choice

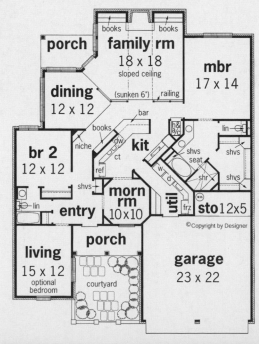

Frost-Proctected Shallow Foundations

Frost-Protected Shallow Foundations (FPSF) provide protection against frost damage without the need for excavating below the frost line. An FPSF has insulation placed strategically around the outside of a foundation to direct heat loss from the building toward the foundation, and also to use the earth's natural geothermal energy.

Traditionally, foundations are protected from frost-heaving damage by placing the footing below the frost line. Because FPSFs are protected from freezing by thermal insulation, bottoms of footings can be just twelve to sixteen inches below grade. This reduces excavation costs, making this an economical alternative for protecting foundations against frost damage.

Insulation around the perimeter of the foundation reduces the amount of heat loss from the warm interior to the cold exterior in the winter, which would normally pass through the slab or floor, and out through the foundation. Heating energy costs are thus reduced.

Courtesy of PATH
www.pathnet.org/homeowners

Price Code C 62037

Total Sq. Ft.: 1,880
Width: 57'
Depth: 61'-4"
Bedrooms: 4
Baths: 2
Garage: 2-car

(For more plan info, visit www.familyhomeplans.com)

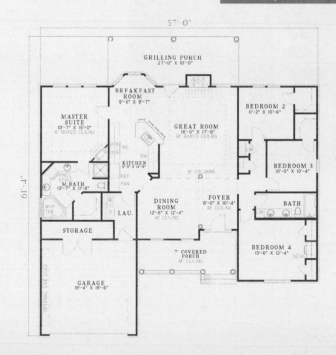

Price Code C   65493

Total Sq. Ft.: 1,883
Width 68'-8"
Depth 41'-8"
Bedrooms: 3
Baths: 2
Garage: 2-car

(For more plan info, visit www.familyhomeplans.com)

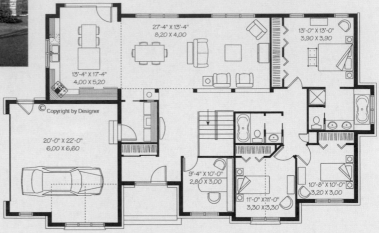

Price Code C   65486

Total Sq. Ft.: 1,885
Main Level: 908'
Upper Level: 977'
Width 36'
Depth 40'
Bedrooms: 3
Baths: 2
Garage: 1-car

(For more plan info, visit www.familyhomeplans.com)

SECOND FLOOR

FIRST FLOOR

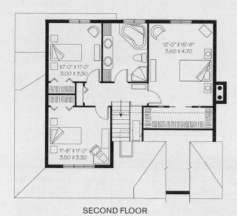

SECOND FLOOR

12'-0" X 15'-8"
3,60 X 4,70

10'-0" X 11'-0"
3,00 X 3,30

11'-8" X 11'-0"
3,50 X 3,30

10'-4" X 11'-0"
3,10 X 3,30

12'-0" X 12'-0"
3,60 X 3,60

13'-0" X 13'-0"
3,90 X 3,90

13'-0" X 18'-8"
3,00 X 5,60

© Copyright by Designer

FIRST FLOOR

Price Code C 65490

Total Sq. Ft.: 1,888
Main Level: 1,095'
Upper Level: 793'
Width 37'
Depth 33'
Bedrooms: 3
Baths: 1.5
Garage: none

(For more plan info, visit www.familyhomeplans.com)

Screened Porch
12' x 12'

Breakfast
13'4" x 11'

Great Room
15'3" x 15'10"

Master
Bedroom
15' x 13'

Bath

Kitchen
13'4" x 13'2"

Dining Room
11'8" x 10'

Foyer

WALK IN
CLOSET

Hall

Bath

Laun.

Porch

Bedroom
11' x 12'6"

Bedroom
12'6" x 11'4"

Two Car
Garage
22'4" x 24'3"

© Copyright by Designer

Price Code C 50075

Total Sq. Ft.: 1,895
Width: 66'
Depth: 69'
Bedrooms: 3
Baths: 2
Garage: 2-car

(For more plan info, visit www.familyhomeplans.com)

smarter homebuilding technologies

Price Code C 69503

Total Sq. Ft.: 1,892
Width: 65'
Depth: 44'
Bedrooms: 3
Baths: 2.5
Garage: 2-car

(For more plan info, visit www.familyhomeplans.com)

This three bedroom, 2½ bath, ranch was inspired by the simple Folk Victorians found throughout rural America—evidenced in the rambling form, simple rooflines, big front porch and bay window details. The interior and open floor plan, however, are totally up-to-date. Bedroom privacy is foremost, as this split plan separates a lovely master suite from the secondary bedrooms on the opposite side of the home.

Editor's Choice

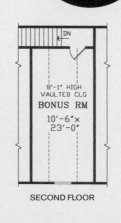

SL GL DRS

BEDRM #2
12'-0"x 11'-0"

10'-5" HIGH
STEPPED CLG
GREAT RM
FIREPLACE
18'-0"x
21'-4"
BUILT-INS

CL   LIN

BATH

CL

BEDRM #3
12'-0"x 11'-0"

FOY

HIGH
CEIL

10'-5" HIGH
STEPPED CLG
DINING RM
13'-0"x
11'-0"

COV. PORCH

SEAT

BKFST RM
10'-0"x
12'-0"

KIT
10'-0"x
11'-0"

REF

S
DW

NICHE

10'-5" HIGH
TRAY CEIL
MSTR BEDRM
13'-0"x 17'-0"
+ BAY

WICL

LIN   MSTR
       BATH

WICL

UP TO OPT
BONUS ROOM

LOCATION OF OPT
BSMT STAIR

LAV

D
W

LAUN
RM

CL

TWO CAR GARAGE

20'-0"x 20'-4" / 24'-0"
+ BAY

© Copyright by Designer

SEAT

FIRST FLOOR

DN

8'-1" HIGH
VAULTED CLG
BONUS RM
10'-6"x
23'-0"

SECOND FLOOR

Packed With Features.
This home is packed with all the features that you've always wanted, all within 1900 s.f. A foyer, formal dining room, and half bath are all extras that you would expect to find in a much larger home. The many available features and flexibility of this home make it the perfect choice for you and your family.

Price Code C   59192

Total Sq. Ft.: 1,900
Width: 69'
Depth: 57'
Bedrooms: 3
Baths: 2.5
Garage: 2-car

(For more plan info, visit www.familyhomeplans.com)

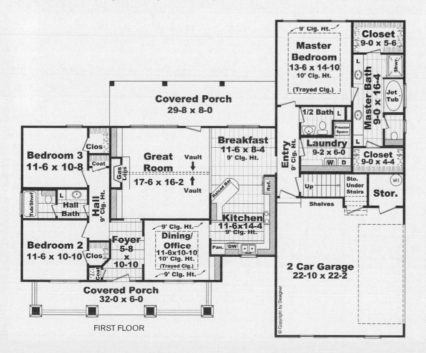

FIRST FLOOR

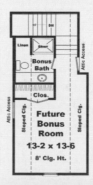

SECOND FLOOR

Price Code C 68236

Total Sq. Ft.: 1,897
Main Level: 1,448'
Upper Level: 449'
Width: 48'
Depth: 46'
Bedrooms: 3
Baths: 2.5
Garage: 2-car

(For more plan info, visit www.familyhomeplans.com)

This traditional two story home offers almost 1,900 square feet of living space. The home features a massive master suite on the first floor, with a huge walk-in closet. A large soaking tub and corner shower combine with dual vanities to make the master bath a great escape. The second floor offers two secondary bedrooms, and a large bathroom. One of the these bedrooms has its own walk-in closet, and there's access to the attic over the garage from the upstairs hallway. Off either side of the front foyer you'll find a dining room and formal living room. The dining room adjoins the kitchen through a cozy butler's pantry, and the living room is separate from the rest of the house, offering a spot for quiet conversation. A kitchen, dining nook, and family room make the perfect spot for family and friends to gather. The family room offers a corner fireplace and vaulted ceiling.

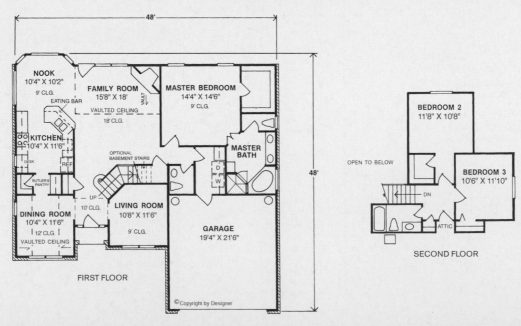

Price Code C   92462

Total Sq. Ft.: 1,897
Main Level: 995'
Upper Level: 902'
Width: 52'
Depth: 40'-4"
Bedrooms: 4
Baths: 3
Garage: 3-car

(For more plan info, visit www.familyhomeplans.com)

Energy Star... What's it all about?

If looking for new household products look for ones that have earned the ENERGY STAR. They meet strict energy efficiency guidelines set by the EPA and US Department of Energy.

ENERGY STAR is a government-backed program helping businesses and individuals protect the environment through superior energy efficiency.

Results are already adding up. Americans, with the help of ENERGY STAR, saved enough energy in 2005 alone to avoid greenhouse gas emissions equivalent to those from 23 million carsall while saving $12 billion on their utility bills.

For the Home

Energy efficient choices can save families about a third on their energy bill with similar savings of greenhouse gas emissions, without sacrificing features, style or comfort. ENERGY STAR helps you make the energy efficient choice.

Courtesy of PATH
www.pathnet.org/homeowners

Price Code C   73279

Total Sq. Ft.: 1,898
Width: 72'
Depth: 44'-8"
Bedrooms: 3
Baths: 2.5
Garage: 3-car

(For more plan info, visit www.familyhomeplans.com)

SECOND FLOOR

Price Code C   65489

Total Sq. Ft.: 1,898
Main Level: 1,195'
Upper Level: 703'
Width 62'
Depth 33'
Bedrooms: 3
Baths: 2
Garage: 2-car

(For more plan info, visit www.familyhomeplans.com)

FIRST FLOOR

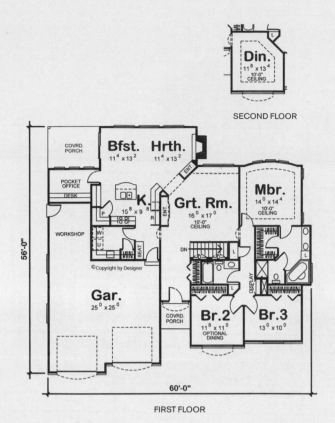

Din.
11⁸ x 13⁴
10'-0"
CEILING

SECOND FLOOR

Bfst.
11⁴ x 13²

Hrth.
11⁴ x 13²

COVRD.
PORCH

POCKET
OFFICE

DESK

Mbr.
14⁰ x 14⁴
10'-0"
CEILING

K.
15⁸ x 9⁸

Grt. Rm.
16⁰ x 17⁰
10'-0"
CEILING

WORKSHOP

56'-0"

Gar.
25⁰ x 25⁰

©Copyright by Designer

DN

Br.2
11⁸ x 11⁰
OPTIONAL
DINING

Br.3
13⁰ x 10⁰

COVRD.
PORCH

DISPLAY

60'-0"

FIRST FLOOR

Price Code C   44003

Total Sq. Ft.: 1,899
Width: 60'
Depth: 56'
Bedrooms: 3
Baths: 2
Garage: 2-car

(For more plan info, visit www.familyhomeplans.com)

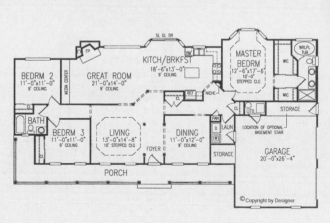

BEDRM 2
11'-0"x11'-0"
9' CEILING

MEDIA CENTER

GREAT ROOM
21'-0"x14'-0"
9' CEILING

KITCH/BRKFST
18'-6"x13'-0"
9' CEILING

MASTER
BEDRM
12'-6"x17'-6"
10'-0"
STEPPED CLG

WIC

WRLPL
TUB

BATH

BEDRM 3
11'-0"x11'-0"
9' CEILING

LIVING
13'-0"x14'-8"
10' STEPPED CLG

FOYER

DINING
11'-0"x12'-0"
9' CEILING

PAN

LAUN

NICHE

WIC

LOCATION OF OPTIONAL
BASEMENT STAIR

STORAGE

PORCH

STORAGE

GARAGE
20'-0"x26'-4"

©Copyright by Designer

Price Code c   69507

Total Sq. Ft.: 1,902
Width: 75'
Depth: 45'
Bedrooms: 3
Baths: 2
Garage: 2-car

(For more plan info, visit www.familyhomeplans.com)

ORDER NOW!   Phone: **1-800-235-5700**   Online: **www.FamilyHomePlans.com**   Order Code: **H6SSM**

Price Code C 99154

Total Sq. Ft.: 1,907
Width: 66'-4"
Depth: 56'
Bedrooms: 3
Baths: 2.5
Garage: 3-car

(For more plan info, visit www.familyhomeplans.com)

Brick and traditional siding grace the exterior of this traditional ranch home. Inside, a vaulted and tiled foyer welcomes you, and straight ahead a fireplace warms the great room. The island kitchen serves the nook and the dining room with ease, and the rear-covered porch is perfect for outdoor grilling. Family bedrooms include a master suite with a private bath and two additional bedrooms that share a hall bath. A three-car garage with storage, laundry room and powder rooms complete the floor plan.

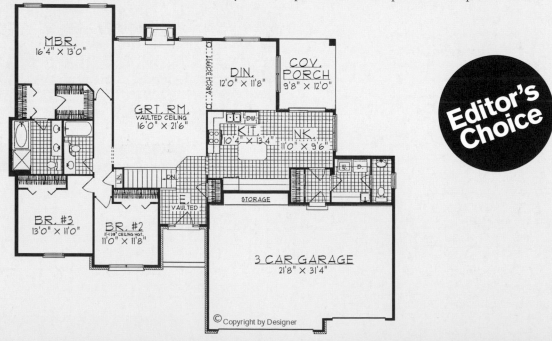

Editor's Choice

ORDER NOW! Phone: **1-800-235-5700** Online: **www.FamilyHomePlans.com** Order Code: **H6SSM**

Price Code C   10785

Total Sq. Ft.: 1,907
Main Level: 1,269'
Upper Level: 638'
Width: 47'
Depth: 39'
Bedrooms: 3
Baths: 2.5
Garage: none

(For more plan info, visit www.familyhomeplans.com)

Take this 1,907 sq. ft. farmhouse for instance with all the components for casual living at hand. For starters, a wraparound porch and geometric back deck bask in fresh air. Interior drama opens with a two-story foyer, and a sky-lit living room that accesses the deck through sliding glass doors. A formal dining room lines up with the centralized kitchen. A main-floor master suite makes life easier. Its walk-in closet and double sinks in the bath are a plus! The upstairs is a jewel with two charmed bedrooms, their own huge walk-ins, large shared bath, and a balcony overview.

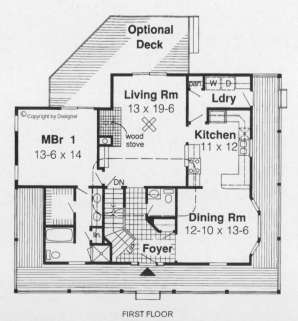

FIRST FLOOR

SECOND FLOOR

Editor's Choice

OPTIONAL LAYOUT

Price Code C 20501

Total Sq. Ft.: 1,908
Main Level: 1,316'
Upper Level: 592'
Width: 39'
Depth: 48'
Bedrooms: 3
Baths: 2

(For more plan info, visit www.familyhomeplans.com)

New-age living is out in front when it comes to fabulous features. 1,908 sq. ft. provides multiple levels, sun-catching walls of windows, huge deck, and so much more. The living room is a showcase with sloping ceilings, and a soaring fireplace—all open to the dining room and island kitchen. A unique demi-landing with steps leads to private areas: laundry area, shared bath and two bright bedrooms with corner windows and walk-in closets. The main stairs lead to the master suite with sloping ceilings, balcony, built-in bookshelves and wide walk-in. The bath has a step-up window tub, double vanities, linen closet and attic access.

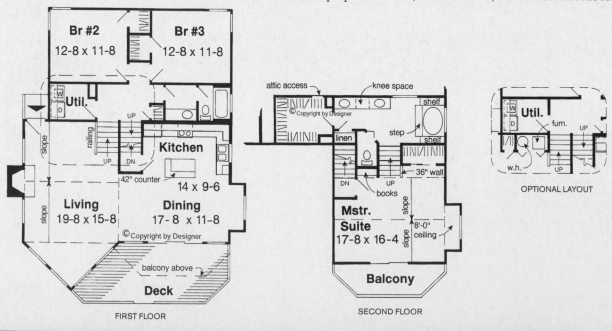

FIRST FLOOR

SECOND FLOOR

OPTIONAL LAYOUT

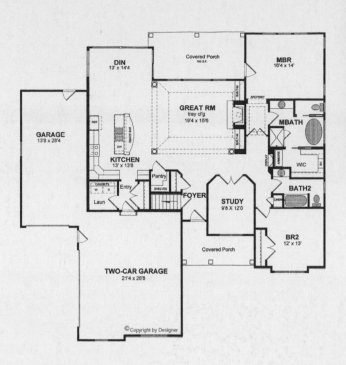

Price Code C   94157

Total Sq. Ft.: 1,912
Width: 64'
Depth: 65'
Bedrooms: 2
Baths: 2
Garage: 3-car

(For more plan info, visit www.familyhomeplans.com)

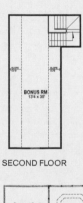

SECOND FLOOR

FIRST FLOOR

Price Code C   94153

Total Sq. Ft.: 1,916
Width: 58'
Depth: 63'-6"
Bedrooms: 2
Baths: 2
Garage: 2-car

(For more plan info, visit www.familyhomeplans.com)

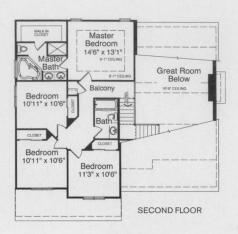

SECOND FLOOR

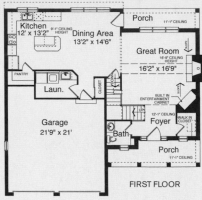

FIRST FLOOR

Price Code C 50106

Total Sq. Ft.: 1,921
Main Level: 968'
Upper Level: 953'
Width: 45'
Depth: 42'-2"
Bedrooms: 4
Baths: 2.5
Garage: 2-car

(For more plan info, visit www.familyhomeplans.com)

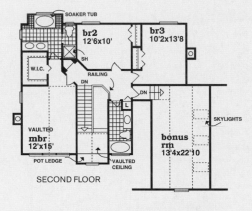

SECOND FLOOR

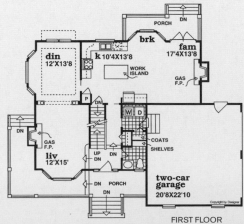

FIRST FLOOR

Price Code C 55004

Total Sq. Ft.: 1,924
Main Level: 1,007'
Upper Level: 917'
Width: 53'
Depth: 44'
Bedrooms: 3
Baths: 2.75
Garage: 2-car

(For more plan info, visit www.familyhomeplans.com)

Price Code C   63001

Total Sq. Ft.: 1,919
Width: 40'
Depth: 62'
Bedrooms: 4
Baths: 2
Garage: 2-car

(For more plan info, visit www.familyhomeplans.com)

Plumbing Manifolds

A new method for residential water distribution is gaining acceptance in the home building industry. Manifold plumbing systems are control centers for hot and cold water that feed flexible supply lines to individual fixtures. Plumbing manifold systems can be installed more quickly than rigid plumbing systems with fewer hidden fittings. Because of its relatively easy installation, this system can save on labor costs.

Plumbing manifolds are mounted in a convenient, accessible location, such as a basement wall or a service closet, to allow access for shut off to individual fixtures. Separated manifold chambers or separate manifolds can serve hot and cold water lines. The cold water manifold is fed from the main water supply line and the hot water manifold is fed from the water heater. Water pressure in manifolds is maintained by the incoming service line. The systems permit several fixtures to be used simultaneously without dramatic pressure or temperature drops.

Courtesy of PATH
www.pathnet.org/homeowners

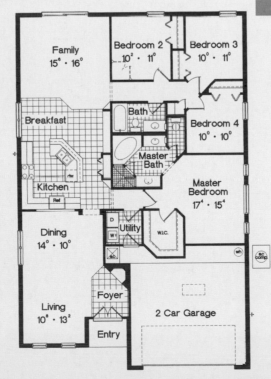

Price Code C 96544

Total Sq. Ft.: 1,925
Main Level: 1,329'
Upper Level: 596'
Width: 64'
Depth: 46'
Bedrooms: 3
Baths: 2.5
Garage: 2-car

(For more plan info, visit www.familyhomeplans.com)

Cozy yet full of amenities, this plan features an inviting great room and a warm fireplace for relaxed entertaining. This two story floor plan offers privacy for the master suite which boasts a wonderful master bath with whirlpool tub, separate shower, and dual vanities. An angled bar is available for added seating, and the utility area is located conveniently off of the kitchen. The second level houses two additional bedrooms, large storage closet, and additional bath. The front porch has plenty of room for sitting. Great for Southern hospitality!

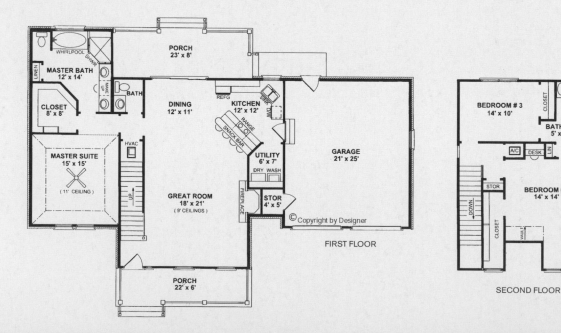

Price Code C 99115

Total Sq. Ft.: 1,926
Width: 69'-8"
Depth: 46'
Bedrooms: 3
Baths: 2.5
Garage: 3-car

(For more plan info, visit www.familyhomeplans.com)

This hip-roofed ranch has an exterior that tastefully mixes brick and siding. The recessed entrance with sidelights creates a formal entry. The foyer opens to a formal dining room with butler's pantry to the right and vaulted great-room to the left. There is a large open kitchen with ample cupboard space, and a spacious breakfast area which leads to the backyard. The spacious main-floor master suite has a large walk-in closet, private bath, and bay windows, overlooking the rear yard. The large triple-tandem garage provides plenty of storage or workshop space. The laundry room is located conveniently on the main level between the garage and the kitchen, and adjoins the guest bath. This home is designed with a basement foundation.

Editor's Choice

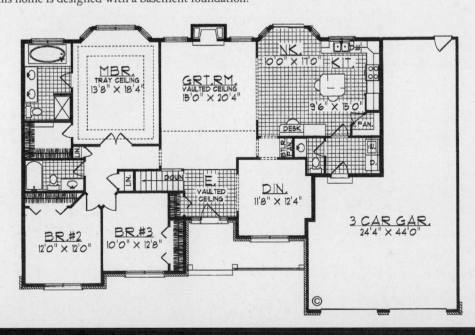

Price Code C 40004

Total Sq. Ft.: 1,927
Width: 64'
Depth: 56'
Bedrooms: 3
Baths: 2.5
Garage: 2-car

(For more plan info, visit www.familyhomeplans.com)

A warming fireplace, flanked by built-in cabinets beneath a cathedral ceiling adds to the ambiance of the great room. The private wing of the owner's suite includes dual walk-in closets, garden tub, shower, linen closet and two lavatories. The two additional bedrooms share a bath with each having a single lavatory vanity and a walk-in closet. They share a tub with shower, commode and a large linen cabinet. Upstairs above the bedrooms there is an additional space consisting of 400 more square feet available to expand.

Editor's Choice

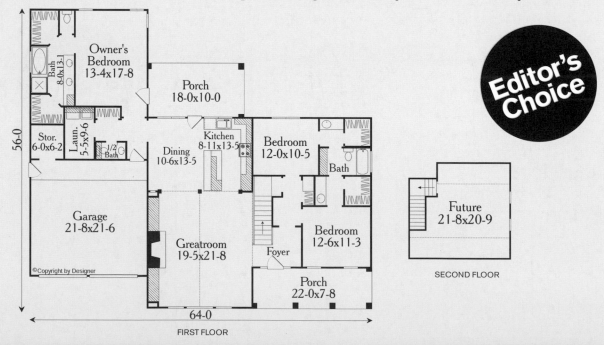

Special Grilling Porch.

A covered porch leads directly to a huge great-room, complete with a tray ceiling, a fireplace and access to a rear grilling porch. The kitchen leads to an interior dining room and to a cozy breakfast nook. The master bedroom connects to a gigantic full bath and room-sized walk-in closet. This home is designed with a slab foundation.

Price Code C   62053

Total Sq. Ft.: 1,930
Width: 52'
Depth: 71'-6"
Bedrooms: 4
Baths: 2
Garage: 2-car

(For more plan info, visit www.familyhomeplans.com)

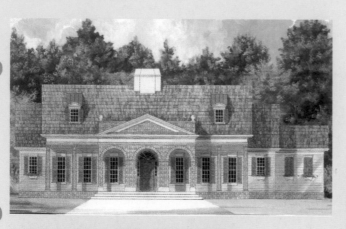

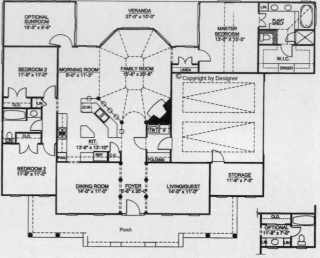

Price Code C   98238

Total Sq. Ft.: 1,931
Width: 69'
Depth: 47'
Bedrooms: 3
Baths: 2
Garage: 2-car

(For more plan info, visit www.familyhomeplans.com)

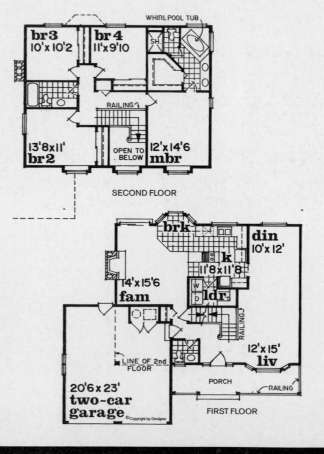

Price Code C   55023

Total Sq. Ft.: 1,938
Main Level: 936'
Upper Level: 1,002'
Width: 47'
Depth: 42'
Bedrooms: 4
Baths: 2.5
Garage: 2-car

(For more plan info, visit www.familyhomeplans.com)

ORDER NOW!   Phone: **1-800-235-5700**   Online: **www.FamilyHomePlans.com**   Order Code: **H6SSM**

Programmable Thermostats

Programmable thermostats save energy by permitting occupants to set temperatures according to whether the house is occupied. These thermostats can automatically store and repeat settings daily and can be set to adjust the temperature setting according to a user's schedule. Programmable thermostats typically offer a number of programming options which may include:

■ Vacation Override, which allows temporary override of the programmed settings.

■ Keyboard Lock, which prevents unauthorized changes to the preprogrammed settings.

■ Low Battery Indicator indicates whether the battery used to hold the programmed schedule is low.

■ An Energy Monitor that can keep track of how many hours the HVAC system has run for any selected time period.

■ An Auto Season Changeover that automatically provides heat or cooling at the onset of the heating and cooling season.

■ A Filter Change Indicator that goes on after a pre-set time period to remind when it is time to clean or replace the filter.

Different types of heating/cooling systems may require different types of programmable thermostats. When purchasing a programmable thermostat, it is necessary to insure the thermostat is compatible with your HVAC system.

Courtesy of PATH
www.pathnet.org/homeowners

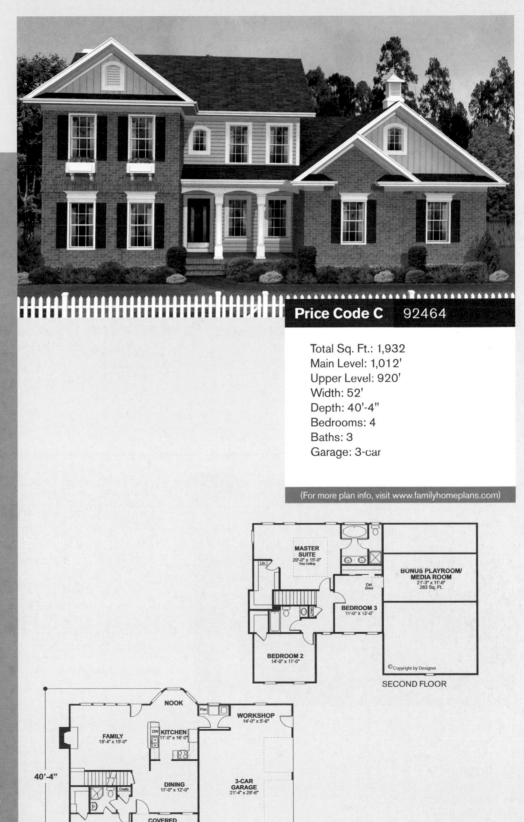

Price Code C 92464

Total Sq. Ft.: 1,932
Main Level: 1,012'
Upper Level: 920'
Width: 52'
Depth: 40'-4"
Bedrooms: 4
Baths: 3
Garage: 3-car

(For more plan info, visit www.familyhomeplans.com)

Price Code C   98223

Total Sq. Ft.: 1,940
Width: 54'-4"
Depth: 50'-8"
Bedrooms: 3
Baths: 2.5
Garage: 3 Drive Under Car

(For more plan info, visit www.familyhomeplans.com)

Price Code C   65488

Total Sq. Ft.: 1,953
Main Level: 1,301'
Upper Level: 652'
Width 58'
Depth 55'
Bedrooms: 3, 4
Baths: 2.5
Garage: 2-car

(For more plan info, visit www.familyhomeplans.com)

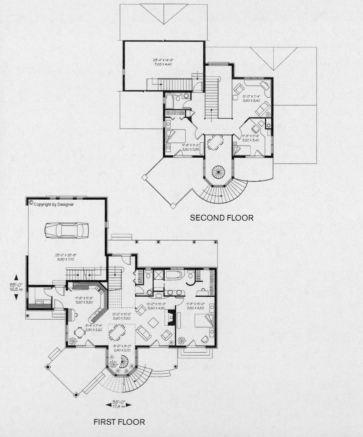

SECOND FLOOR

FIRST FLOOR

Price Code C 44015

Total Sq. Ft.: 1,951
Bedrooms: 3
Baths: 2
Garage: 2-car
Width: 70'
Depth: 50'-8"

(For more plan info, visit www.familyhomeplans.com)

A tasteful exterior presentation of brick and stucco previews the stylish interior of this smartly designed 3-bedroom home. Just inside, the entry is flanked by convenient built-in seats. A few steps more reveal the great room's expansive views to the outside, pleasantly shaded by a deep covered porch. The kitchen is open to the great room, breakfast area and hearth room. Adjacent to the hearth room, a computer area with built-in desk provides a convenient spot to pay bills and do homework. The opposing side of the home features the sleeping quarters - an opulent master suite and two secondary bedrooms with shared bath. In the garage, space is set aside for a workshop area.

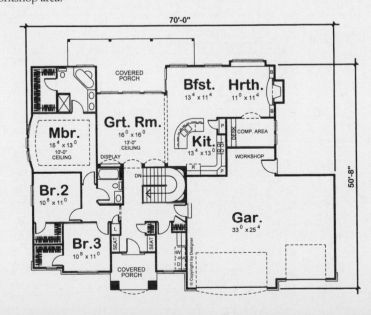

comfortable views

When comfort is a key consideration and view is vital, set your sights on homes like this fabulous design, with easy-going porches, dormers and big, bright windows. This home's creative blend of American Four-Square and Country styling provides 2,089 sq. ft. of living space. Four bedrooms, plus two and one half baths offer abundant room for daily living and weekend entertaining. The formal entry hall leads through French doors to a layout loaded with illuminating features, including a solarium that radiates into the family room with fireplace and into the dining room. The kitchen with island can host a hungry crowd. The breakfast nook opens to a breezy side porch. The media room (or bedroom #4) looks onto the front porch and the treasured view. Upstairs, the master bedroom's walk-in closet features a window. The bedroom itself enjoys double windows, a fireplace, and a spa-style bathroom with a corner platform tub beneath a window. Bedroom #2 features a built-in workstation. Bedroom #3 sleeps cozily in the oversized dormer. Both bedrooms border a windowed full bath.

Above: The skylit kitchen offers plenty of workspace and accessed a side porch. Top and Bottom Right: The pampering master suite is enhanced by a romantic fireplace and luxurious bath.

FIRST FLOOR

SECOND FLOOR

Price Code D   65135

Total Sq. Ft.: 2,089
Main Level: 1,146'
Upper Level: 943'
Bedrooms: 3
Bathrooms: 2.5
Garage: 2-car
Width: 56'
Depth: 38'

(For more plan info, visit www.familyhomeplans.com)

Price Code C 86108

Total Sq. Ft.: 1,957
Width: 46'-8"
Depth: 70'-6"
Bedrooms: 4
Baths: 4
Garage: 2-car

(For more plan info, visit www.familyhomeplans.com)

A cozy cottage built for two or three or four or more. Designed for all seasons, this home works like a charm. Winter nights before the fireplace with hot chocolate and a good book, summer evenings on the terrace dining out beneath the stars, romance, family and friends- this home encompasses all with warmth and good cheer.

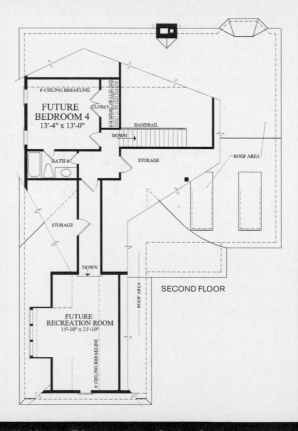

FIRST FLOOR

STORAGE AREA

Price Code C   94158

Total Sq. Ft.: 1,962
Width: 66'
Depth: 51'-4"
Bedrooms: 3
Baths: 2
Garage: 2-car

(For more plan info, visit www.familyhomeplans.com)

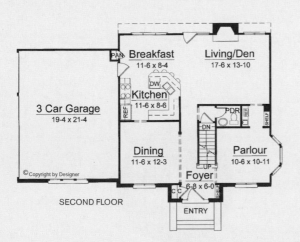

SECOND FLOOR

FIRST FLOOR

Price Code C   72022

Total Sq. Ft.: 1,967
Main Living: 1,002'
Upper Living: 965'
Width: 50'
Depth: 35'
Bedrooms: 3
Baths: 2.5
Garage: 3-car

(For more plan info, visit www.familyhomeplans.com)

Price Code C   63002

Total Sq. Ft.: 1,963
Width: 58'
Depth: 66'-8"
Bedrooms: 3
Baths: 2
Garage: 2-car

(For more plan info, visit www.familyhomeplans.com)

Double pillars on this home's covered porch grab attention. The front door opens to the family room, where a fireplace adds a warm glow to the light streaming in from the windows. Elegant columns and a decorative ceiling enhance the dining room, which has direct access through a door into the kitchen. The kitchen shares an angled bar with the nook, while built-ins and a pantry add to its already ample work space. The split-bedroom design allows privacy for all family members.

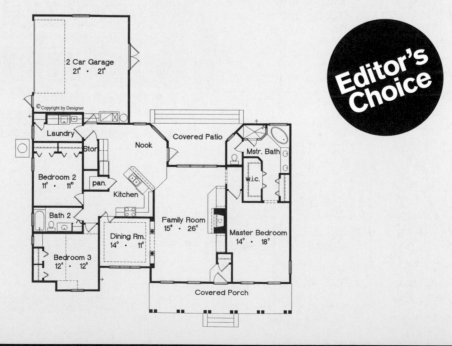

Editor's Choice

Radiant Floor Heating
(Dry System Hydronic)

Radiant heat installed beneath a finished floor that isn't embedded in concrete.

Dry system radiant flooring is radiant heat installed beneath a finished floor without material poured over the tubing. Several manufacturers offer dry radiant systems that position radiant floor tubing above floor, between two layers of plywood, or below floor under the subfloor. Hydronic radiant floor systems pump heated water through tubing positioned in loops beneath the finished floor. The heated water flowing through the tubes heats the surrounding air and flooring material.

Radiant floor systems allow even heating throughout the entire floor. The heat radiates from the floor and warms objects near the floor as opposed to forced hot air that tends to rise to the ceiling. Radiant floors eliminate dust, draft, and noise problems associated with forced air systems. They can be more aesthetically pleasing than other forms of heating because there are no heat registers or radiators to obstruct interior designs. Manufacturers claim radiant floor heating saves 20 to 40 percent on monthly heating bills.

Courtesy of PATH
www.pathnet.org/homeowners

Price Code C   92461

Total Sq. Ft.: 1,963
Width: 57'-8"
Depth: 57'-6"
Bedrooms: 3
Baths: 2
Garage: 2-car

(For more plan info, visit www.familyhomeplans.com)

A tasteful execution of style with columns and gables mark the exterior of this lovely home. Open arrangements between the dining room, family room and kitchen/breakfast area invite plenty of interaction. A screened porch to the rear opens onto a spacious deck for outdoor living options. The master is secluded for privacy and features a sitting room and his and her walk-in closets. Added space is optional with an upstairs bonus room.

Editor's Choice

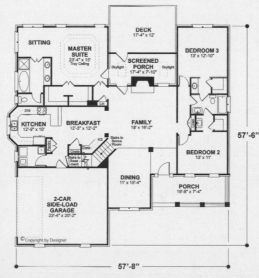

FIRST FLOOR

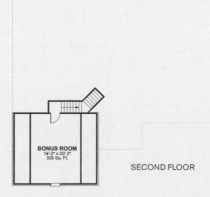

SECOND FLOOR

Price Code C   96527

Total Sq. Ft.: 1,972
Width: 76'
Depth: 61'
Bedrooms: 3
Baths: 2
Garage: 2-car

(For more plan info, visit www.familyhomeplans.com)

Looking for classy sophistication and lots of storage? This beautiful home has it all! Stunning 12-foot ceilings carry your eyes into the gigantic great room with fireplace. The great room and dining room offer a spacious view of the tranquil yard and porch areas. The utility area offers more space than ever with plenty of room for a washer, dryer, and extra freezer. Added storage areas are found throughout this plan in the utility room, study, foyer, bedrooms, and garage.

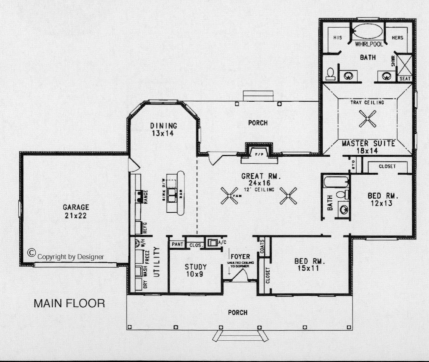

MAIN FLOOR

Price Code C 40033

Total Sq. Ft.: 1,974
Width: 72'
Depth: 55'-2"
Bedrooms: 3
Baths: 2.5
Garage: 2-car

(For more plan info, visit www.familyhomeplans.com)

A palladian window and covered porch enhance this home's sense of "welcome." Inside, guests are greeted by views into the formal dining room and great room. Vistas from the great room include the skylit rear covered porch, and patio beyond. A spacious kitchen/breakfast area serves casual dining with an island snack bar. Bedrooms are situated for privacy, with the well-appointed master suite tucked away from living areas. A generous laundry area, along with storage space in the garage, provide added sensibility to this design.

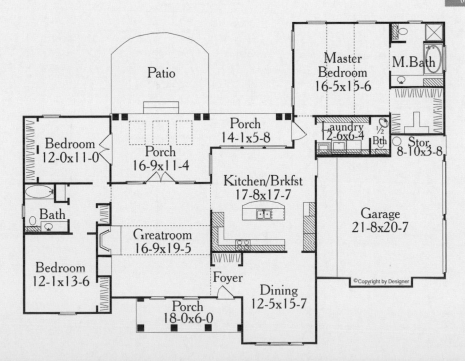

Editor's Choice

Price Code C 86103

Total Sq. Ft.: 1,990
Width: 60'
Depth: 67'-2"
Bedrooms: 4
Baths: 3.5
Garage: 2-car

(For more plan info, visit www.familyhomeplans.com)

FIRST FLOOR

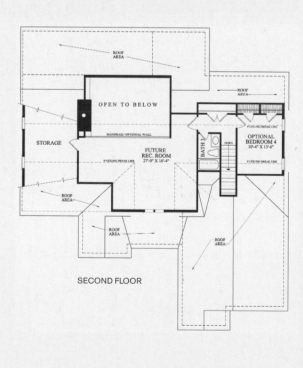

SECOND FLOOR

Price Code C 92427

Total Sq. Ft.: 1,982
Width: 63'
Depth: 58'
Bedrooms: 3
Baths: 2.5
Garage: 3-car

(For more plan info, visit www.familyhomeplans.com)

This home's lovely siding exterior is accented with areas of wood shingles, a "bayed" living room, and an irresistible front porch. Its radius top windows, luxurious master suite, a large screened porch, and the addition of a 386 square foot bonus room, are sure to make this 1,982 square foot home hard to top. The exquisite master suite boasts a vaulted ceiling, a sitting area, and a large walk-in closet. Also adorning the family room, living room, and screened porch are vaulted ceilings, and a tray ceiling in the dining room. Other rooms have 9' ceilings. Just off the kitchen are stairs leading to the enormous bonus room, measuring 11'-4" x 30'-8". The spacious secondary bedrooms each measure approximately. 13' x 11', have walk-in closets, and share a "Jack and Jill" bath.

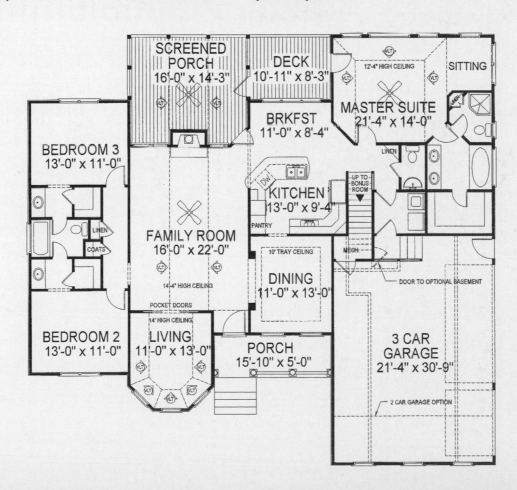

Price Code C 86106

Total Sq. Ft.: 1,985
Main Living Area: 1,348'
Upper Living Area: 637'
Width: 34'-7"
Depth: 57'
Bedrooms: 4
Baths: 4

(For more plan info, visit www.familyhomeplans.com)

How does my garden grow? In nooks and crannies, beside the picket fences and in carefully planned areas all around this cherished home. The warm charm and detail of this home instantly catches the eye.

FIRST FLOOR

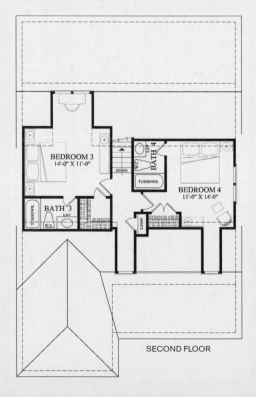

SECOND FLOOR

Price Code C 97405

Total Sq. Ft.: 1,984
Main Level: 1,487'
Upper Level: 497'
Width: 62'
Depth: 42'-6"
Bedrooms: 3
Baths: 2.5
Garage: 2-car

(For more plan info, visit www.familyhomeplans.com)

The French Country exterior of this home makes you comfortable before you even enter. And you'll know why as soon as you enter. The openness of the kitchen, dining and living areas make this a great spot for entertaining family and friends. A gorgeous master suite has it all — a huge sleeping area, enormous bath with dual sinks, and a large walk in closet. And, it's nicely separated from the rest of the home. The second floor has two great bedrooms and a full bath with dual vanities. The top story also offers two optional attic storage areas. A hallway open to below joins the two sides of the second floor.

Editor's Choice

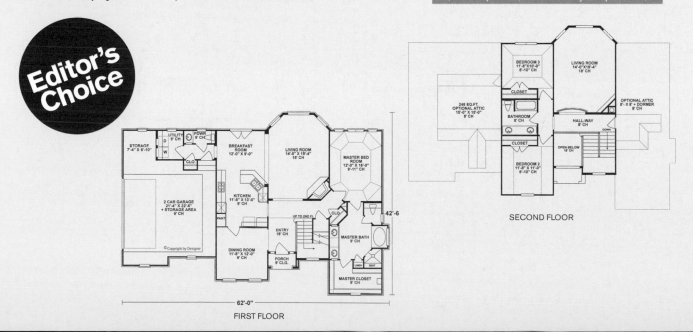

FIRST FLOOR

SECOND FLOOR

smarter **homebuilding** technologies

Price Code C 92446

Total Sq. Ft.: 1,992
Width: 66'-2"
Depth: 62'
Bedrooms: 3
Baths: 3
Garage: 2-car

(For more plan info, visit www.familyhomeplans.com)

This elegant country porch style home is both classic and contemporary. From the inviting front porch to the rear screened porch and deck, this home provides dramatic spaces, luxurious appointments and true flexibility. Just beyond the porch, the entry is lit by the open dormer above. Directly ahead is a spacious octagonally shaped family room with a 19'-9" high ceiling. The rear wall holds a gas fireplace with an entertainment center above and an arched clerestory window. French doors with transoms lead to a favorite area—the rear porch with its 6' spa and outdoor kitchenette. The intriguing master suite directly accesses the screened porch, a sitting room, luxurious bath, and "his and hers" walk-in closets.

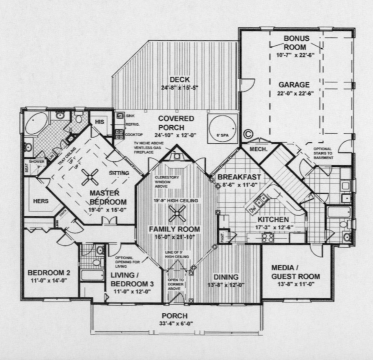

Sprayed Foam Insulation

Foam insulation that is sprayed into place and then expands to fill cavities

Sprayed foam insulation is sprayed into wall cavities and expands to fill all the nooks and crannies. This very effective insulation does not shrink, sag, settle, or biodegrade. By acting as an air barrier, sprayed foam insulation provides insulation and air sealing in one step. It is ideal for filling small spaces where cutting fiberglass batt insulation to fit can be difficult and labor-intensive.

Sprayed foam materials cost more than traditional fiberglass batt insulation. However, since sprayed foam forms both an insulation and an air barrier, it can be cost competitive with batt insulation because it eliminates the steps for air-tightness detailing (such as caulking, applying housewrap and vapor barrier, and taping joints). As a result, it also reduces construction time and the number of specialized contractors. In addition, most foam insulation products have a higher R-value per inch than fiberglass batt insulation. This increases energy efficiency by allowing downsizing of the heating and cooling system equipment.

Courtesy of PATH
www.pathnet.org/homeowners

Price Code C   92421

Total Sq. Ft.: 1,992
Width: 63'
Depth: 57'-2"
Bedrooms: 3
Baths: 2.5
Garage: 3-car

(For more plan info, visit www.familyhomeplans.com)

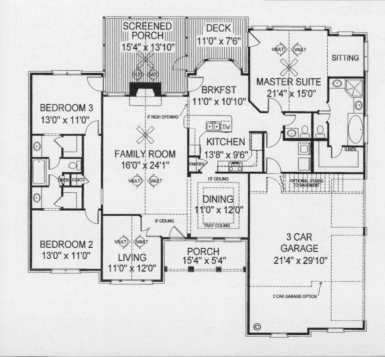

Price Code C **63101**

Total Sq. Ft.: 1,993
Width: 58'
Depth: 72'-4"
Bedrooms: 3
Full Baths: 2
Garage: 2-car

(For more plan info, visit www.familyhomeplans.com)

A stately brick elevation complete with front porch and dormers creates a warmth that is hard to beat in this 1,993 sq. ft. plan. This open plan has won many parade of homes awards, and has been a best seller. With the minimum of wasted hallway space, the rooms all benefit. The traditional split living and dining rooms create openness and the family room welcomes all.

Price Code C 69508

Total Sq. Ft.: 1,994
Width: 77'-10"
Depth: 54'
Bedrooms: 4
Baths: 2
Garage: 2-car

(For more plan info, visit www.familyhomeplans.com)

This charming, country influenced split bedroom ranch plan offers a more formal, balanced facade. Victorian detailed bay windows flank each side of a brick faced center section, set under a deep covered porch. Round top windows in this section add lots of light to the entry and flanking rooms. Ten-foot-high first floor ceilings prevail throughout the living area in the center section, as well as in the master bedroom.

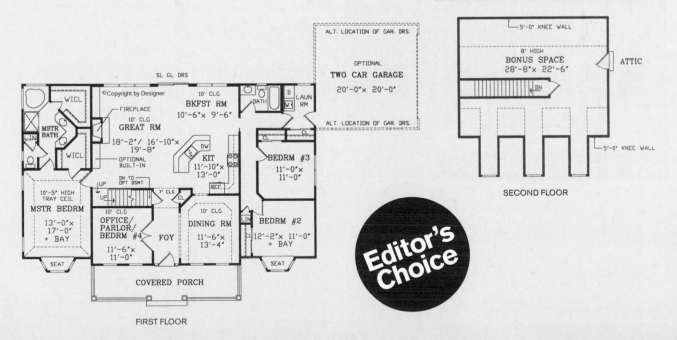

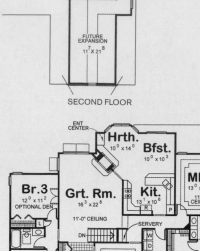

SECOND FLOOR

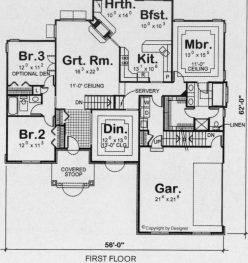

FIRST FLOOR

Price Code C 97912

Total Sq. Ft.: 1,995
Width: 56'
Depth: 62'
Bedrooms: 3
Baths: 2
Garage: 2-car

(For more plan info, visit www.familyhomeplans.com)

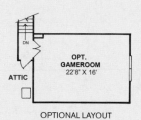

OPT. GAMEROOM
22'8" X 16'

ATTIC

OPTIONAL LAYOUT

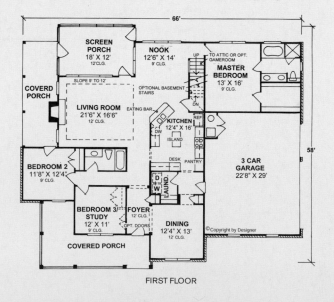

FIRST FLOOR

Price Code C 68161

Total Sq. Ft.: 1,995
Width: 66'
Depth: 58'
Bedrooms: 3
Baths: 2
Garage: 3-car

(For more plan info, visit www.familyhomeplans.com)

Price Code C   20230

Total Sq. Ft.: 2,056
Main Level: 1,422'
Upper Level: 634'
Width: 44'
Depth: 54'
Bedrooms: 4
Baths: 2.5
Garage: 2-car

(For more plan info, visit www.familyhomeplans.com)

We're confident this 1,995-sq.-ft. layout meets even the highest standards. Peaked dormers bring beautiful balance to the exterior. The covered porch enters a sophisticated interior. A formal dining room lines up with a unique double-door kitchen and bright breakfast area with bumped-out picture window. Soaring ceilings add depth to the great room, and a corner fireplace adds warmth. Wind around the main-floor to the master bedroom with dramatic windowing and personal his and her walk-ins. The master bath has double vanities. An open railing along the staircase rises to balcony level where two of three bedrooms feature walk-in closets. The shared bath has lots of room.

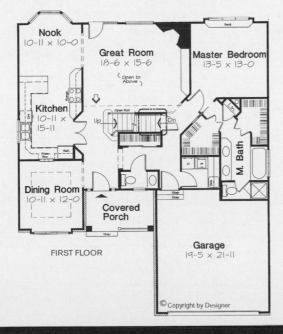

FIRST FLOOR

OPTIONAL LAYOUT

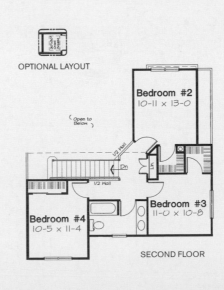

SECOND FLOOR

J.N. HANSEN S.D.G.

Price Code C 63049

Total Sq. Ft.: 1,997
Width: 64'
Depth: 57'
Bedrooms: 3
Baths: 2.5
Garage: 2-car

(For more plan info, visit www.familyhomeplans.com)

Ideal for the year-round gardener, this design features a built-in greenhouse illuminated by three skylights, or the space could be used as a sun-room. The huge kitchen with its central cook top island, the breakfast nook and the vaulted family room are inviting for family gatherings. Bedroom #2 and the study each access a full bath. The den could be used as a third bedroom. A split plan, the master bedroom features a super-sized walk-in closet. The luxury-filled master bathroom looks directly into a private garden. Upstairs, bonus space can be finished as needed, and would make an ideal media room or guest suite.

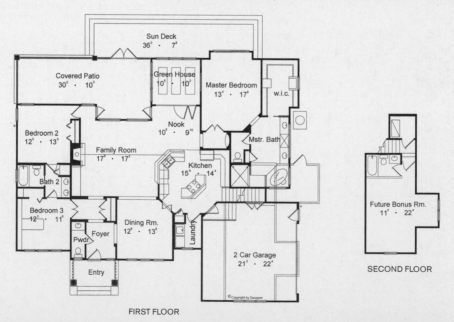

FIRST FLOOR

SECOND FLOOR

Ventilation Control Systems

Increase energy efficiency, reduce moisture condensation problems, and increase indoor air quality

Today's energy efficient homes do a great job of keeping conditioned air in. The downside is that reduced ventilation and air exchange with the outside can result in poor indoor air quality and possible health problems. Even air systems that are designed with fresh air intake do not provide ventilation or exhaust when they are not running.

Economical and affordable ventilation control systems mix the house air with fresh outdoor air and can increase energy efficiency, reduce moisture condensation problems, and increase indoor air quality.

There are many types of ventilation control systems available. Most manufacturers of ventilation equipment will also offer a control unit. Controls can be as simple as a twist-timer that is operated manually. Or, some units provide automatic control and are adjustable for cycle duration and time between cycles. These systems help bring in fresh air while removing stale air in addition to helping equalize pressure and temperature in homes.

Courtesy of PATH
www.pathnet.org/homeowners

Round-top windows and a pillared stoop enhance the sophisticated design of this well-planned 1½-story home. Inside, a formal dining room and office/parlor greet guests at the foyer. An open arrangement allows an open exchange between the great room, kitchen and breakfast room. The secluded master suite enjoys privacy from the four secondary bedrooms—two on the main level and two more upstairs.

Price Code C   69509

Total Sq. Ft.: 1,996
Width: 61'-6"
Depth: 66'-6"
Bedrooms: 5
Baths: 2.5
Garage: 2-car

(For more plan info, visit www.familyhomeplans.com)

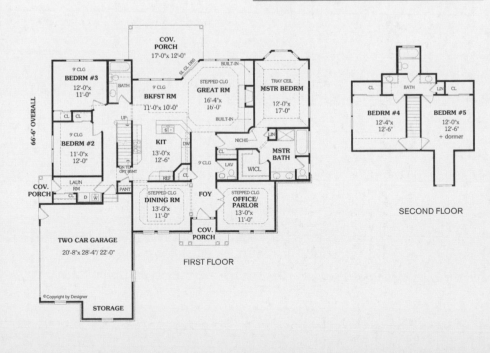

FIRST FLOOR

SECOND FLOOR

country retreat

Intimate, yet unconfined, this marvelous design embraces a highly versatile layout across 2,283 sq. ft. Bright and open, this plan invites family to spread out, or gather in easy-going comfort. An ample entry hall radiates a hearty welcome and streamlines to a private home office and light-filled family room with fireplace. A galley kitchen feeds into the breakfast area where sliding doors lead to an open-air porch. A dining room and a comfortable living room with cathedral ceiling flow elegantly into one another and share a balcony porch. A lofty upper-level mezzanine features three spacious bedrooms and two bathrooms. The master suite has a walk-in closet for two, bath with double sinks, separate shower and tub, and recessed windowing that bathes the room in light. Auxiliary bedrooms have a large bath nestled between them. Tucked away on the side of the house, there is a roomy two-car garage. A full basement awaits transformation to personal gym, or play area.

PHOTOS COURTESY OF DESIGNER.

Price Code E 65138

Total Sq. Ft.: 2,283
Main Level: 1,274'
Upper Level: 1,009'
Width: 50'
Depth: 46'
Bedrooms: 3
Baths: 2.5
Garage: 2-car

(For more plan info, visit www.familyhomeplans.com)

Top Left: The living room at the front of the home is graced by the beauty of an elliptical arch topped window. Right: The master suite's pampering bath provides a spot for peace and quiet. Above Right and Bottom Right: Sunshine brightens the breakfast area and kitchen.

SECOND FLOOR

FIRST FLOOR

Price Code C 40014

Total Sq. Ft.: 1,997
Width: 56'-4"
Depth: 67'-4"
Bedrooms: 4
Baths: 2.5
Garage: 2-car

(For more plan info, visit www.familyhomeplans.com)

Beautiful style and simple construction enhance this four bedroom plan. The kitchen has many amenities including an island snack bar and a large walk-in pantry. The skylit rear porch is great for enjoying outdoors and is easily accessed from several areas of the home. A spacious 10-foot ceiling shelters this great design.

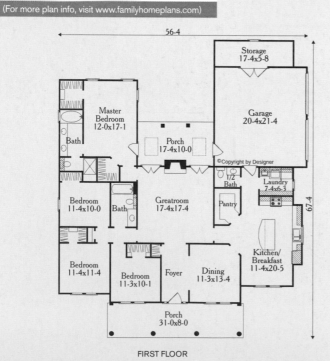

FIRST FLOOR

ALTERNATE FIRST FLOOR

Editor's Choice

Price Code C 44002

Total Sq. Ft.: 1,998
Width: 70'-4"
Depth: 62'-8"
Bedrooms: 2
Baths: 2
Garage: 3-car

(For more plan info, visit www.familyhomeplans.com)

Angles and arches enhance the interior aspects of this airy one-story home. Upon entry, interior views open to an intriguing dining area and expansive views of the great room. The great room interacts with the kitchen and is brightened by generous glass to the rear. The master suite pampers with large-home amenities and offers privacy from active areas. On the opposite side of the home, a secondary bedroom enjoys an equally secluded location. A bench and storage closet lend practicality to the entry from the garage, not to be outdone by the sensibly spacious laundry area.

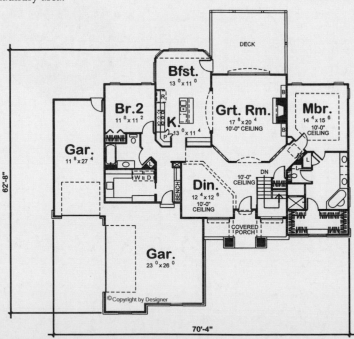

REAR EXTERIOR

Price Code D 59023

Total Sq. Ft.: 2,001
Width: 64'
Depth: 58'-10"
Bedrooms: 3
Baths: 2.5
Garage: 2-car

(For more plan info, visit www.familyhomeplans.com)

This very unique design maximizes every inch of its usable space. Three spacious bedrooms and two-and-a-half baths provide plenty of room for that growing family. Practicality abounds with a large utility room and walk-in closets in every bedroom. A sunroom and covered porch expand living areas to enjoy those evening sunsets. The great room adjoins space for that home office that you have always wanted.

Editor's Choice

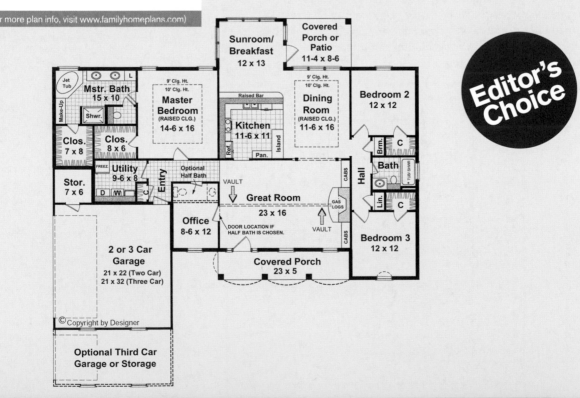

Price Code D   59024

Total Sq. Ft.: 2,002
Width: 64'-6"
Depth: 61'-4"
Bedrooms: 3
Baths: 2.5
Garage: 2-car

(For more plan info, visit www.familyhomeplans.com)

This home elicits the charming appeal of a quaint cottage that you might find in an old village in the English countryside! A trio of arches on the front porch welcomes friends and family inside, where the great room, warmed by a beautiful fireplace, flows gently into the dining room and kitchen area. Bedrooms are separated for privacy, and the master suite pampers with a full array of amenities, including his and her walk-in closets. A generously sized laundry area lies just inside from the garage along with a flexible nursery/office space. Abundant storage space is found adjacent to the 2-car garage which offers the option of a third bay.

Covered Porch or Patio
23 x 10

Breakfast
11-6 x 7

Master Bath
15 x 10

9' CLG. HT.

Master Bedroom
(RAISED CLG.)
14-6 x 16

10' CLG. HT.

Dining Room
(RAISED CLG.)
11-6 x 16

9' CLG. HT.

Bedroom 2
12-6 x 12

Jet Tub

Make-Up

Shwr.

Kitchen
11-6 x 11

Island

DW

Raised Bar

R

Pan.

Clos.
7 x 8

Clos.
8 x 6

Clos.

Bath

Clos.

Utility
9-6 x 8

Entry

Optional Half Bath

Great Room
23 x 16

Gas Logs

VAULT

Hall

Cabs.

Stor.
7 x 10

DOWN TO BASEMENT

Office/ Nursery
8-6 x 12

VAULT

Cabs.

Lin.

Clos.

Bedroom 3
12-6 x 12

Covered Porch
23 x 6

2 or 3 Car Garage
21 x 22 (Two Car)
21 x 32 (Three Car)

©Copyright by Designer

THIRD CAR GARAGE or STORAGE
NOTE: OVERALL DIMENSIONS DO NOT INCLUDE OPTIONAL THIRD CAR GARAGE.

smarter homebuilding technologies

Price Code D   86107

Total Sq. Ft.: 2,404
Main Living Area: 2,012'
Upper Living Area: 392'
Width: 59'-10"
Depth: 64'-8"
Bedrooms: 4
Baths: 3
Garage: 2-car

(For more plan info, visit www.familyhomeplans.com)

A stitch in time... it seems that Grace always, always made it - one stitch here, one stitch there (where needed) in the fabric of her life. Grace loved people and shared what little she could. This cottage is the home she dreamed of, but never had. In her dream, her gardens would be blazing with color and her kitchen fragrant with her famous apple dumplings. Though Grace never realized her dream, her daughter, in her mother's memory, made Grace's dream come true. Love passed down thrives like a well-tended flower and continues to bloom. Grace would be so proud.

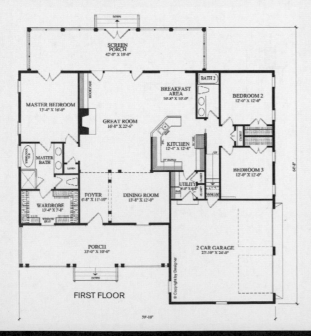

FIRST FLOOR

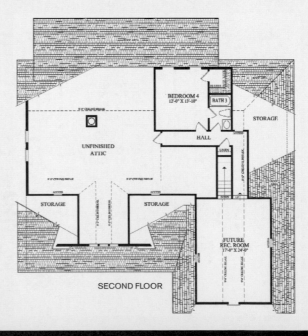

SECOND FLOOR

Price Code D 75003

A blend of brick and siding balance the front of this tastefully designed 4-bedroom, one-story home. A pleasant porch invites guests inside with views of the great room, complete with corner fireplace and views to the rear covered patio. The kitchen, served by a breakfast bar, is open to the main living areas. Bedrooms are separated for maximum privacy. In the master suite two walk-in closets flank an oval soaking tub. The secondary bedrooms are set apart by a central bath.

Total Sq. Ft.: 2,018
Width: 64'-10"
Depth: 56'-2"
Bedrooms: 4
Baths: 2
Garage: 2-car

(For more plan info, visit www.familyhomeplans.com)

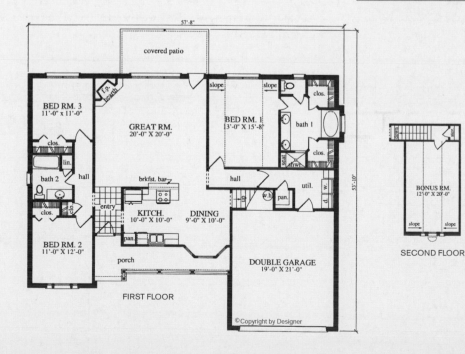

FIRST FLOOR

SECOND FLOOR

©Copyright by Designer

Price Code D 86109

Total Sq. Ft.: 2,020
Main Living Area: 1,424'
Upper Living Area: 596'
Width: 45'
Depth: 55'-2"
Bedrooms: 3
Baths: 2.5
Garage: 2-car

(For more plan info, visit www.familyhomeplans.com)

We all come home, but how differently today than yesterday. From a team of six white horses to sedans, suv's, jeeps, trucks and sports cars, oh how times have changed, however…the desire to come home remains the same. Familiar places, special memories, family, friends, holidays and good times - all of these and more nostalgically draw us home time and time again - to our own cozy little home.

FIRST FLOOR

SECOND FLOOR

This home's elegant brick exterior is accented with a "Palladian" window, multi-level trim and an inviting front porch. The exceptional master suite, with direct access to the deck, a sitting area, full-featured bath, and spacious walk-in closet, create a true "Master's Retreat." A bay window brightens the breakfast room which accesses a deep screened porch. Eyes are drawn upward in awe as vaulted or tray ceilings adorn the living, family room, dining, and master suite. Other rooms have 9' ceilings.

Price Code D   92463

Total Sq. Ft.: 2,071
Width: 63'
Depth: 63'
Bedrooms: 3
Baths: 2.5
Garage: 3-car

(For more plan info, visit www.familyhomeplans.com)

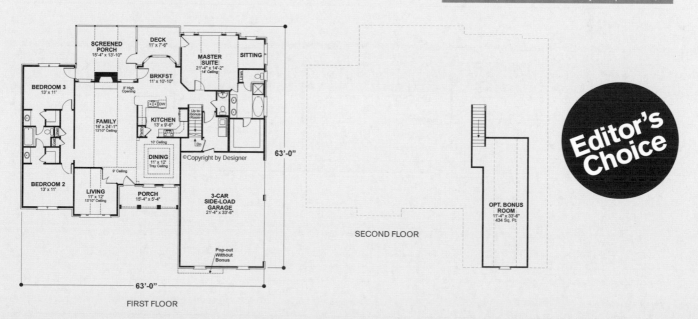

FIRST FLOOR

SECOND FLOOR

Editor's Choice

Price Code D 92444

Total Sq. Ft.: 2,097
Width: 70'-2"
Depth: 59'
Bedrooms: 3
Baths: 3
Garage: 3-car

(For more plan info, visit www.familyhomeplans.com)

Elegant round columns "dress up" this three bedroom, three bath, Southern Country porch design. It's classic irresistible styling makes it perfect for almost any neighborhood. The large vaulted family room, enormous country kitchen and its 452 square foot bonus area make this home feel so much more spacious than one might expect of a 2,097 square foot design. The sumptuous master suite includes a double tray ceiling, a sitting area, a large walk-in closet, and luxurious bath. The country kitchen is open to the vaulted family room. A French door leads to the vaulted screened porch. The patio or deck is accessible from both the screened porch and master bedroom. The dining room is adorned with a decorative round column and tray ceiling. Bedrooms #2 and #3 each feature walk-in closets and individual baths.

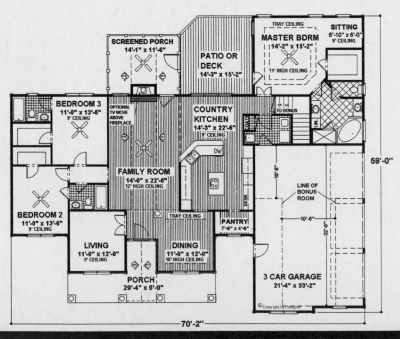

Price Code D   92465

This design is what we choose to call an "Elegant Country" style. This 1-1/2 story home is a simple design but becomes irresistible with its full-surround porch and symmetrical dormers. If you can bear to leave the delightful porch for a while to go inside, you'll find a somewhat contemporary design with lively angles, room brightening clerestory windows and spacious open areas. This is a "master on main level" plan with lots of glass, an open family room, kitchen and eating area, and very little wasted space. Upstairs are two sizeable bedrooms and a loft. Bedroom #2 has a walk-in closet with a pass-through to attic storage and built-in bookcase. Bedroom #3 has a built-in desk and bookshelves. A special convenience is the laundry chute just outside bedroom #2. The ceilings on the main level are 9 feet high except for the clerestory areas above the master bedroom, family room, eating area and dining area which soar to approximately 18 feet. Upstairs ceilings are 8 feet high.

Total Sq. Ft.: 2,098
Main Level: 1,512'
Upper Level: 586'
Width: 63'-4"
Depth: 86'-6"
Bedrooms: 3
Baths: 2.5
Garage: 3-car

(For more plan info, visit www.familyhomeplans.com)

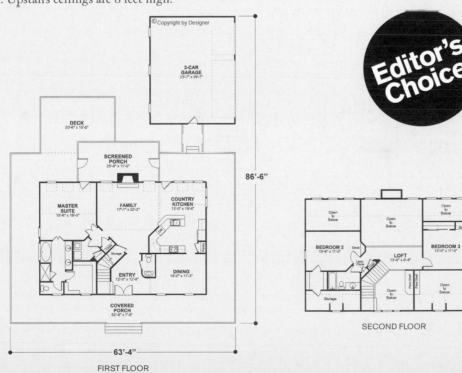

Editor's Choice

ORDER NOW!   Phone: **1-800-235-5700**   Online: **www.FamilyHomePlans.com**   Order Code: **H6SSM**

Price Code D 65862

Total Sq. Ft.: 2,091
Width 76'-9"
Depth 71'-5"
Bedrooms: 3
Baths: 2.5
Garage: 2-car

(For more plan info, visit www.familyhomeplans.com)

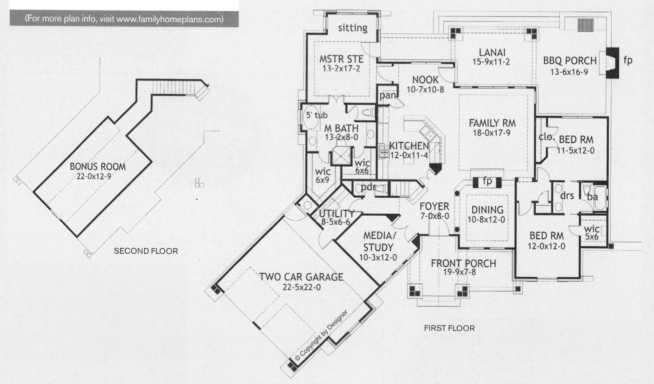

BONUS ROOM
22-0x12-9

SECOND FLOOR

sitting

MSTR STE
13-2x17-2

LANAI
15-9x11-2

BBQ PORCH
13-6x16-9

fp

NOOK
10-7x10-8

5' tub

M BATH
13-2x8-0

pan

FAMILY RM
18-0x17-9

clo.

BED RM
11-5x12-0

KITCHEN
12-0x11-4

wic
6x6

wic
6x9

pdr

fp

drs

ba

UTILITY
8-5x6-6

FOYER
7-0x8-0

DINING
10-8x12-0

BED RM
12-0x12-0

wic
5x6

MEDIA/
STUDY
10-3x12-0

TWO CAR GARAGE
22-5x22-0

FRONT PORCH
19-9x7-8

© Copyright by Designer

FIRST FLOOR

Price Code D   92443

Total Sq. Ft.: 2,184
Width: 71'-2"
Depth: 58'-1"
Bedrooms: 3
Baths: 3
Garage: 2-car

(For more plan info, visit www.familyhomeplans.com)

This sophisticated southern country home, with its updated facade and spacious interior design, is both flexible and dramatic. Three full baths, a screened porch and a 379 square foot bonus room are just a few of its irresistible features. The luxurious master suite includes a double tray ceiling, a sitting area, his and hers walk-in closets, and exquisite bath. The country kitchen is open to the vaulted family room. A French door leads to the vaulted screened porch. The patio or deck is accessible from both the screened porch and master bedroom. A decorative square column and tray ceiling adorn the elegant dining room. Bedrooms #2 and #3 each feature walk-in closets and individual baths.

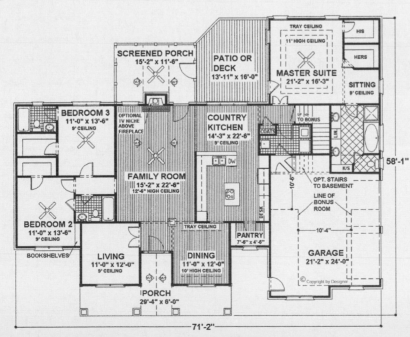

Price Code D 96829

Total Sq. Ft.: 2,198
Main Level: 1,201'
Upper Level: 997'
Width: 67'
Depth: 48'
Bedrooms: 4
Baths: 2.5
Garage: 2-car

(For more plan info, visit www.familyhomeplans.com)

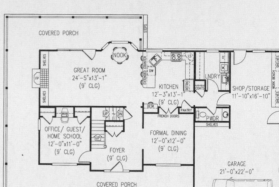

SECOND FLOOR

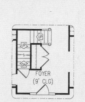

OPTIONAL LAYOUT

FIRST FLOOR

Price Code E 96815

Total Sq. Ft.: 2,266
Main Level: 1,216'
Upper Level: 1,050'
Width: 64'-6"
Depth: 47'-7"
Bedrooms: 4
Baths: 3.5
Garage: 2-car

(For more plan info, visit www.familyhomeplans.com)

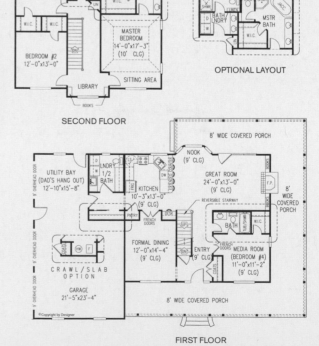

SECOND FLOOR

OPTIONAL LAYOUT

FIRST FLOOR

Price Code E   65145

Total Sq. Ft.: 2,292
Main Level: 1,246'
Upper Level: 1,046'
Width: 58'
Depth: 42'-2"
Bedrooms: 3
Baths: 2.5
Garage: 2-car

(For more plan info, visit www.familyhomeplans.com)

Whether water-front, mountain, or curbside, this 2,292 sq.ft. plan is versatile enough to play vacation hideaway or full family home as it harbors three to four generous bedrooms, 2.5 baths, and a host of other amenities, including two fireplaces—one in the living room and one in the master suite. With abundant windowing, and a grand wrap-around porch that embraces three sides of the house, this layout makes the most of scenic vistas. Plus, important family gathering spaces like the kitchen, breakfast area and family rooms practically own the outdoor view. Convenience is a key component as well, with the laundry facility and half-bath within easy reach. The full basement can easily convert to a roomy play area or personal gym.

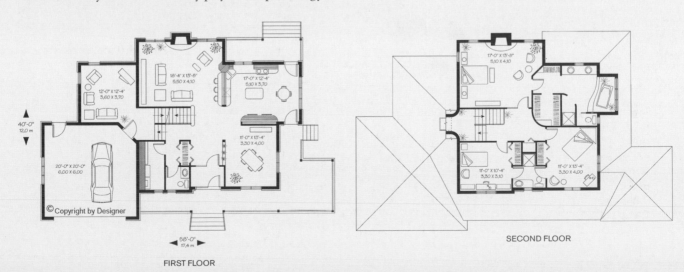

FIRST FLOOR

SECOND FLOOR

Price Code E 59214

Total Sq. Ft.: 2,336
Width: 73'
Depth: 74'
Bedrooms: 4
Baths: 2.5
Garage: 2-car

(For more plan info, visit www.familyhomeplans.com)

Country Charm. This charming country home offers much more than just great style. It also features a floorplan designed for the busy lifestyles of families today. The large great room features a gas log fireplace, trayed ceilings, and provides a perfect place to entertain guests. The well-equipped kitchen features a raised bar, large pantry, and easy access to the neighboring dining room. The master suite features a large walk-in closet, dual lavatories, jet tub, separate shower, and enclosed toilet. The other three bedrooms all include large closets. This home also features great porch areas for outdoor entertaining and a large two car garage complete with separate storage space. Make this your family's next home!

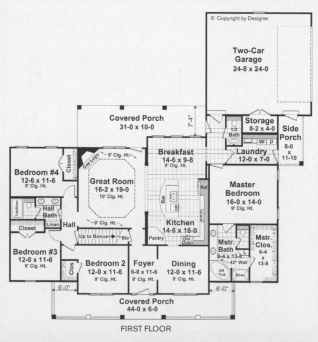

FIRST FLOOR

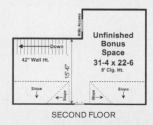

SECOND FLOOR

Price Code D   86104

Being of incisive line, thought, style and effect, the understated appeal of this Cottage is reminiscent of a simpler life. Times when neighbor greeted neighbor, doors were left unlocked and a helping hand was near. We can have that again. Choose your neighborhood, plan your home you've made a wise decision.

Total Sq. Ft.: 2,151
Width: 61'
Depth: 55'-8"
Bedrooms: 4
Full Baths: 3
Garage: 2-car

(For more plan info, visit www.familyhomeplans.com)

FIRST FLOOR

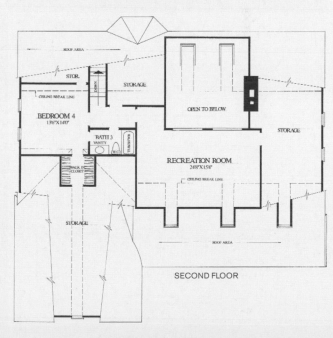

SECOND FLOOR

Price Code D 24734

Total Sq. Ft.: 2,114
Main Living Area: 1,127'
Upper Living Area: 987'
Width: 74'
Depth: 41'-6"
Bedrooms: 3
Baths: 2.5
Garage: 2-car

(For more plan info, visit www.familyhomeplans.com)

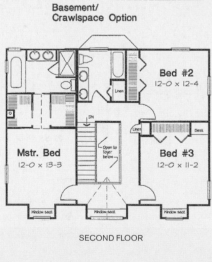

Basement/
Crawlspace Option

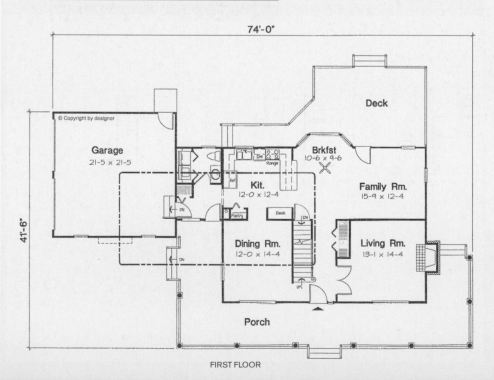

FIRST FLOOR

SECOND FLOOR

Price Code D 59212

Total Sq. Ft.: 2,140
Width: 71'
Depth: 77'
Bedrooms: 5
Baths: 2.5
Garage: 2-car

(For more plan info, visit www.familyhomeplans.com)

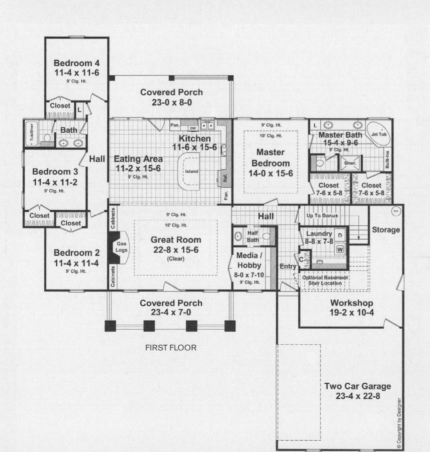

Bedroom 4
11-4 x 11-6
9' Clg. Ht.

Closet

L

Bath

Tub/Shwr.

Covered Porch
23-0 x 8-0

Pan.

DW

Kitchen
11-6 x 15-6

9' Clg. Ht.
10' Clg. Ht.

L

Master Bath
15-4 x 9-6
9' Clg. Ht.

Jet Tub

Shwr.

Built-Ins

Hall

Eating Area
11-2 x 15-6
9' Clg. Ht.

Island

Ref.

Pan.

Master Bedroom
14-0 x 15-6

Bedroom 3
11-4 x 11-2
9' Clg. Ht.

Closet

Closet

Cabinets

Cabinets

Gas Logs

9' Clg. Ht.
10' Clg. Ht.

Great Room
22-8 x 15-6
(Clear)

Hall

Half Bath

Media / Hobby
8-0 x 7-10
9' Clg. Ht.

Entry

C

Closet 7-6 x 5-8   Closet 7-6 x 5-8

Up To Bonus

Laundry
8-8 x 7-8

W

Storage

Bedroom 2
11-4 x 11-4
9' Clg. Ht.

Optional Basement Stair Location

Covered Porch
23-4 x 7-0

Workshop
19-2 x 10-4

FIRST FLOOR

© Copyright by Designer

Two Car Garage
23-4 x 22-8

SECOND FLOOR

Attic Access

Sloped Clg.

Bonus Room
14-0 x 33-4
8' Clg. Ht.

Sloped Clg.

17'-0"

Price Code D   77080

Total Sq. Ft.: 2,143
Main Living Area: 1,535'
Upper Living Area: 585'
Width: 55'
Depth: 42'
Bedrooms: 4
Full Baths: 3
Garage: 2-car

(For more plan info, visit www.familyhomeplans.com)

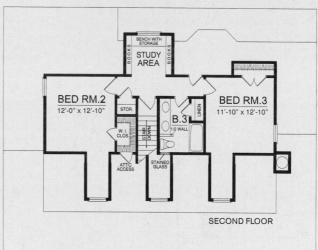

SECOND FLOOR

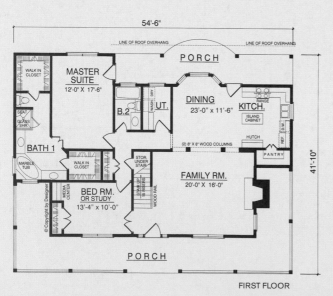

FIRST FLOOR

Price Code D 86303

Total Sq. Ft.: 2,215
Width: 69'-10"
Depth: 60'-6"
Bedrooms: 4
Full Baths: 4
Garage: 2-car

(For more plan info, visit www.familyhomeplans.com)

Miss Margaret has lived here all her life - along with her brothers, sisters, cousins, and grandparents. This has been their home forever. It is with many fond memories that she bids a final farewell and wishes happiness and joy for the new family ready to begin their sojourn within.

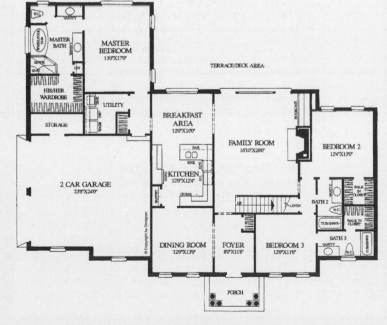

FIRST FLOOR

SECOND FLOOR

ORDER FORM

PRICE GUIDE

Price Level	1 Set	4 Sets	8 Sets	Vellums	PDF Files	CADD Files	Material List	Additional Sets
A	$ 515.00	$585.00	$685.00	$765.00	$ 765.00	$1,165.00	$ 75.00	$50.00
B	$ 545.00	$ 615.00	$715.00	$795.00	$795.00	$1,245.00	$ 75.00	$50.00
C	$ 575.00	$ 645.00	$745.00	$825.00	$ 825.00	$1,275.00	$ 75.00	$50.00
D	$ 605.00	$ 675.00	$775.00	$855.00	$ 855.00	$1,405.00	$ 85.00	$50.00
E	$ 635.00	$ 705.00	$805.00	$885.00	$ 885.00	$1,435.00	$ 85.00	$50.00
F	$ 665.00	$ 735.00	$835.00	$915.00	$ 915.00	$1,515.00	$ 85.00	$50.00
G	$ 695.00	$ 765.00	$865.00	$945.00	$ 945.00	$1,545.00	$ 85.00	$50.00
H	$ 740.00	$ 810.00	$910.00	$990.00	$ 990.00	$1,590.00	$ 95.00	$50.00
I	$ 785.00	$ 855.00	$955.00	$1,035.00	$ 1,035.00	$1,635.00	$ 95.00	$50.00
J	$ 830.00	$ 900.00	$1,000.00	$1,080.00	$ 1,080.00	$1,680.00	$ 95.00	$50.00
K	$ 875.00	$ 945.00	$1,045.00	$1,125.00	$ 1,125.00	$1,725.00	$ 95.00	$50.00
L	$ 935.00	$ 1,005.00	$1,105.00	$1,185.00	$ 1,185.00	$1,785.00	$105.00	$50.00
M	$ 995.00	$ 1,065.00	$1,165.00	$1,245.00	$ 1,245.00	$1,845.00	$105.00	$50.00
N	$1,115.00	$ 1,185.00	$1,285.00	$1,365.00	$ 1,365.00	$1,965.00	$115.00	$50.00

* Not all plans offer CADD files, PDF files and materials lists.

** Prices subject to change.

To order your plan on-line
using our secure server, visit:
www.familyhomeplans.com

To order your home plans by phone
or if you have questions call
1-800-235-5700

SHIPPING
(Standard for any home plan purchase)

US Orders:	Ground	$25
	2nd	$40
	Overnight	$50
CANADA:	Ground	$45
	Expedited	$90
International:	3-4 Weeks	$120

Plan orders will ship out the following business day.

CALL: (800) 235-5700 FAX: (866) 454-9101

We accept all major credit cards.
Payment may also be made via PayPal™

For a **FREE** subscription to FAMILY HOME PLANS newsletter visit
http://www.familyhomeplans.com/newsletter

Order Code No. H6SSM

Ignoring Copyrights Laws Can Be a $100,000 Mistakes

What You Can't Do
U.S. copyright laws allow for statutory penalties of up to $100,000 per incident for copyright infringement involving any of the copyrighted plans found in this publication. The law can be confusing. So, for your own protection, take the time to understand what you can and cannot do when it comes to home plans.

You Cannot Duplicate Home Plans
Purchasing a bond copy and making additional sets by reproducing the original is illegal. If you need more than one set of a particular home plan, you must purchase them.

You Cannot Copy Any Part of a Home Plan to Create Another
Creating your own plan by copying even part of a home design found in this publication without permission is called "creating a derivative work" and is illegal.

You Cannot Build a Home Without a License
You must have a specific permission or license to build a home from a copyrighted design, even if the finished home has been changed from the original plan. It is illegal to build one of the homes found in this publication without a license.

Blueprint Order Information

Reversed Home Plans

Right Reading Reverse ($135.00 charge) is a process that Reverses the house plan and still retains Readable text. The house plans with this option are computer generated, drawn with a CADD (computer aided drafting) program. The designer can "flip" the house plan with the computer software and in-turn, the text comes out readable.

Mirror Reverse ($50.00 charge) is a process that takes the original house plan drawings and makes a backwards copy. The text is backwards because is was not "flipped" with a computer aided drafting program. The mirror reverse option is a very common practice in the building industry. We recommend that if you decide to order a plan mirror reversed, that you request no more that half of the total number of sets mirror reversed. For example, let's say you order 5 sets of blueprints total; we would recommend that you request no more than 3 sets mirror reversed (2 sets the regular way, 3 sets mirrored reversed). Remember that the text on the mirror reversed sets is backwards, you will need a couple of sets readable for reference. Not available for a 1 Set of Blueprints order.

Remember to Order Your Materials List

For obtaining faster, more accurate bids, materials list give the quantity, dimensions and specifications for the major materials needed to build your home. Materials Lists are available for all home plans except as otherwise indicated, but can only be ordered with a set of home plans. Electrical, plumbing and HVAC specifications are not included. Call **800-235-5700** for pricing.

How Many Sets of Plans Will You Need?
The Standard 8-Set Construction Package

Our experience shows that you'll speed up every step of construction and avoid costly building errors by ordering enough sets to go around. Each tradesperson wants a set—the general contractor and all subcontractors: foundation, electrical, plumbing, heating/air conditioning, and framers. Don't forget your lending institution, building department, and, of course, a set for yourself.
* Recommended For Construction *

To Reorder, Call 800-235-5700

If you find after your initial purchase that you require additional sets of plans, a materials list, or other items, you may purchase them from us at special reorder prices (please call for pricing details) provided that you reorder within six months of your original order date. There is a $28 reorder processing fee that is charged on all reorders. For more information on reordering plans, please contact our Sales Department.

An Important Note About Building Code Requirements

All plans are drawn to conform to one or more of the industry's major national building standards. However, due to the variety of local building regulations, your plan may need to be modified to comply with local requirements—snow loads, energy loads, seismic zones, etc. Do check them fully and consult your local building officials. A few states require that all building plans used be drawn by an architect registered in that state. While having your plans reviewed and stamped by such an architect may be prudent, laws requiring non-conforming plans like ours to be completely redrawn forces you to unnecessarily pay very large fees. If your state has such a law, we strongly recommend you contact your state representative to protest. The rendering, floor plans, and technical information contained within this publication are not guaranteed to be totally accurate. Consequently, no information from this publication should be used either as a guide to constructing a home or for estimating the cost of building a home. Complete blueprints must be purchased for such purposes.

Customer Service/Exchanges Call 800-895-3715

If for some reason you have a question about your existing order, please call **800-895-3715**. Your plans are custom printed especially for you once you place your order. For that reason we cannot accept any returns. If for some reason you find that the plan you have purchased from us does not meet your needs, then you may exchange that plan for any other plan in our collection. We allow you 30 days from your original invoice date to make an exchange. At the time of the exchange, you will be charged a processing fee of 50% of the total amount of your original order, plus the original shipping amount. Call our Customer Service Department for more information. Please Note: Reproducible Vellums can only be exchanged if they are unopened. No exchanges allowed for PDF or CADD file orders.

Important Shipping Information

Please refer to the shipping charts on the order form for service availability for your specific plan number. Our delivery service must have a street address or Rural Route Box number—never a post office box. (PLEASE NOTE: Supplying a P.O. Box number will only will delay the shipping of your order.) Use a work address if no one is home during the day. Orders being shipped to APO or FPO must go via First Class Mail. Please include the proper postage. For our International Customers, only Certified bank checks and money orders are accepted and must be payable in U.S. currency. For speed, we ship international orders Air Parcel Post, or we can email PDF or CADD files. Please refer to the chart for the correct shipping cost.

Important Canadian Shipping Information

To our friends in Canada, we have a plan design affiliate in Penticton, BC. This relationship will help you avoid the delays and charges associated with shipments from the United States. Moreover, our affiliate is familiar with the building requirements in your community and country. We prefer payments in U.S. currency.

See http://www.familyhomeplans.com for contact information.

PAGE	PLAN NUMBER	SQUARE FEET	PAGE	PLAN NUMBER	SQUARE FEET	PAGE	PLAN NUMBER	SQUARE FEET
8	59040	800	54	97113	1416	103	97740	1593
9	40025	923	55	74001	1428	103	99682	1595
10-11	65015	1468	56	62131	1451	104	62086	1597
12	65643	984	57	82009	1452	104	92424	1598
13	59043	1000	58-59	69505	1489	105	65619	1600
14	75002	1565	60	47005	1437	105	82008	1598
15	92438	1050	60	55031	1455	106-7	69506	1679
16	55022	1064	61	65487	1457	108	59057	1600
17	55015	1108	61	96516	1458	108	62399	1600
18	34003	1146	62	93165	1472	109	72018	1605
19	65394	1147	63	97137	1461	109	94522	1606
20	65648	1191	64	24706	1470	110	94624	1615
21	68231	1195	65	86105	1473	111	97760	1611
22	55026	1204	66	55028	1479	112	94683	1618
22	20001	1255	68	50099	1483	113	65246	1625
23	55029	1215	69	40026	1492	114	82012	1627
23	55017	1298	69	44017	1492	115	96561	1628
24	55000	1230	70	50081	1498	116	55027	1634
24	65638	1244	70	99106	1495	117	62219	1636
25	55025	1260	71	59050	1500	118	44010	1641
25	68232	1263	71	94517	1500	119	24717	1642
26	65681	1266	72	59146	1509	120	75000	1636
26	96559	1277	73	40027	1501	120	93100	1642
27	65492	1281	74	93130	1508	121	86100	1684
28	55030	1299	75	50038	1509	121	96513	1648
28	92431	1296	76	94691	1510	122	24725	1661
29	44008	1304	77	72019	1515	122	96824	1698
29	68233	1333	78	82026	1525	123	50021	1651
30	35008	1291	79	65495	1530	123	79007	1688
31	24700	1312	80	71022	1532	124	10674	1600
32	34600	1328	81	40028	1532	124	79005	1643
33	92458	1343	82	62036	1538	125	42503	1792
34	47001	1363	83	24721	1539	126	65682	1672
34	62115	1374	84-85	99682	1595	126	24729	1663
35	94688	1363	86	40006	1539	127	68172	1675
36	24402	1346	87	93161	1540	128	24738	1554
37	44012	1372	88	55011	1543	129	40005	1680
39	65001	1480	89	40029	1551	130	82010	1684
40	20156	1359	89	44009	1547	131	59901	1634
40	65617	1375	90	82026	1525	132-3	65409	1727
41	99673	1380	90	99654	1554	134	34029	1686
42	44014	1381	91	34602	1560	136	40010	1688
42	76012	1370	92	62277	1560	137	65866	1698
43	44018	1388	93	24705	1562	138	72023	1694
43	50083	1390	94	68188	1575	138	92460	1695
44	61008	1387	94	68234	1563	139	40017	1698
44	59002	1400	95	65085	1572	139	94156	1696
45	61296	1407	96	10748	1540	140	50042	1698
45	94690	1401	97	24242	1595	140	92690	1698
46	55002	1405	98	24701	1625	141	68235	1699
47	44007	1412	99	55016	1578	141	94602	1704
48	34601	1415	99	55001	1541	142	50006	1707
49	68226	1416	100	44011	1589	142	63093	1704
50	92459	1420	100	44016	1588	143	62208	1723
51	65418	1432	101	63083	1590	143	34077	1757
52	24711	1434	102	92433	1593	144	86101	1738
53	50098	1442	102	97178	1591	145	94151	1716

PAGE	PLAN NUMBER	SQUARE FEET	PAGE	PLAN NUMBER	SQUARE FEET	PAGE	PLAN NUMBER	SQUARE FEET
146	72020	1725	189	59017	1802	234	96544	1925
147	40034	1726	190	94155	1802	235	99115	1926
148	50040	1727	191	96541	1815	236	40004	1930
149	40030	1730	192	50100	1824	237	62053	1930
150	62177	1760	192	24651	1821	238	98238	1931
151	99123	1732	193	94654	1819	238	55023	1938
152	94603	1737	194	44019	1830	239	92464	1932
153	62321	1732	194	65684	1828	240	65488	1953
154	10839	1738	195	34031	1831	240	98223	1940
155	75004	1749	196	63113	1831	241	40015	1955
155	98240	1746	197	94152	1832	242-3	65135	2183
156	62035	1750	198	40016	1836	244	86108	1957
156	98224	1751	198	96819	1840	245	72022	1967
157	59010	1751	199	44006	1850	245	94158	1962
157	59011	1751	199	65411	1844	246	63002	1963
158	63090	1758	200	59019	1855	247	92461	1963
158	93191	1756	201	59018	1852	248	96527	1972
159	50104	1751	202	71031	1855	249	40033	1974
160-1	65177	1936	203	94623	1857	250	86103	1990
162	74000	1760	203	99174	1859	251	92427	1982
162	94160	1760	204	68170	1867	252	86106	1985
163	68139	1762	206	93107	1868	253	94705	1984
163	93133	1763	206	94521	1865	254	92446	1992
164	59114	2000	207	65634	1868	255	92421	1992
165	94518	1765	208	63114	1868	256	63101	1993
166	68204	1765	209	10515	2044	257	69508	1994
166	94159	1765	210	40031	1875	258	68161	1995
167	86102	1762	210	50056	1874	258	97912	1995
167	94519	1768	211	75006	1876	259	20230	1995
168	50015	1770	212-3	65125	2037	260	63040	1007
169	24714	1771	214	96560	1878	261	69509	1996
170	44000	1772	215	62190	1875	262-3	65138	2283
170	96525	1771	216	63224	1879	264	40014	1997
171	50105	1775	217	40032	1879	265	44002	1998
171	72024	1775	217	94607	1880	266	59023	2001
172	63111	1782	218	65624	1891	267	59024	2002
172	59148	1800	219	62037	1880	268	86107	2012
173	44001	1780	220	65486	1885	269	75003	2018
174	44004	1783	220	65493	1883	270	86109	2020
174	92420	1787	221	50075	1895	271	92463	2071
175	24610	1785	221	65490	1888	272	92444	2097
176	20198	1792	222	69503	1892	273	92465	2098
177	65683	1792	223	59192	1900	274	65862	2091
177	99680	1793	224	68236	1897	275	92443	2184
178	65491	1795	225	92462	1897	276	96815	2266
178	82013	1797	226	65489	1898	276	96829	2198
179	93176	1795	226	73279	1898	277	65145	2292
180	59012	1799	227	44003	1899	278	59214	2336
180	65622	1800	227	69507	1902	279	86104	2151
181	65625	1800	228	99154	1907	280	24734	2114
182-3	65431	1980	229	10785	1907	281	59212	2140
184	59015	1800	230	20501	1908	282	93483	2156
185	59068	1800	231	94153	1916	283	86303	2215
186	93143	1802	231	94157	1912			
187	44005	1802	232	63001	1919			
188	93193	1802	232	50106	1921			
188	94642	1802	233	55023	1924			